Blazor Web Development Cookbook

Tested recipes for advanced single-page application
scenarios in .NET 9

Pawel Bazyluk

Blazor Web Development Cookbook

Group Product Manager: Kaustubh Manglurkar

Publishing Product Manager: Chayan Majumdar

Book Project Manager: Sonam Pandey

Senior Editor: Rashi Dubey

Technical Editor: Simran Ali

Copy Editor: Safis Editing

Indexer: Manju Arasan

Production Designer: Shankar Kalbhor

Senior DevRel Marketing Executive: Nivedita Pandey

First published: November 2024

Production reference: 1071124

Published by Packt Publishing Ltd.

Grosvenor House

11 St Paul's Square

Birmingham

B3 1RB, UK

ISBN 978-1-83546-078-8

www.packtpub.com

To everyone who supported me throughout the years. To my family - for always being my safe place. To my friends - for inspiring and challenging me. To my partner-in-crime - who always believes we can achieve more. I love you all. Thank you for being the pillars of my journey.

- Pawel Bazyluk

Contributors

About the author

Pawel Bazyluk is a seasoned Software Engineer with expertise in Blazor and .NET technologies. With a career spanning over a decade, Pawel has dedicated himself to mastering a diverse range of programming languages. In 2019, when Blazor started to surface, he realized its potential and has been positioning himself as a Blazor expert since. His innovative and user-centered approach to development has been key in solving numerous complex challenges for the companies he works with. Pawel's journey in the tech industry is also marked by his enthusiasm for sharing knowledge and mentoring, making him a valued member of the developer community. His insights into Blazor and web development have gained recognition on LinkedIn and various tech forums.

I want to thank everyone who helped bring that book to reality. The Team at Packt - thank you for your guidance and for taking a chance on me. My technical reviewers - Wojtek, Christian, and Sebastian - thank you for your time and patience. The Team at Inspeerity - thank you for rooting for me and giving me space to focus on writing. And to my partner - thank you for making sure I don't forget to eat and get enough sleep.

About the reviewers

Christian Stage is a dedicated IT professional and passionate Blazor developer. During his studies at the IT University of Copenhagen, he developed a keen interest in .NET, Python, machine learning, and physical computing.

Christian's fascination with Blazor began as a Student Developer at Copenhagen Business School's System Center Endpoint Team. He later became the Lead Developer at PreSeed Ventures (PSV), where he played a pivotal role in delivering a custom lead-generation tool using Blazor. Currently, as a Consultant at Netcompany, he is an active participant in the responsible digitalization of Denmark and has participated in the teaching of Blazor basics to new employees.

Sebastiaan Dammann is a seasoned web developer with over 12 years of experience. He began his career at a small sustainability agency, working with ASP.NET Web Forms and ASP Classic. For the past decade he has been working at the digital sustainability team at EY – the last number of years as lead developer. Since .NET 5 Sebastiaan has been developing enterprise applications using Blazor. Since the advent of .NET 5, he has been at the forefront of developing enterprise applications using Blazor. He is a language polygot, developing in Java, C#, C++, ASM, and TypeScript/Javascript.

Sebastiaan is passionate about 3D printing, writing on his personal blog, contributing to open source software, and raising his children Christina, Hannah and Isabella.

Wojciech Kasa is a seasoned software architect with nearly 20 years of professional experience. He specializes in distributed systems and Domain-Driven Design. Throughout his career he has held leadership roles, guiding teams in the design and implementation of high-performance, scalable systems.

He has a wonderful wife and two sons.

Aaron Piotrowski was trained as a 3D Artist and later converted to a full stack developer after finding that programming could take the conceptualization and imagery he created to fully functioning interactive applications. Having worked on everything from game animation, to custom frontend feature design and implementation for Fortune 500 and national brands, Angular web-app creation, and AR/VR projects on iOS, Android, HTC Vive and the Oculus Go, Aaron is a well rounded technology connoisseur. He can often be found in the office discussing Apple's latest releases or debating the advantages of different technologies. Ultimately, he's interested how innovative solutions can solve problems and create value for users.

Table of Contents

2

Synchronous and Asynchronous Data Binding 29

3

Taking Control of Event Handling 47

4

Enhancing Data Display with Grids   71

5

Managing Application State   97

6

Building Interactive Forms   125

7

Validating User Input Forms   143

8

Keeping the Application Secure   169

9

Exploring Navigation and Routing   199

10

Integrating with OpenAI 217

Index 249

Other Books You May Enjoy 256

Preface

Blazor is a powerful web framework introduced by Microsoft that allows developers to build interactive and modern web applications using **C#** and **.NET** instead of relying on JavaScript. Blazor bridges the gap between front-end and back-end development, offering a unified programming model that makes it easier to create full-featured web applications with a consistent and robust language stack. With Blazor, you can choose to host your application statically on the server; have a server-side interactivity through **SignalR**; build a client-side interface running directly in the browser, using **WebAssembly**; or mix all approaches however you see fit.

While you can easily find resources introducing Blazor basics and fundamental concepts, this book takes you deeper into advanced techniques and best practices for building enterprise-grade Blazor applications. The goal is to equip you with the tools to build robust, secure, scalable, and maintainable solutions. We will focus on practical, real-world examples and walk through the recipes you need to tackle the most common development challenges, leveraging the powerful features that Blazor offers.

The solutions and tricks in this cookbook come from or are inspired by two primary sources:

- my years of experience developing Blazor applications across various industries, countries, and domains
- Blazor community and insights from leading Blazor developers and experts

As Blazor continues to evolve, it is increasingly recognized as a game-changer in the .NET ecosystem, especially with the growing trend of full-stack C# development. As more companies adopt Blazor for their web development needs, the demand for skilled Blazor developers is rapidly increasing. This book will not only help you stay ahead of the curve but also ensure that you can confidently build and maintain Blazor applications that meet modern web standards.

I hope you find the book both insightful and practical. Your feedback is incredibly valuable to me, and I would be glad to hear about your experience. If you found the content helpful or if it made a difference in your projects, please consider leaving a review. Additionally, feel free to connect with me on LinkedIn or reach out via social media to share your thoughts, suggestions, or simply to discuss how the book has impacted your work. Your insights will help shape future editions and continue the conversation within the developer community.

Who this book is for

This book is intended for developers and software architects proficient in C# and .NET and already have experience in web development. Ideally, you must have a basic understanding of Blazor as we only skim through fundamentals to set the stage for the advanced topics.

The three main personas who will benefit from this content are:

- web developers who want to leverage their C# and .NET skills to build modern, interactive web applications using Blazor

- software architects looking to design and implement scalable, maintainable web applications using Blazor as part of their technology stack

- all Blazor enthusiasts who have a foundational understanding of Blazor and wish to deepen their knowledge by exploring advanced techniques, best practices, and real-world scenarios

What this book covers

Chapter 1, Working with Component-Based Architecture, introduces the architectural design of Blazor and explains the concept of a component. It also covers components parameterization, reusability and dynamic customization.

Chapter 2, Synchronous and Asynchronous Data Binding, is a comprehensive guide on advanced data binding techniques – application interactivity cornerstone. It explores two-way binding patterns and showcases practical case studies for asynchronous binding and input throttling, essential for efficient data exchange with external sources.

Chapter 3, Taking Control of Event Handling, covers everything there is to know about event handling in Blazor. It guides through working with event delegates, lambda expressions, capturing event arguments and leveraging Blazor-native `EventCallback`. It demonstrates techniques to control default event behaviors and propagation and building fully customized events. It also covers UX/UI tips for maintaining user awareness and interface responsiveness when handling long-running events.

Chapter 4, Enhancing Data Display with Grids, demonstrates how to enhance data representation with grids and attach actions to rows, columns, or individual cells. It also contains an example of infinite-scroll implementation and strategies for handling big datasets effectively with pagination and virtualization.

Chapter 5, Managing Application State, explores all corners of state management, from REST-like route patterns to support bookmarkable state, through in-memory and injectable state containers and to persisting state in the browser to prevent loss in higher latency scenarios. It also covers a practical implementation of globally injected state and components dynamically responding to the state changes.

Chapter 6, Building Interactive Forms, focuses on form handling by utilizing Blazor's built-in components and the importance of securing forms, particularly in public-facing applications, by implementing antiforgery tokens and preventing cross-site request forgery attacks.

Chapter 7, Validating User Input Forms, showcases the form validation strategies. It covers implementing both in-memory and client-side validation for simple and complex object types and guides through integrating asynchronous server-side validation for robust data integrity. Moreover, it contains UI/UX tips, enabling conditional form submission based on validation states and enhancing user experience with toast notifications for validation messages.

Chapter 8, Keeping the Application Secure, highlights techniques for handling authentication and authorization, starting with JWT token support, through role-based authorization, and implementing custom policies for fine-grained control. It also covers creating a custom authentication provider to manage unique identity scenarios and building tenant-specific authorization logic.

Chapter 9, Exploring Navigation and Routing, guides through navigation and routing intricacies from supporting routes from external assemblies and securing routes with type constraints to centralizing the routing to enhance deep linking across the application. It's also a practical guide to leveraging navigation events to cancel long-running requests to preserve memory and preventing accidental navigation to safeguard unsaved user inputs.

Chapter 10, Integrating with OpenAI, explores the integration of the Azure OpenAI service into a Blazor app and leveraging the possibilities of AI models. It showcases how to setup and manage the AI services and guides through creating a smart support ticket creator, leveraging smart pasting and smart input area. It also contains a walkthrough of adding an AI-powered chat bot to the application.

To get the most out of this book

You will need to have an understanding of the basics of Blazor, as well as fundamentals of web development. On top of that, you're required to have an IDE that supports .NET and Blazor development as well as a browser that supports WebAssembly and modern CSS and HTML (which all modern web browsers do). You also need to have a .NET 9 SDK and runtime installed on your machine.

Software/Hardware covered in the book	OS Requirements
.NET 9	Windows, Mac OS X, and Linux (Any)
Blazor	Visual Studio, Visual Studio Code, Rider (Any)
Azure	

If you are using the digital version of this book, we advise you to type the code yourself or access the code via the GitHub repository (link available in the next section). Doing so will help you avoid any potential errors related to the copying and pasting of code.

Download the example code files

You can download the example code files for this book from GitHub at https://github.com/PacktPublishing/Blazor-Web-Development-Cookbook. In case there's an update to the code, it will be updated on the existing GitHub repository.

We also have other code bundles from our rich catalog of books and videos available at https://github.com/PacktPublishing/. Check them out!

Conventions used

There are a number of text conventions used throughout this book.

Code in text: Indicates code words in text, database table names, folder names, filenames, file extensions, pathnames, dummy URLs, user input, and Twitter handles. Here is an example: "We intentionally designed Provider to match the ItemsProvider signature required by the Virtualize component, ensuring compatibility and seamless integration."

A block of code is set as follows:

```
<div class="ticket">
    <div class="name">Adult</div>
    <div class="price">10.00 $</div>
</div>
```

Any command-line input or output is written as follows:

```
dotnet new blazor -o BlazorCookbook.App -int Auto --framework net9.0
```

Bold: Indicates a new term, an important word, or words that you see onscreen. For example, words in menus or dialog boxes appear in the text like this. Here is an example: "Start Visual Studio and select **Create a new project** from the welcome window."

> **Tips or important notes**
> Appear like this.

Sections

In this book, you will find several headings that appear frequently (*Getting ready*, *How to do it...*, *How it works...*, *There's more...*, and *See also*).

To give clear instructions on how to complete a recipe, use these sections as follows:

Getting ready

This section tells you what to expect in the recipe and describes how to set up any software or any preliminary settings required for the recipe.

How to do it...

This section contains the steps required to follow the recipe.

How it works...

This section usually consists of a detailed explanation of what happened in the previous section.

There's more...

This section consists of additional information about the recipe in order to make you more knowledgeable about the recipe.

See also

This section provides helpful links to other useful information for the recipe.

Get in touch

Feedback from our readers is always welcome.

General feedback: If you have questions about any aspect of this book, mention the book title in the subject of your message and email us at customercare@packtpub.com.

Errata: Although we have taken every care to ensure the accuracy of our content, mistakes do happen. If you have found a mistake in this book, we would be grateful if you would report this to us. Please visit www.packtpub.com/support/errata, selecting your book, clicking on the Errata Submission Form link, and entering the details.

Piracy: If you come across any illegal copies of our works in any form on the Internet, we would be grateful if you would provide us with the location address or website name. Please contact us at copyright@packt.com with a link to the material.

If you are interested in becoming an author: If there is a topic that you have expertise in and you are interested in either writing or contributing to a book, please visit authors.packtpub.com.

Share Your Thoughts

Once you've read Blazor *Web Development Cookbook*, we'd love to hear your thoughts! Scan the QR code below to go straight to the Amazon review page for this book and share your feedback.

https://packt.link/r/183546078X

Your review is important to us and the tech community and will help us make sure we're delivering excellent quality content.

Download a free PDF copy of this book

Thanks for purchasing this book!

Do you like to read on the go but are unable to carry your print books everywhere?

Is your eBook purchase not compatible with the device of your choice?

Don't worry, now with every Packt book you get a DRM-free PDF version of that book at no cost.

Read anywhere, any place, on any device. Search, copy, and paste code from your favorite technical books directly into your application.

The perks don't stop there, you can get exclusive access to discounts, newsletters, and great free content in your inbox daily

Follow these simple steps to get the benefits:

1. Scan the QR code or visit the link below

https://download.packt.com/free-ebook/9781835460788

2. Submit your proof of purchase
3. That's it! We'll send your free PDF and other benefits to your email directly

Working with Component-Based Architecture

1

Welcome to *Blazor Web Development Cookbook*. This book will be your comprehensive guide to enhancing your skills in building dynamic and scalable web applications with Blazor. It offers a collection of practical solutions and techniques for tackling the most common challenges in web development. In each chapter, we'll dive into different areas of application development. This book is packed with detailed examples and actionable tips. We'll explore a range of topics – from optimizing components, through managing **application state** to increasing your application's interactivity and security. Having such a resource will allow you to gain development velocity and focus on addressing business requirements.

In this chapter, you'll learn about the core principles of component-based architecture in Blazor. We'll start by creating a basic **component** and progress to more complex aspects such as parameterization for reusability and handling required parameters. We'll also explore advanced topics, such as building components with customizable content, implementing generic components, and increasing **loose coupling** with DynamicComponent.

By the end of this chapter, you'll be able to implement and optimize components in **Blazor**. Understanding **component-based architecture** is foundational in building more sophisticated, interactive, and responsive web applications. It's also essential for writing scalable, maintainable, and reusable code.

We're going to cover the following recipes in this chapter:

- Initializing a project
- Creating your first basic component
- Declaring parameters on a component
- Detecting render mode at runtime
- Ensuring that a parameter is required
- Passing values from the parent component with CascadingParameter

- Creating components with customizable content
- Making components generic
- Decoupling components with `DynamicComponent`

Technical requirements

You don't need any paid tools or add-ons to kick off your Blazor journey. To aid with this, we've decided to limit the dependencies for the recipes in this book. You can pick up any topic independently whenever you need to.

For this chapter, you'll need the following:

- A modern IDE. We'll be using Visual Studio 17.12.0, but any other is also fine, so long as it supports development in .NET 9.
- A modern web browser.
- The .NET 9 SDK. If it wasn't part of your IDE installation, you can get it from `https://dotnet.microsoft.com/en-us/download/dotnet/9.0`.

You can find all the code examples for this chapter on GitHub at: `https://github.com/PacktPublishing/Blazor-Web-Development-Cookbook/tree/main/BlazorCookbook.App.Client/Chapters/Chapter01`.

Initializing a project

With .NET 9, the .NET team focused on improving the quality, stability, and performance of Blazor applications. Thankfully, there are no breaking changes between .NET 8, so you can safely raise the target framework of your application. However, with .NET 8, Blazor got a whole new solution type and rendering experience, so we'll review the steps required to initialize a new project here.

Let's initialize a **Blazor Web App** with a per-component rendering scope. It's a strategic choice for our cookbook as it enables me to highlight various render mode caveats while we explore different areas of web development.

Getting ready

In this recipe, we'll showcase initializing the project with the GUI provided as part of Visual Studio. So, start your IDE and dive in.

If you're using the **.NET CLI** in your environment, I'll provide equivalent commands in the *There's more...* section.

How to do it...

Perform the following steps to initialize the Blazor Web App project:

1. Start Visual Studio and select **Create a new project** from the welcome window:

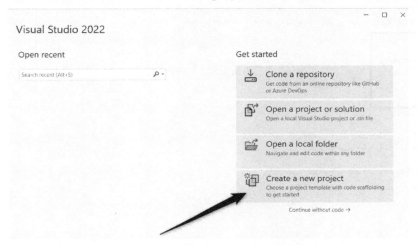

Figure 1.1: Navigating to the project creation panel

2. Use the search bar at the top of the next panel to narrow the list of available project types, select **Blazor Web App**, and confirm your choice by clicking **Next**:

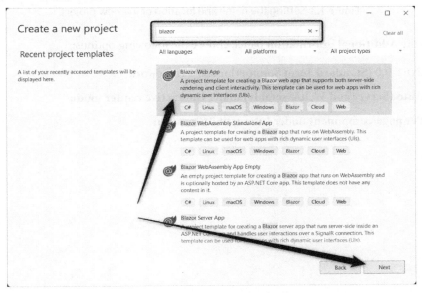

Figure 1.2: Selecting Blazor Web App from the available project types

3. On the **Configure your new project** panel, define the project's name and location and confirm these details by clicking **Next**:

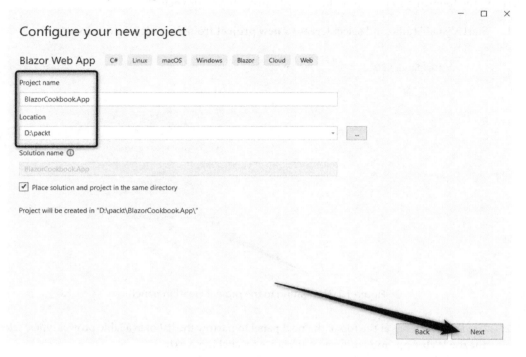

Figure 1.3: Setting the name and location of the new project

4. On the **Additional information** panel, choose the following options:

    *   **.NET 9.0 (Standard Term Support)** under **Framework**
    *   **Auto (Server and WebAssembly)** under **Interactive render mode**
    *   **Per page/component** under **Interactivity location**

On top of that, check the **Include sample pages** checkbox. Confirm your choice by clicking **Create**:

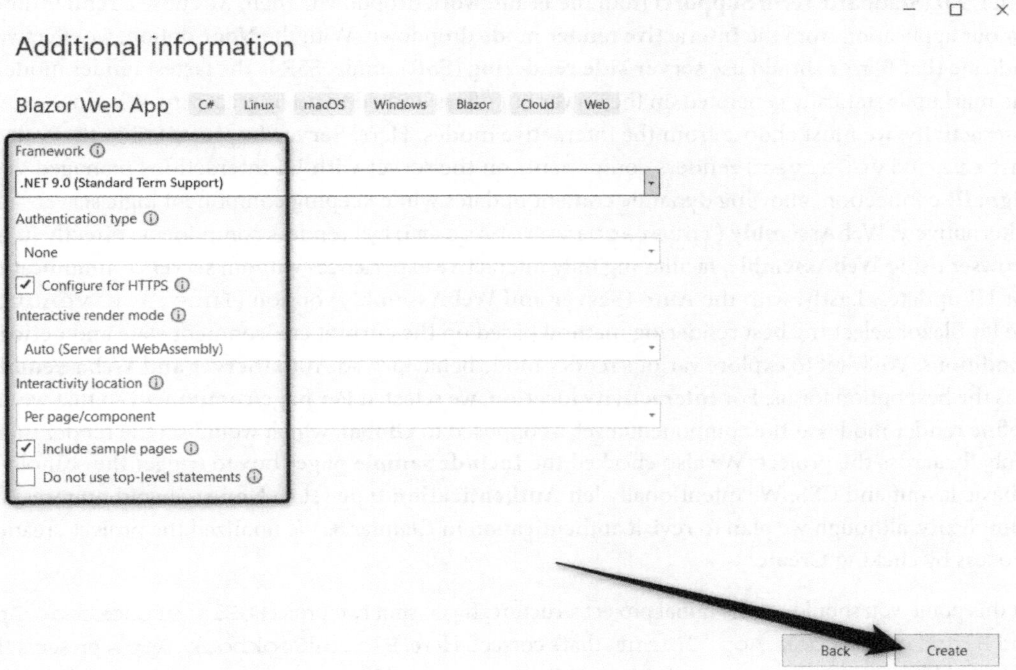

Additional information

Blazor Web App   C#   Linux   macOS   Windows   Blazor   Cloud   Web

Framework ⓘ

.NET 9.0 (Standard Term Support)   ▾

Authentication type ⓘ

None   ▾

☑ Configure for HTTPS ⓘ

Interactive render mode ⓘ

Auto (Server and WebAssembly)   ▾

Interactivity location ⓘ

Per page/component   ▾

☑ Include sample pages ⓘ
☐ Do not use top-level statements ⓘ

Back   Create

Figure 1.4: Configuring the project's framework and interactivity

Here's what your initial solution structure will look like:

Solution 'BlazorCookbook.App' (2 of 2 projects)
▷ **BlazorCookbook.App**
▷ BlazorCookbook.App.Client

Figure 1.5: Initial project structure

How it works...

In *step 1*, we started Visual Studio and selected the **Create a new project** option from the welcome menu. Since Visual Studio comes with many project templates preinstalled, in *step 2*, we utilized the search bar at the top of the panel and, by searching for the `blazor` keyword, we quickly found and selected **Blazor Web App** from the results list. We proceeded to the next stage by clicking the **Next** button. In *step 3*, we defined the project name and location. For this book, I chose `BlazorCookbook.App` and `D:\packt`. We continued the setup process by clicking **Next**.

In *step 4*, we configured the project. Considering that we'll focus on Blazor in .NET 9, we chose **.NET 9.0 (Standard Term Support)** from the **Framework** dropdown. Then, we chose a **render mode** for our application from the **Interactive render mode** dropdown. With the **None** option, we effectively indicate that Blazor should use **server-side rendering** (**SSR**) mode. SSR is the fastest render mode as the markup is statically generated on the server but offers limited to no interactivity. When we expect interactivity, we must choose from the interactive modes. Here, **Server** (represented in the code as `InteractiveServer`) renders components on the server with UI interactions managed via a **SignalR** connection, allowing dynamic content updates while keeping component logic server-side. Alternatively, **WebAssembly** (`InteractiveWebAssembly`) renders components directly in the browser using **WebAssembly**, facilitating fully interactive experiences without server communication for UI updates. Lastly, with the **Auto (Server and WebAssembly)** option (`InteractiveAuto`), we let Blazor select the best rendering method based on the current environment state and network conditions. We want to explore various render mode behaviors, so **Auto (Server and Webassembly)** was the best option for us. For **Interactivity location**, we selected **Per page/component** so that we can define render modes at the component level, as opposed to **Global**, which would set the render mode globally across the project. We also checked the **Include sample pages** box to trigger the scaffold of a basic layout and CSS. We intentionally left **Authentication type** set to **None** to avoid unnecessary complexity, although we plan to revisit authentication in *Chapter 8*. We finalized the project creation process by clicking **Create**.

At this point, you should see the initial project structure. If you spot two projects, `BlazorCookbook.App` and `BlazorCookbook.App.Client`, that's correct. Here, `BlazorCookbook.App` represents the server-side components of our application, while `BlazorCookbook.App.Client` is the client-side part that compiles into WebAssembly code. Everything that's placed in `BlazorCookbook.App.Client` will be transmitted to the user's browser, so you shouldn't place any sensitive or confidential information there. Since `BlazorCookbook.App` references `BlazorCookbook.App.Client`, there's no need to duplicate code, regardless of how it's rendered initially.

There's more...

If your IDE doesn't have a GUI similar to Visual Studio, you can leverage the cross-platform .NET CLI. Navigate to your working directory and run the following command to initialize a Blazor Web App project with the same configuration that was outlined in *step 4*:

```
dotnet new blazor -o BlazorCookbook.App -int Auto --framework net9.0
```

Creating your first basic component

A component is a self-contained chunk of the **user interface** (**UI**). A component in Blazor is a .NET class with markup, created as a **Razor** (`.razor`) file. In Blazor, components are the primary building blocks of any application and encapsulate markup, logic, and styling. They enable code reusability and increase code maintainability and testability. This modular approach streamlines the development process greatly.

For our first component, we'll create a `Ticket` component that renders a tariff name and a price when the user navigates to a page.

Getting ready

Before you dive into creating the first component, in your Blazor project, create a `Recipe02` directory – this will be your working directory.

How to do it...

Follow these steps to create your first component:

1. Navigate to the `Recipe02` directory that you just created.

2. Use the **Add New Item** feature and create a Razor component:

Figure 1.6: Adding a new Razor component prompt

3. In the `Ticket` component, add supporting HTML markup:

```
<div class="ticket">
    <div class="name">Adult</div>
    <div class="price">10.00 $</div>
</div>
```

4. Add a new `Offer` component. Use the `@page` directive to make it navigable and render the `Ticket` component within:

```
@page "/ch01r02"
<Ticket />
```

How it works...

In *step 1*, we navigated to `Recipe02` – our working directory. In *step 2*, we leveraged a built-in Visual Studio prompt to create files and create the first component: `Ticket`. While building components in the Razor markup syntax, we named our component file `Ticket.razor`. In *step 3*, we added simple markup to `Ticket` – we rendered **Adult** and **10.00 $**, which describe a given ticket. In *step 4*, we created our first page – the `Offer` page. In Blazor, any component can become a page with the help of a @page directive, which requires a fixed path argument starting with /. The @page "/ch01r02" directive enables navigation to that component. In the Offer markup, we embedded Ticket using the **self-closing tag** syntax – a simpler, more convenient equivalent of the explicit opening and closing tags (<Ticket></Ticket>). However, we can only utilize it when the component doesn't require any additional content to render.

There's more...

While componentization in Blazor offers numerous benefits, it's essential to know when and how much to use it. Components are a great way to reuse representation markup with various data objects. They significantly enhance code readability and testability. However, caution is necessary – you can overdo componentization. Using too many components leads to increased reflection overhead and unnecessary complexities in managing render modes. It's especially easy to overlook when you're refactoring grids or forms. Ask yourself whether every cell must be a component and whether you need that input encapsulated. Always weigh what you might gain from higher markup granularity with the performance cost it brings.

Declaring parameters on a component

In Blazor, component parameters allow you to pass data into components. It's the first step in making your application dynamic. Component parameters are like method parameters in traditional programming. You can utilize the same primitive, as well as the reference and complex types. This results in code flexibility, simplified UI structures, and high markup reusability.

Let's create a parametrized component that represents a ticket so that we can display any incoming tariff and price without unnecessary code duplication or markup incoherence.

Getting ready

Before you dive into component parameterization, do the following:

- Create a Recipe03 directory – this will be your working directory
- Copy the Ticket component from the *Creating your first basic component* recipe or copy its implementation from the Chapter01/Recipe02 directory of this book's GitHub repository

How to do it...

To declare parameters on your component, start with these foundational steps:

1. In the Ticket component, declare parameters in the @code block:

```
@code {
    [Parameter] public string Tariff { get; set; }
```

```
    [Parameter] public decimal Price { get; set; }
    [Parameter]
    public EventCallback OnAdded { get; set; }
}
```

2. Modify the `Ticket` markup so that you can render values from parameters:

```
<div class="ticket">
    <div class="name">@Tariff</div>
    <div class="price">
        @(Price.ToString("0.00 $"))
    </div>
    <div class="ticket-actions">
        <button @onclick="@OnAdded">
            Add to cart
        </button>
    </div>
</div>
```

3. Create an `Offer` page and enhance it so that it renders in `InteractiveWebAssembly` mode:

```
@page "/ch01r03"
@rendermode InteractiveWebAssembly
```

4. Below the functional directives in the `Offer` component, add two parametrized instances of `Ticket`. Implement an `Add()` method as a placeholder for interactivity:

```
<Ticket Tariff="Adult" Price="10.00m"
        OnAdded="@Add" />
<Ticket Tariff="Child" Price="5.00m"
        OnAdded="@Add" />

@code {
    private void Add()
        => Console.WriteLine("Added to cart!");
}
```

How it works...

In *step 1*, we extended the `Ticket` component with a `@code` block, which Blazor recognizes as a container for the C# code. Within this `@code` block, we used the `Parameter` attribute to mark properties that are settable externally, such as method arguments in C#. In our example, we used a string for a ticket tariff and a decimal for its price. For the last parameter, we used the `EventCallback` type. It's a Blazor-specific `struct` that carries an invokable action with an additional benefit. When you change the UI state, you should use the `StateHasChanged()` life cycle method to notify

Blazor that something happened. By design, `EventCallback` triggers `StateHasChanged()` automatically, so you can't omit it accidentally. In *step 2*, we rebuilt the `Ticket` markup based on parameter values that we accessed using the @ symbol. That symbol signaled to the compiler that we were switching to dynamic C# code. If you pair it with round brackets, you can embed complex code blocks as well, as we did when we formatted the price in a money format.

In *step 3*, we created a navigable `Offer` page. This time, on top of the @page directive, we also declared a @rendermode directive, which allowed us to control how our component renders initially. We can choose from any of the render modes that a Blazor Web App supports, but as we expect some interactivity on the page, we opted for `InteractiveWebAssembly` mode. In *step 4*, in the @code block of `Offer`, we implemented an `Add()` placeholder method that simulates adding a ticket to the cart. We also implemented the `Offer` markup, where we rendered two `Ticket` instances with different parameters. You pass parameter values similarly to standard HTML attributes such as `class` or `style`. Blazor automatically recognizes that you're calling a component, not an HTML element. Finally, we rendered **Adult** and **Child** tickets and attached the `Add()` method to the exposed `EventCallback` parameter.

There's more...

You must be aware that the number of parameters can directly affect the rendering speed. That's because the renderer uses reflection to resolve parameter values. Over-reliance on reflection can significantly hinder performance. You can optimize that process by overriding the `SetParametersAsync()` method of the component life cycle, though that's an advanced operation. Instead, you should focus on keeping the parameters list concise or introducing wrapper classes where necessary.

Earlier in this chapter, we declared a specific render mode for a component when your Blazor application is set to expect interactivity at the page or component level. However, when you enable interactivity globally, you can still exclude certain pages from interactive routing. You'll find it useful for pages that depend on standard request/response cycles or reading or writing HTTP cookies:

```
@attribute [ExcludeFromInteractiveRouting]
```

To enforce static server-side rendering on a page, you must add the `ExcludeFromInteractiveRouting` attribute, using the @attribute directive, at the top of the page. In this case, you no longer add the @rendermode directive as it's dedicated to declaring interactive render modes.

Detecting render mode at runtime

Understanding where and how your component renders is crucial for optimizing performance and tailoring user experience. Blazor allows you to detect the render location, interactivity, and assigned render mode at runtime. You can query whether the component is operating in an interactive state or just prerendering. These insights open up new possibilities for debugging, performance optimization, and building components that adapt dynamically to their rendering context.

Let's hide the area with tickets in the `Offer` component to prevent user interactions, such as adding tickets to the cart, until the component is ready and interactive.

Getting ready

Before you explore render mode detection, do the following:

- Create a `Recipe04` directory – this will be your working directory
- Copy the `Offer` and `Ticket` components from the *Declaring parameters on a component* recipe or copy their implementations from the `Chapter01/Recipe03` directory of this book's GitHub repository

How to do it...

Follow these steps:

1. Navigate to the `Offer` component and update the path attached to the `@page` directive to avoid routing conflicts:

    ```
    @page "/ch01r04"
    @rendermode InteractiveWebAssembly
    ```

2. Below the component directives, add some conditional markup to indicate that the component is getting ready based on the value of the `RendererInfo.IsInteractive` property:

    ```
    @if (!RendererInfo.IsInteractive)
    {
        <p>Getting ready...</p>
        return;
    }
    @* existing markup is obscured, but still down here *@
    ```

How it works...

In *step 1*, we navigated to the `Offer` component and updated the path that was assigned to the `@page` directive. Blazor doesn't allow duplicated routes, so we triggered a conflict since we copied the `Offer` component with a route from the *Declaring parameters on a component* recipe.

In *step 2*, we introduced a conditional markup block below the component directives. We leveraged the `RendererInfo` property that the `ComponentBase` class exposes, allowing us to track the component rendering state. The `RendererInfo` property has two properties:

- The `RendererInfo.Name` property tells us where the component is currently running and returns the following options:

  - `Static`: This indicates that the component is running on the server without any interactivity

  - `Server`: This indicates that the component is running on the server and will be interactive after it fully loads

  - `WebAssembly`: This indicates that the component is running in the client's browser and becomes interactive after loading

  - `WebView`: This indicates that it's dedicated to .NET MAUI and native devices

- The `RendererInfo.IsInteractive` property shows whether the component is in an interactive state or not (such as during prerendering or static SSR)

We leveraged the `RendererInfo.IsInteractive` property to detect whether the interactivity is ready. If it isn't, we display a **Getting ready...** message to inform users they should wait.

Ensuring that a parameter is required

The `EditorRequired` attribute indicates to your IDE that passing data to the component is functionally critical. This attribute triggers data validation at compile time, creating a quick feedback loop and enhancing code quality. Utilizing the `EditorRequired` attribute ensures neither you nor anyone from your team will fall into errors due to missing parameters. You can simplify your code by skipping initial parameter value validation. Using the `EditorRequired` attribute leads to robust and predictable component behavior throughout the application.

Let's enhance the `Ticket` component parameters so that Blazor treats them as required. You'll also learn how to configure your IDE so that you can flag any missing required parameters as compilation errors.

Getting ready

Before setting up the required parameters, do the following:

- Create a `Recipe05` directory – this will be your working directory

- Copy the `Ticket` and `Offer` components from the previous recipe or copy their implementation from the `Chapter01/Recipe04` directory of this book's GitHub repository

How to do it...

Ensure parameters are required in your component by following these steps:

1. Navigate to the @code block of the Ticket component and extend attribute collection on parameters with the EditorRequired attribute:

```
@code {
    [Parameter, EditorRequired]
    public string Tariff { get; set; }
    [Parameter, EditorRequired]
    public decimal Price { get; set; }
    [Parameter]
    public EventCallback OnAdded { get; set; }
}
```

2. Now, navigate to the .csproj file of the project where you're keeping your components.

3. Add the RZ2012 code to the WarningsAsErrors section:

```
<Project Sdk="Microsoft.NET.Sdk.Web">
  <PropertyGroup>
    <TargetFramework>net9.0</TargetFramework>
    <ImplicitUsings>enable</ImplicitUsings>
    <WarningsAsErrors>RZ2012</WarningsAsErrors>
  </PropertyGroup>
  <!-- ... -->
</Project>
```

4. In the Offer markup, modify the Ticket instances by removing the OnAdded parameter from both. Additionally, remove the Price parameter from the second instance:

```
<Ticket Tariff="Adult" Price="10.00m" />
<Ticket Tariff="Child" />
```

5. Compile your application so that you can see your IDE flagging the omitted but required Price parameter:

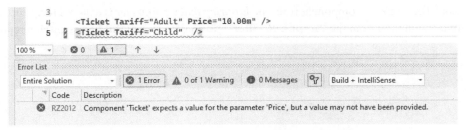

Figure 1.7: IDE flags missing the Price parameter as a compilation error

How it works...

In *step 1*, we enhanced the `Tariff` and `Price` parameters of the `Ticket` component with the `EditorRequired` attribute. This prompts your IDE to expect these values during compilation and flag the missing ones as warnings by default. I suggest that you raise that severity. In *step 2*, you navigated to the `.csproj` file of your project. Here, as outlined in *step 3*, you either found or added the `WarningsAsErrors` section and included the `RZ2012` code within. In *step 4*, we broke the `Offer` markup a little. We removed the `OnAdded` parameter from both `Ticket` instances and the `Price` parameter from one of them. Now, any compilation attempt will end with an error, similar to the one shown in *step 5*. This makes it practically impossible to miss required assignments and encounter related rendering errors. Notice that as we didn't mark the `OnAdded` parameter with the `EditorRequired` attribute, the compiler will treat it as optional and allow it to be skipped.

Passing values from the parent component with CascadingParameter

Sharing parameters across multiple components is a common scenario in web applications. It boosts performance as data can be shared rather than being requested from an external source by each component. It also simplifies the code, especially in parent-child scenarios. In Blazor, that's where the concept of `CascadingParameter` comes into play. Its counterpart, `CascadingValue`, allows you to provide a value that cascades down the component tree. This pair enables child components to receive and use this shared data or state. This approach solves the challenge of passing information through component hierarchies without complex plumbing or tightly coupled communication.

Let's implement a `Cart` service and pass it downward in a cascading fashion so that we can intercept it within the offer area represented by `Ticket` components. We'll also render the `Cart` summary – fully decoupled from the `Ticket` behavior.

Getting ready

Before we start exploring how to pass the cascading value, do the following:

- Create a `Recipe06` directory – this will be your working directory
- Copy the `Ticket` component from the *Ensuring that a parameter is required* recipe or copy its implementation from the `Chapter01/Recipe05` directory of this book's GitHub repository.

How to do it...

Follow these steps to implement `CascadingParameter` for value sharing:

1. Add a `Cart` class and declare supporting `Content` and `Value` properties. Extend `Cart` so that you can communicate state changes by requiring a fallback `Action` property with a primary constructor and implement the basic `Add()` method that triggers this notification:

    ```
    public class Cart(Action onStateHasChanged)
    {
        public List<string> Content { get; init; } = [];
        public decimal Value { get; private set; }
        public int Volume => Content.Count;
        public void Add(string tariff, decimal price)
        {
            Content.Add(tariff);
            Value += price;
            onStateHasChanged.Invoke();
        }
    }
    ```

2. Create a `SellingTickets` component so that our tickets can be sold:

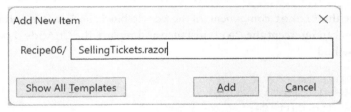

Figure 1.8: Adding a new SellingTickets component

3. Use the `@rendermode` attribute to declare that `SellingTickets` operates in `InteractiveWebAssembly` mode and a `@page` directive to enable routing:

    ```
    @page "/ch01r06"
    @rendermode InteractiveWebAssembly
    ```

4. In the `@code` block of `SellingTickets`, declare the `Cart` object and initialize it within the `OnInitialized()` life cycle method:

    ```
    @code {
        protected Cart Cart;
        protected override void OnInitialized()
        {
            Cart = new(() =>
    ```

```
            InvokeAsync(StateHasChanged));
    }
}
```

5. In the `SellingTickets` markup, add the `CascadingValue` wrapper with the `Cart` instance as its value. Declare two sellable tickets within the cart's operational scope, leveraging the `Ticket` component:

```
<CascadingValue Value="Cart">
    <Ticket Tariff="Adult" Price="10.00m" />
    <Ticket Tariff="Child" Price="5.00m" />
</CascadingValue>
```

6. Below the `Cart` area of the `SellingTickets` markup, append additional markup to display the `Cart` summary:

```
<div class="cart-summary">
    <div class="cart-content">
        Items: @Cart.Volume
    </div>
    <div class="cart-value">Price: @Cart.Value</div>
</div>
```

7. Navigate to the `Ticket` component. In the `@code` block, declare `CascadingParameter` so that you can intercept the `Cart` instance and replace the `OnAdded` parameter with an `Add()` method:

```
@code {
    [CascadingParameter]
    public Cart Cart { get; set; }
    public void Add() => Cart.Add(Tariff, Price);
}
```

8. In the `Ticket` markup, replace the `@onclick` button action so that you can execute the new `Add()` method:

```
<div class="ticket-actions">
    <button @onclick="@Add">Add to cart</button>
</div>
```

How it works...

In *step 1*, we implemented the `Cart` class. We declared a `Value` property to hold the current cart value and a `Content` collection to store added ticket tariffs. We also implemented a parameterless `Volume` method to calculate the amount of tickets currently in the cart. Then, we implemented an `Add()` method that, in addition to the normal logic for adding to the cart, is responsible for communicating those changes to external objects by invoking the `onStateHasChanged` delegate, which is passed using the **primary constructor** pattern. That way, we ensured `Cart` initialization requires us to provide an action to execute upon state changes.

In *step 2*, we created a `SellingTickets` component. In *step 3*, we declared it to render in `InteractiveWebAssembly` mode and leveraged the `@page` directive to enable routing. In *step 4*, in the `@code` block of `SellingTickets`, we declared a `Cart` instance. We initialized `Cart` as part of the overridden `OnInitialized()` life cycle method and, as an invokable `Action` delegate responsible for applying state changes, we passed in the `StateHasChanged()` life cycle method. With that in place, any change in the `Cart` object will prompt Blazor to recalculate DOM changes at the level of the `SellingTicket` component. To avoid any threading or race condition issues, we wrapped the `StateHasChanged()` method in the `InvokeAsync()` component base method. In *step 5*, we implemented the `SellingTickets` markup. We used a `CascadingValue` component and assigned `Cart` as its value. We also declared `CascadingValue` content by adding two `Ticket` instances, representing tickets available for sale. In *step 6*, we extended the `SellingTickets` markup further by adding a section that contained the summary of the cart, showing its current size and value.

In *step 7*, we navigated to the `@code` block of the `Ticket` component and declared `CascadingParameter` there. Blazor will intercept this parameter's value as it cascades from a parent component. Notably, we didn't use `EditorRequired` here – as Blazor resolves the cascading value just in time, it would have no impact on compilation. With `Cart` available in the scope of the `Ticket` component, we replaced the existing `OnAdded` parameter with an `Add()` method that invokes `Cart.Add()` directly. In *step 8*, we updated the `Ticket` markup by replacing the outdated `@onclick` assignment on the existing button with a reference to the newly implemented `Add()` method.

There's more...

So, why does the `Cart` implementation require an `Action` delegate to work? Here, `StateHasChanged()` is a component life cycle method, so it triggers DOM re-rendering scoped to that component and its nested children. Since adding to the cart happens at the `Ticket` component level and invokes `StateHasChanged()`, there's no impact on the parent `SellingTickets` component, and the `Cart` summary section remains unchanged! Having the `Action` delegate allows the `Cart` object to persist a reference to the origin component and thus trigger a DOM update at any level of the component tree.

Creating components with customizable content

Creating components with customizable content in Blazor applications is another level in building flexible and reusable UI elements. This approach allows you to design functional components that can be adapted to various content needs and data types. We'll utilize the `RenderFragment` feature to address it. The `RenderFragment` feature represents a segment of UI content. It allows components to accept arbitrary HTML markup as a parameter. That's how you can achieve higher flexibility. You can repurpose a single component structure with different content, enhancing the modularity and reusability of your code base.

Let's create a `Ticket` component with a customizable display of ticket details while keeping a fixed button so that you can add the ticket to a cart.

Getting ready

Before you start implementing a component with customizable content, do the following:

- Create a `Recipe07` directory – this will be your working directory
- Copy the `Chapter01/Data` directory, which contains the `Samples` and `TicketViewModel` objects required for this recipe, next to the working directory

How to do it...

Follow these steps to build a component with customizable content:

1. Create a new `Ticket` component. We'll use this to display individual ticket details.

2. In the `@code` block of `Ticket`, add the `Id` and `ChildContent` parameters and an `Add()` placeholder method that simply writes a console message displaying the ID of the ticket that was added to the cart:

    ```
    @code {
        [Parameter, EditorRequired]
        public Guid Id { get; set; }
        [Parameter, EditorRequired]
        public RenderFragment ChildContent { get; set; }
        public void Add()
            => Console.WriteLine($"Ticket {Id} added!");
    }
    ```

3. As the `Ticket` markup, render the `ChildContent` value and a button to trigger the `Add()` method:

    ```
    <div class="ticket">
        <div class="ticket-info">@ChildContent</div>
        <div class="ticket-actions">
            <button @onclick="@Add">Add to cart</button>
        </div>
    </div>
    ```

4. Create a routable `Offer` component that renders in `InteractiveWebAssembly` mode. Add a `@using` directive so that the `Samples` object can be referenced:

```
@page "/ch01r07"
@using
    BlazorCookbook.App.Client.Chapters.Chapter01.Data
@rendermode InteractiveWebAssembly
```

5. As markup of the `Offer` component, while leveraging the `Ticket` component, render a `Samples.Adult` ticket tariff and price and a `Samples.FreeAdmission` ticket with just a tariff name since it's free to do so:

```
<Ticket Id="@Samples.Adult.Id">
    @Samples.Adult.Tariff (@Samples.Adult.Price)
</Ticket>
<Ticket Id="@Samples.FreeAdmission.Id">
    <div class="free-ticket">
        @Samples.FreeAdmission.Tariff
    </div>
</Ticket>
```

How it works...

In *step 1*, we created a new `Ticket` component and implemented its `@code` block in *step 2*. Then, we declared a set of required parameters – `Id` to add a ticket to the cart and `ChildContent`, which is of the `RenderFragment` type, to hold the custom markup for a `Ticket` instance. We leveraged the `EditorRequired` attribute and made both parameters required. In *step 3*, we implemented the `Ticket` markup. We embedded the `ChildContent` value to render ticket details by placing it the same as any other parameter. We also added a button that allows the user to add a ticket to the cart by leveraging the `Add()` method.

In *step 4*, we created an `Offer` component. We utilized the `@page` directive to make it routable and declared it so that it rendered in the `InteractiveWebAssembly` mode. On top of that, we added a `@using` directive with the namespace of the `Samples` object so that we could reference it within the `Offer` component (the namespace can vary depending on the structure and name of your solution). In *step 5*, we implemented the `Offer` markup and saw the `RenderFragment` object in action. For an adult ticket with a price tag, we rendered both its tariff and price. For the free admission ticket, we chose to render only the tariff name. Blazor will inject the custom markup in place of the `ChildContent` parameter, within the `Ticket` component, while retaining and reusing the interactive button implementation, regardless of the customized content.

There's more...

You can use a `RenderFragment` object to encapsulate common parts of your components. The testing and maintainability of your code will skyrocket. Another reason to leverage them is that a static `RenderFragment` instance positively impacts performance.

You might have noticed that when a `RenderFragment` parameter is named `ChildContent`, the compiler automatically recognizes and assigns its value. You can still opt to declare `<ChildContent>` `</ChildContent>` explicitly but there's no need to complicate your code.

However, you might encounter scenarios where you need more than one customizable section within a component. Fortunately, Blazor allows you to have multiple `RenderFragment` parameters. To implement that, you must explicitly declare both `RenderFragment` values using markup element syntax within your component. This approach enables even higher modularity and adaptability of your UI. For instance, you could have `Details` and `Actions` content to structure your component with multiple customizable areas. You can see that in the following code blocks.

Here's the `Ticket` component, which allows us to customize the `Details` and `Actions` areas:

```
<div class="ticket">
    <div class="ticket-info">@Details</div>
    <div class="ticket-actions">@Actions</div>
</div>
@code {
    [Parameter, EditorRequired]
    public RenderFragment Details { get; set; }
    [Parameter, EditorRequired]
    public RenderFragment Actions { get; set; }
}
```

Here's the `Ticket` component in action, with customized `Details` and `Actions` areas:

```
<Ticket>
    <Details>
        @Samples.Adult.Tariff (@Samples.Adult.Price)
    </Details>
    <Actions>
        <button @onclick="@(() => Add(Samples.Adult.Id))">
            Add to cart
        </button>
    </Actions>
</Ticket>
```

Making components generic

A **generic class** in C# is a class that's defined with a placeholder type, allowing it to operate with any data type. This flexibility enables the creation of a single class that can adapt its behavior to a variety of data types, enhancing code reusability and efficiency. Generic components in Blazor applications are a similar concept. These components are highly reusable across different contexts and data types. They abstract away specific details, allowing high adaptability to various data or functionalities with minimal changes. This approach significantly reduces code duplication. With that flexibility, you can achieve even higher delivery velocity. The most common scenario where you'll see generic components shine is repetitive data display, especially grids.

Let's create a generic `Grid` component that can render objects of any type by using the provided row template.

Getting ready

Before you start implementing the generic grid, do the following:

- Create a `Recipe08` directory – this will be your working directory
- Copy the `Chapter01/Data` directory, which contains the `Samples` and `TicketViewModel` objects required for this recipe, next to the working directory

How to do it...

Follow these steps to build and use your generic component:

1. Create a `Grid` component. At the top of the file, declare it as generic with the `@typeparam` attribute:

```
@typeparam T
```

2. In the `@code` block of the `Grid` component, declare parameters for data source and table area customization. The source and row template must be generic:

```
@code {
    [Parameter, EditorRequired]
    public IList<T> Data { get; set; }
    [Parameter, EditorRequired]
    public RenderFragment Header { get; set; }
    [Parameter, EditorRequired]
    public RenderFragment<T> Row { get; set; }
}
```

3. For the `Grid` markup, add a standard HTML table with the `Header` content rendered where the table header is. For the table body, iterate over `Data` and render the `Row` template for each element:

```
<table class="grid">
    <thead>
        @Header
    </thead>
    <tbody>
        @foreach (var item in Data)
            @Row(item)
    </tbody>
</table>
```

4. Create a routable `Offer` component that renders in `InteractiveWebAssembly` mode and uses the `Samples` assembly so that `Samples` can be referenced later:

```
@page "/ch01r08"
@using
    BlazorCookbook.App.Client.Chapters.Chapter01.Data
@rendermode InteractiveWebAssembly
```

5. In the `@code` block of `Offer`, implement an `Add()` placeholder method that writes a simple action confirmation to `Console`:

```
public void Add(TicketViewModel ticket)
    => Console.WriteLine($"Ticket {ticket.Id} added!");
```

6. In the markup of the `Offer` component, use the `Grid` component and pass in `Samples.Tickets` as the data source for `Grid`:

```
<Grid Data="@Samples.Tickets">
    @* you will add areas here *@
</Grid>
```

7. Implement the required `Header` area inside the `Grid` instance in the `Offer` markup:

```
<Header>
    <tr>
        <td>Ticket code</td>
        <td>Tariff</td>
        <td>Price</td>
        <td></td>
    </tr>
</Header>
```

8. Inside the `Grid` instance, in the `Offer` markup, implement the required `Row` template so that elements of the `TicketViewModel` type can be rendered:

```
<Row>
    <tr>
        <td>@context.Id</td>
        <td>@context.Tariff</td>
        <td>@context.Price</td>
        <td @onclick="() => Add(context)">
            Add to Cart
        </td>
    </tr>
</Row>
```

How it works...

We started this recipe by implementing the foundation for creating a generic component. In *step 1*, we created a `Grid` component and added the `@typeparam` attribute at the top. We also specified the name for the parameter type placeholder – much like you would in backend development. We chose to call it T. Blazor recognized `@typeparam` and now allows us to operate on T inside the component. The IDE will also apply all validations that generic modules require. In *step 2*, we implemented the `@code` block of the `Grid` component by adding a `Data` parameter that will hold elements to render and two `RenderFragment` parameters, enabling `Grid` customization. You can learn more about `RenderFragment` in the *Creating components with customizable content* section. Notably, the `Data` collection isn't the only generic object. The `Row` parameter, which contains a row template, is also generic, which means it will expect a data object of type T for initialization. In *step 3*, we implemented the `Grid` markup. We rendered the `Header` value inside the `<thead>` tags, where the table header normally goes; for the table body, we used a `foreach` loop to iterate over the `Data` collection and rendered the `Row` template for each element.

In *step 4*, we created a routable `Offer` component to test our grid. As we expected interactivity, we declared that `Offer` rendered in `InteractiveWebAssembly` mode. We also leveraged the `Samples` object, so we exposed the required assembly with the `@using` directive. In *step 5*, we implemented an `Add()` placeholder method within the `@code` block of the `Offer` component to test the `Grid` component's interactivity. In *step 6*, we started implementing the `Offer` markup. We embedded the `Grid` component and passed the `Samples.Tickets` array as the value of the `Data` parameter. In *step 7*, we declared the content of `Header`, which in our case is a set of columns representing `TicketViewModel` properties and an additional column where we placed action buttons. The real rendering magic happened in *step 8*. As the `Row` template expects a `TicketViewModel` object, we can access `TicketViewModel` properties in the markup with a `@context` directive and place them in table columns matching the `Header` declaration.

There's more...

The power of the generic component lies in its agnosticism to the data type you'll use. It simply knows how to construct a template, and where to place customizable content. It's up to you to define markup to present data properties.

You might find yourself in need of nesting multiple generic components. To do so, you'll have to define all required `RenderFragment` parameters. However, a key challenge here is going to be distinguishing each generic context. In that case, you must assign custom names to the context of each generic component using the `Context` parameter. This parameter is inherited automatically, streamlining the process and enhancing the readability of your code.

Even though our example doesn't require nesting, we can still leverage the `Context` naming feature to enhance the code's readability:

```
<Grid Data="@Data.Tickets" Context="ticket">
    ...
    <Row>
        <tr>
            <td>@ticket.Id</td>
            ... *
        </tr>
    </Row>
</Grid>
```

Remember that the more intuitive your code is, the easier it is to navigate and update, especially when you're working in team environments or returning to the code after some time.

Decoupling components with DynamicComponent

Decoupling is a design principle that enhances the flexibility and maintainability of your applications. It comes down to reducing direct dependencies between various parts of your code. Blazor offers an elegant solution for rendering components dynamically. In this recipe, we'll explore the strategic use of `DynamicComponent`. It allows you to render components dynamically at runtime based on certain conditions or parameters. You're not required to specify the component type in the markup at compile time explicitly. Heads up – most compilation validators won't apply here.

Let's implement the fully decoupled and dynamic prompting of success and failure notifications when the user adds a ticket to the cart, based on that ticket's availability.

Getting ready

Before you dive into implementing `DynamicComponent`, do the following:

- Create a `Recipe09` directory – this will be your working directory
- Copy the `Offer` and `Grid` components from the *Making components generic* recipe or copy their implementation from the `Chapter01/Recipe08` directory of this book's GitHub repository
- Copy the `Chapter01/Data` directory, which contains the `Samples` and `TicketViewModel` objects required in this recipe, next to the working directory

How to do it...

Follow these steps to learn how to create more modular and independent components using `DynamicComponent`:

1. Add a new `Alerts` directory to your project.

2. Within the `Alerts` directory, create the `AddedToCart` and `SoldOut` components:

Figure 1.9: Project structure with newly added alert components and sample objects

3. Navigate to the `AddedToCart` component and add a successful alert markup:

```
<div class="alert alert-success" role="alert">
    Added to cart successfully.
</div>
```

4. Navigate to the `SoldOut` component. Declare a `Tariff` parameter and add a danger alert markup by using the `Tariff` value:

```
<div class="alert alert-danger" role="alert">
    Ticket @Tariff is sold out!
</div>
@code {
    [Parameter] public string Tariff { get; set; }
}
```

5. Navigate to the `Offer` component and, in the @code block, declare additional `AlertType` and `AlertParams` variables:

```
protected Type AlertType;
protected Dictionary<string, object> AlertParams;
```

6. Inside the @code block of `Offer`, replace the `Add()` method's implementation to validate ticket availability and display a designated notification:

```
public void Add(TicketViewModel ticket)
{
    AlertType = ticket.AvailableSeats == 0 ?
        typeof(Alerts.SoldOut) :
        typeof(Alerts.AddedToCart);
    AlertParams = new();

    if (ticket.AvailableSeats == 0)
    {
        AlertParams.Add(
            nameof(ticket.Tariff),
            ticket.Tariff
        );
    }
}
```

7. In the `Offer` markup, below the existing `Grid` instance, add a conditional rendering of `DynamicComponent` while leveraging the resolved values of the `AlertType` and `AlertParams` variables:

```
@if (AlertType is null) return;
<DynamicComponent Type="@AlertType"
                  Parameters="@AlertParams" />
```

How it works...

In *step 1*, we added an `Alerts` directory where we could place different alert components. In *step 2*, we created the `AddedToCart` and `SoldOut` components, representing success and failure notifications when adding a ticket to the cart. In *step 3*, we focused on implementing the `AddedToCart` component, which renders an `alert-success` class with an **Added to cart successfully** message. In *step 4*, we implemented the `SoldOut` component, which renders an `alert-danger` class and renders the sold-out ticket tariff.

In *step 5*, we added two critical variables that `DynamicComponent` leverages. The first is `AlertType`, of the `Type` type, which determines the type of component to render. The second is `AlertParams`, a dictionary that allows us to dynamically pass parameter values to the loaded component. In *step 6*, we resolved the state of the requested ticket. We checked seat availability and decided whether to use the `SoldOut` or `AddedToCart` component. When seats are unavailable, we conditionally add the `Tariff` parameter to our dynamic collection of parameters. Finally, in *step 7*, we embedded the `DynamicComponent` component in the `Offer` markup. If the `AlertType` value is unset, we skip rendering it. Otherwise, we append the dynamically resolved markup.

Notice that we utilized the built-in `typeof()` and `nameof()` functions to declare the type and parameters of the current notification. If you want or need to take decoupling even further, you can initialize them purely from `string` variables. That's especially powerful when you're working in architecture such as **micro-frontends**.

2

Synchronous and Asynchronous Data Binding

In this chapter, we will explore various facets of data binding in Blazor. **Binding** is a cornerstone in modern web development. We'll start with the fundamentals of binding values with DOM elements. Then, we will progress to binding specific DOM events, ensuring that your Blazor application is highly interactive and responsive. Most commercial applications will require integration with an external data provider. With that, you will have to perform asynchronous actions. We will explore how to pair them with bindings as well.

Further, we'll cover customizing getters and setters, allowing for greater data handling flexibility. We will also cover the `bind-Value` binding pattern, which should simplify most of your binding scenarios. Lastly, we will implement a commercial scenario of seamless binding with an external data provider. That comes in handy when implementing search modules or data persistence mechanisms.

However, we will fully skip building forms or using Blazor-native components that can simplify binding – we cover that in *Chapter 6*, which covers *building interactive forms*.

By the end of this chapter, you will gain a deep understanding of data binding in Blazor. It will enable you to build more dynamic and user-friendly web applications. All interactivity you'll come to implement will come down to binding. You'll have recipes at hand to handle those synchronous and asynchronous scenarios.

Here's the list of recipes we'll cover in this chapter:

- Binding values with markup elements
- Binding to a specific DOM event
- Performing asynchronous actions after binding
- Customizing get and set binding logic
- Simplifying binding with the `bind-Value` pattern
- Binding with an external data provider

Technical requirements

As we will be exploring fundamental concepts of Blazor and web development, you won't need any paid add-ons or additional tools. You will, however, need the following:

- A modern IDE (of your choice)
- A modern web browser (supporting **WebAssembly**)
- A Blazor project

All the code examples (and data samples) that you'll see next can be found in a dedicated GitHub repository at:

```
https://github.com/PacktPublishing/Blazor-Web-Development-Cookbook/
tree/main/BlazorCookbook.App.Client/Chapters/Chapter02
```

Binding values with markup elements

In this recipe, we introduce the foundational concept of data binding in Blazor applications. This feature bridges the gap between the user interface and the application's data or state. A deep understanding of this concept will allow you to level up the interactivity of your projects. We start with mastering the basics.

Let's bind a simple text field to a backing variable to see the data flowing from the user interface to the backend.

Getting ready

Before you dive into binding, create a `Recipe01` directory – this will be your working directory.

How to do it...

Follow these steps to bind a C# value with a markup element:

1. Add a routable `IntroduceYourself` component that renders in an `InteractiveWebAssembly` mode:

    ```
    @page "/ch02r01"
    @rendermode InteractiveWebAssembly
    ```

2. Inside the `@code` block of `IntroduceYourself`, initialize a `User` variable to store the user input value:

    ```
    @code {
        protected string User = string.Empty;
    }
    ```

3. In the `IntroduceYourself` markup, add a call to action and an input field with a `@bind` attribute assigned to the `User` variable:

```
<h3>What's your name?</h3>
<input class="form-control w-50" @bind="@User" />
```

4. As part of the `IntroduceYourself` markup, construct a little logic to dynamically display a greeting once the user fills the input field:

```
@if (string.IsNullOrWhiteSpace(User)) return;

<hr />
<h1>Hello @User!</h1>
```

How it works...

We kick off the recipe with a routine step in Blazor development – the creation of a new component. In *step 1*, we execute a routine step in Blazor development – we create a new `IntroduceYourself` component and declare its render mode. In our case, we opt for `InteractiveWebAssembly`. In *step 2*, we jump to the `@code` block of `IntroduceYourself` and initialize a `User` backing field – crucial for our data-binding operation.

The actual binding magic starts in *step 3*. We move to the `IntroduceYourself` markup and, next to a call to action, we embed an `input` element and leverage Blazor's native `@bind` attribute for the first time. The `@bind` attribute enables a two-way data binding – not only assigning the input value to the `User` backing field but also ensuring that the UI is updated to reflect this change. In *step 4*, we add another section of the `IntroduceYourself` markup – we display the current `User` value when a user fills the input. That will help us to visualize the behavior of our binding.

The two-way binding, facilitated by the `@bind` attribute, simplifies the implementation of user interactivity. It is a go-to method for most simple binding cases, where you don't need to execute additional logic. Notably, by default, this binding occurs when the user exits the input box, but that's fully customizable. We will explore and clarify this behavior and its underlying mechanics in the next recipe.

Binding to a specific DOM event

Now, we will dive into targeted and efficient handling of user interactions in Blazor applications. While general data binding is crucial, binding specific actions to specific **DOM events** takes your application's interactivity to the next level. This approach allows for a more controlled and responsive user experience. You can directly link an event, such as a click or a key press, to a corresponding C# method or action. You'll learn how to identify and bind to these events and which events are bindable.

Let's implement a simple text field but trigger binding as the user types, not when they exit the field, which is the default behavior.

Getting ready

Before exploring binding on a specific event, do the following:

- Create a `Recipe02` directory – this will be your working directory
- Copy your `IntroduceYourself` component from the *Binding values with markup elements* recipe or copy its implementation from the `Chapter02/Recipe01` directory of the GitHub repository

How to do it...

To bind to a specific DOM event, follow these instructions:

1. Navigate to the `@code` block in your `IntroduceYourself` component.

2. Alongside the existing `User` variable, initialize a new `Greeting` variable. We will use it to hold a greeting for the user:

   ```
   protected string User = string.Empty,
                   Greeting = string.Empty;
   ```

3. Implement the `IsGreetingReady` and `IsUserFilled` methods, which allow you to evaluate the state of the `User` and `Greeting` variables:

   ```
   private bool IsGreetingReady
       => !string.IsNullOrWhiteSpace(Greeting);
   private bool IsUserFilled
       => !string.IsNullOrWhiteSpace(User);
   ```

4. Add a `SayHello()` method that prepares a greeting message:

   ```
   private void SayHello() => Greeting = $"Hello {User}";
   ```

5. In the `IntroduceYourself` markup, extend the input field binding by adding `@bind:event="oninput"`:

   ```
   <input class="form-control w-50"
          @bind="@User"
          @bind:event="oninput" />
   ```

6. Extend the input field binding further by attaching a `SayHello()` behavior to the `@onfocusout` event:

   ```
   <input class="form-control w-50" @bind="@User"
          @bind:event="oninput"
          @onfocusout="@SayHello" />
   ```

7. Remove any existing checks of the User value from the previous implementation and implement a conditional greeting rendering based on the state-checking methods:

```
@if (IsGreetingReady)
{
    <h1>@Greeting</h1>
    return;
}
@if (IsUserFilled)
{
    <h1>Introducing @User...</h1>
}
```

How it works...

In this recipe, we're enhancing the IntroduceYourself component to make it more interactive and engaging. Our goal is to enable the component to greet the user and display the progress of the user name input.

In *step 1*, we navigate to the IntroduceYourself component, and in *step 2*, we go straight to the @code block and initialize an additional Greeting variable to store the generated greeting message. That sets the stage for our dynamic user interaction. In *step 3*, we introduce IsUserFilled and IsGreetingReady parameterless methods that check the state of the User and Greeting variables and allow us to simplify the markup code and make our logic more readable. Moving on to *step 4*, we add another method – SayHello(). We will invoke SayHello() when the user finishes typing their name to generate a greeting and assign it to the Greeting variable. It adds a personalized touch to the user experience.

Step 5 is where we take control of the binding logic. You can trigger binding on any event applicable in script-based frameworks, such as oncopy, onpaste, or onblur. We chose the oninput event for this example. We override the default binding event with @bind:event="oninput" and enable User value live updates as the user types. Notice the lowercase syntax of the @bind:event attribute, as Razor is a case-sensitive language framework. In *step 6*, we take interactivity a step further. We use a native Blazor reference to the @onfocusout event and when the user navigates away from the input field, we invoke the SayHello() method, effectively generating the greeting message.

Finally, in *step 7*, we implement a little rendering logic to ensure that the greeting is displayed only when the user has finished typing. Until then, the message **Introducing...** is generated. That way, we provide a clear indicator of UI interactivity and progress.

There's more...

It's important to know that Blazor allows you to intercept all event arguments. You can accomplish this by adding a parameter that matches the event argument type corresponding to the triggered event.

For instance, let's consider `DragEventArgs`. When a user is dragging elements into or within your application, you can intercept cursor positions and any active keyboard combinations.

Here's how simple it is to intercept a dragging event:

```
public void OnDragging(DragEventArgs args) { /*...*/ }
```

Similarly, with `InputFileChangeEventArgs`, you can access the details of the file that the user has uploaded. It also exposes the `IBrowserFile` object, which you can use to stream the content to your servers.

Here's how you can intercept details of a file uploaded by a user:

```
public void OnFileInput(InputFileChangeEventArgs args)
{
    var droppedFile = args.File;
    // ...
}
```

The capability to intercept specific events and details of those actions opens possibilities for more advanced and nuanced event handling in your Blazor applications.

Performing asynchronous actions after binding

Asynchronous actions are pivotal in modern web applications, especially when dealing with data-intensive operations such as fetching data from an **API** or database. It's also crucial that your application remains responsive as it's executing a long-running task. In this recipe, I'll guide you through data binding when working with asynchronous tasks. You will learn how to integrate asynchronous actions, allowing non-blocking UI updates and smoother user experiences.

Let's enable an **auto-complete** feature on a simple input field and generate a list of suggestions as the user types their name.

Getting ready

Before diving into the auto-complete implementation, do the following:

- Create a `Recipe03` directory – this will be your working directory
- Copy your `IntroduceYourself` component from the *Binding to a specific DOM event* recipe or copy its implementation from the `Chapter02/Recipe02` directory of the GitHub repository
- Next to `Recipe03`, copy the `Chapter02/Data` directory from the GitHub repository, containing the `SuggestionsApi` class required in this recipe

How to do it...

Follow these steps to trigger asynchronous actions after data binding:

1. Open the `Program` file of your application and register the `SuggestionsApi` service to enable communication with the API:

```
builder.Services.AddTransient<SuggestionsApi>();
```

2. Navigate to the `@code` block of the `IntroduceYourself` component and clean up the section, so only the `User` variable is still there:

```
@code {
    protected string User = string.Empty;
}
```

3. Inside the `@code` block, inject the `SuggestionsApi` service and initialize a `Suggestions` collection that will hold the autocomplete results:

```
[Inject] private SuggestionsApi Api { get; init; }
protected IList<string> Suggestions = [];
```

4. Still within the `@code` block, implement a new asynchronous `AutocompleteAsync()` method responsible for calling the API and updating the `Suggestions` collection based on user input:

```
private async Task AutocompleteAsync()
{
    Suggestions = string.IsNullOrWhiteSpace(User) ?
        [] : await Api.FindAsync(User);

    await InvokeAsync(StateHasChanged);
}
```

5. In the `IntroduceYourself` markup, find the `input` field and replace the `@onfocusout` assignment with the `@bind:after` attribute that triggers the `AutocompleteAsync()` method:

```
<input class="form-control w-50" @bind=@User
       @bind:event="oninput"
       @bind:after="@AutocompleteAsync" />
```

6. Below `input`, under the `<hr />` separator, clear out the existing greeting and introduction sections and construct a fast-return when suggestions are currently unavailable:

```
<hr />
@if (!Suggestions.Any()) return;
```

7. Lastly, at the end of the `IntroduceYourself` markup, render the `Suggestions` collection received from the API response.

```
<h5>Did you mean?</h5>
@foreach (var name in Suggestions)
{
    <div>@name</div>
}
```

How it works...

In *step 1*, we add a `SuggestionsApi` service to the **dependency injection** container of our application. That makes `SuggestionsApi` readily available for injection across the application, ensuring we can utilize it wherever needed. Similar to other .NET web frameworks, Blazor can manage services with three lifetimes – singleton, scoped, and transient:

- **Singleton** services are created once per application and shared across all components and requests.

- **Transient** services are created anew each time they are requested, which makes them perfect for lightweight, stateless services (i.e. API integrations).

- **Scoped** services are a little trickier. In client-side applications, scoped services generally behave like singleton services because there is no connection context to differentiate sessions. However, that changes when an `OwningComponentBase` component comes into play. `OwningComponentBase` is a base class for components ensuring that the component and its dependencies are disposed of gracefully when Blazor destroys the component instance.

In *step 2*, we move on to the `IntroduceYourself` component and clear out the greeting implementation, so only the `User` variable remains. In *step 3*, we inject `SuggestionsApi` into our `IntroduceYourself` component and initialize a `Suggestions` collection to store the results from calls we make to the API. Moving on to *step 4*, we implement the `AutocompleteAsync()` asynchronous method, playing a crucial role in simplifying the logic within the markup. `AutocompleteAsync()` checks whether the user has entered any input and calls the API's `FindAsync()` method to fetch suggestions; otherwise, it short-circuits the operation, returning an empty array.

In *step 5*, we enhance the markup of `IntroduceYourself`. We refine the binding logic on the input field, by removing the `@onfocusout` event and replacing it with the `@bind:after` directive, which invokes the `AutocompleteAsync()` method immediately after the binding completes. With this setup, we ensure that a new set of auto-suggestions is requested from the API each time the user modifies the input. Finally, in *step 6* and *step 7*, we introduce additional markup to display the results of the auto-complete operation. We render a list of found names, starting with the same set of characters that the user entered, if the API returns any.

There's more...

In our example, we utilized the `[Inject]` attribute to inject `SuggestionsApi` into a component. However, Blazor provides additional methods for service injection. Let's review all of them:

- You will commonly use the `[Inject]` attribute when injecting services within the `@code` block of a `.razor` file:

```
@code {
    [Inject] private SuggestionsApi Api { get; init; }
}
```

- You would also use the `[Inject]` attribute if you were adopting a code-behind approach, where you separate your Blazor component's logic in a `.cs` file:

```
public partial class IntroduceYourself
{
    [Inject] private SuggestionsApi Api { get; init; }
}
```

- When working in a code-behind fashion, you can also leverage a **constructor injection** pattern and avoid using any attributes at all:

```
public partial class IntroduceYourself(
    SuggestionsApi Api) { }
```

- Lastly, Blazor allows injecting services directly within the component's markup – in that case, you would use the `@inject` directive:

```
@page "/ch02r01"
@inject SuggestionsApi Api
```

All those methods serve the same purpose but accommodate various coding styles and preferences. None is better than the other, so choose what best fits the structure and organization of your code base.

Customizing get and set binding logic

Data binding is not just about connecting a UI element to a data source. It's also about how data is retrieved and updated. Customizing these `get` and `set` operations makes state management and data flow more flexible. In this recipe, I'll guide you through the caveats of using `get` and `set` explicitly and executing asynchronous logic when setting values. These mechanisms will allow you to simplify your code and take even greater control of the interactivity of your Blazor application.

Let's implement a simple text field with explicit `get` and `set` operations so we can execute additional, asynchronous logic as binding is commencing.

Getting ready

This time, we will take a shortcut with preparations for this upcoming recipe:

- Create a `Recipe04` directory – this will be your working directory
- Copy your `IntroduceYourself` component from the *Performing asynchronous actions after binding* recipe or copy its implementation from the `Chapter02/Recipe03` directory of the GitHub repository
- Next to `Recipe04`, copy the `Chapter02/Data` directory from the GitHub repository, containing the objects required in this recipe

How to do it...

To customize `get` and `set` binding logic, follow these instructions:

1. Locate the `input` field within the `IntroduceYourself` component's markup. Keep the `@bind:event` directive but replace others with custom `@bind:get` and `@bind:set` logic:

```
<input class="form-control w-50" @bind:event="oninput"
       @bind:get="@User"
       @bind:set="@AutocompleteAsync" />
```

2. Navigate to the `@code` block of `IntroduceYourself` and adapt the `AutocompleteAsync()` method to align with a setter pattern, enforced by the `@bind:set` directive:

```
private async Task AutocompleteAsync(string value)
{
    User = value;
    Suggestions = string.IsNullOrWhiteSpace(User) ?
        [] : await Api.FindAsync(User);

    await InvokeAsync(StateHasChanged);
}
```

How it works...

In *step 1*, we update the binding logic on the `input` field. We keep the `oninput` event because we want our methods to execute as the user types but we replace the other directives with `@bind:get` and `@bind:set`. We use `@bind:get` to specify where Blazor should retrieve the input value from – which in our case is just a reference to the `User` variable. With the `@bind:set` directive, we define the logic to execute when Blazor binds the input value to the component's state. That's when we trigger the `AutocompleteAsync()` method. At this point, your IDE should highlight a compilation error.

Typically, a `set` method in C# receives a `value` object by default:

```
private string _userName;
public string UserName
{
    get => _userName;
    set => _userName = value;
}
```

In Blazor, the method used for `@bind:set` must follow a similar pattern. The difference is that we can define the name of the incoming `value` object, offering greater control and clarity. So, in *step 2*, we extend `AutocompleteAsync()` by adding a `value` parameter and keeping it in line with the conventional `get-set` pattern. Pay extra attention to the parameter type consistency. Since we bound `input` to the `User` object of type `string`, the `AutocompleteAsync()` method also expects a string. If, for instance, you were binding to an `Age` variable of type `int`, your binding method would need to accept an `int` parameter.

There's more...

So why do `@bind:after` and `@bind:set` both exist if they do virtually the same thing? The execution time of each event is critical. When you need to execute additional logic, often asynchronous, using the default binding operation, `@bind:after`, should be your choice as it spares you the complexity of persisting the incoming value manually. On the other hand, `@bind:set` provides more flexibility as it's executed upon setting the binding value. It enables the integration of validation logic, including asynchronous operations, into the binding process. Crucially, `@bind:set` allows you to assess the incoming value and, based on the outcome of any validation, decide whether to discard or accept it before it becomes part of the component state. Both features are invaluable for ensuring data integrity and implementing sophisticated validation mechanisms in your Blazor applications.

Simplifying binding with the bind-Value pattern

The `bind-Value` pattern is a game-changer in simplifying the linking process of your UI elements to data properties. It enhances the clarity and conciseness of your code by reducing the boilerplate often associated with handling two-way data binding. In this recipe, I will guide you through a practical example, showcasing the pattern's utility in creating more maintainable and simple code, ultimately enhancing your development workflow.

Let's implement a component that allows binding directly to its parameters in a structure similar to the standard binding to HTML elements.

Getting ready

Before we start implementing a component that enables the `bind-Value` pattern, do the following:

- Create a `Recipe05` directory – this will be your working directory
- Next to `Recipe05`, copy the `Chapter02/Data` directory from the GitHub repository, containing `SkillLevel` and `DataSeed`, required in this recipe

How to do it...

Follow these steps to apply the `bind-Value` binding pattern:

1. Create an `IntroductionForm` component and add the required assembly reference at the top:

    ```
    @using BlazorCookbook.App.Client.Chapters.Chapter02.Data
    ```

2. In the `@code` block of `IntroductionForm`, declare a `string` parameter for Name. Alongside it, add `EventCallback<string>` to communicate changes to the Name value:

    ```
    [Parameter]
    public string Name { get; set; }
    [Parameter]
    public EventCallback<string> NameChanged { get; set; }
    ```

3. Similarly, right below `Name` and `NameChanged`, add a `Skill` and an `EventCallback<SkillLevel>` parameters to manage the skill level state:

    ```
    [Parameter]
    public SkillLevel Skill { get; set; }
    [Parameter]
    public EventCallback<SkillLevel> SkillChanged { get; set; }
    ```

4. Still within the `@code` block, implement a method invoking the `NameChanged` callback and propagating changes to the Name value:

    ```
    private Task OnNameChanged()
        => NameChanged.InvokeAsync(Name);
    ```

5. Lastly, complete the `@code` block with another method, handling changes of the `Skill` value, that retrieves the `ChangeEventArgs` parameter and sets the skill level based on the resolved value and underlying `DataSeed.SkillLevels` data source:

    ```
    private Task OnSkillChanged(ChangeEventArgs args)
    {
        var id = int.Parse(args.Value.ToString());
        var skill = DataSeed.SkillLevels
    ```

```
        .SingleOrDefault (it => it.Id == id);
    return SkillChanged.InvokeAsync(skill);
}
```

6. In the `IntroductionForm` markup, below `@using`, add a section where the user can input their name. Declare the binding to occur on the `oninput` event and set it to trigger the `OnNameChanged` method after the binding is complete:

```
<h5>What's your name?</h5>
<input class="form-control w-50 mb-1" @bind="@Name"
       @bind:event="oninput"
       @bind:after=@OnNameChanged />
```

7. Add another markup section below allowing you to select the user's skill level. Utilize the `DataSeed.SkillLevels` data source to populate the selection options and ensure that the binding of selection changes occurs with the `onchange` event:

```
<h5>What's your skill level?</h5>
<select class="form-control w-50 mb-1"
        @onchange="@OnSkillChanged">
    <option value="0">-</option>
    @foreach (var level in DataSeed.SkillLevels)
    {
        <option value="@level.Id">
            @level.Title
        </option>
    }
</select>
```

8. Create a new `IntroduceYourself` routable component, rendering in an `InteractiveWebAssembly` mode, and reference the data objects assembly:

```
@using BlazorCookbook.App.Client.Chapters.Chapter02.Data
@page "/ch02r05"
@rendermode InteractiveWebAssembly
```

9. In the `@code` block, initialize `Name` and `Skill` variables to capture the user input and generate the greeting:

```
protected string Name { get; set; }
protected SkillLevel Skill { get; set; }
```

10. Still within the @code block, implement an `IsGreetingReady` method, allowing you to check whether the greeting is ready to render:

```
private bool IsGreetingReady
    => !string.IsNullOrWhiteSpace(Name)
    && Skill is not null;
```

11. In the `IntroduceYourself` markup, embed `IntroductionForm` and leverage the `bind-Value` pattern to dynamically bind the `Name` and `Skill` parameters to the corresponding target variables:

```
<IntroductionForm @bind-Name="@Name"
                  @bind-Skill="@Skill" />
```

12. Complete the `IntroduceYourself` markup by adding a section separator and conditional rendering of the user greeting, when it's ready:

```
<hr />
@if (!IsGreetingReady) return;
<h5>Welcome @Name on level @Skill.Title!</h5>
```

How it works...

In *step 1*, we create an `IntroductionForm` component and reference the assembly with sample data at the top. In *step 2*, we define a pair of parameters of type `string` and `EventCallback<string>`, that we will bind to the form, and we intentionally call them `Name` and `NameChanged` respectively. In *step 3*, we add a similar pair to handle the skill level and name them `Skill` and `SkillChanged` respectively. The pairing of a value of type T and a matching `EventCallback<T>` handler forms the basis of the `bind-Value` pattern. Similar to recognizing `ChildContent` implicitly, when working with `RenderFragment`, Blazor's code generators recognize T and `EventCallback<T>` and compile the @bind-Value directive. In *step 4*, we declare an `OnNameChanged()` method to invoke the intended `EventCallback` and propagate the changes in `Name`. To handle value changes of the `Skill` parameter, we implement a bit more complex logic in *step 5*. We intercept a `ChangeEventArgs` object that carries the selected option's value, which we use to retrieve the corresponding `SkillLevel` object from the `DataSeed.SkillLevels` collection. We then pass this value to the intended `EventCallback` handler.

With the logic in place, in *step 6*, we proceed to the `IntroductionForm` markup. We add a simple `input` field and bind it to the `Name` parameter. We also hook up the `OnNameChanged()` method, so it's triggered after the binding completes. In *step 7*, we construct a `select` field to allow the user to choose their skill level. We render a neutral option, displaying -, and skill options from the `DataSeed.SkillLevels` collection. We wire the @onchanged event of the `select` field to the `OnSkillChanged()` method.

In *step 8*, we create a routable `IntroduceYourself` component that renders in an `InteractiveWebAssembly` mode. We also reference the sample data assembly, leveraging the `@using` directive. In *step 9*, we initialize a `@code` block within the `IntroduceYourself` component and declare `Name` and `Skill` backing properties for binding and generating the user's greeting. In *step 10*, we implement a simple `IsGreetingReady` method that checks whether both `Name` and `Skill` have meaningful values and a greeting can be safely generated.

In *step 11*, we jump to the `IntroduceYourself` markup and witness the `bind-Value` pattern in action. Since `IntroductionForm` exposes `Name` and `Skill` parameters with pattern-matching event callbacks, we can dynamically bind them using `@bind-Name` and `@bind-Skill`. Your IDE will recognize this pattern automatically and should even suggest these directives. We finalize the markup in *step 12* by adding a conditional rendering of a greeting message built from the current `Name` and `Skill` values.

The `bind-Value` pattern encapsulates binding logic and validation within a component, greatly simplifying unit testing and enhancing the parent component's cleanliness and robustness. It only requires the parent component to provide backing variables, streamlining the development process. It's even more powerful as all the binding directives that we've covered (`@bind:after`, `@bind:get`, `@bind:set`), you can also pair with the `bind-Value` pattern.

Binding with an external data provider

When building web applications that interact with external data sources, it's common to trigger API calls in response to user input. However, this can lead to a flood of requests, straining the API and degrading the user's experience. To address that challenge, we'll implement input **throttling** – a technique that moderates the rate at which requests are sent based on user input. In this recipe, I will guide you through setting up input throttling in a Blazor component, ensuring efficient and responsible usage of external APIs. You'll create more robust and user-friendly applications capable of handling a heavy load of user interactions without overwhelming your data providers.

Let's implement a simple text field that uses throttling to limit calls to the external API and seamlessly waits for a user to finish typing.

Getting ready

Before you dive into throttling implementation, do the following:

- Create a `Recipe06` directory – this will be your working directory
- Next to `Recipe06`, copy the `Chapter02/Data` directory from the GitHub repository, containing a `SuggestionsApi` class required in this recipe
- Copy the `IntroduceYourself` component from the `Chapter02/Recipe03` directory of the GitHub repository

How to do it...

To implement throttling when calling an external API, follow these steps:

1. Open the `Program` file of your application and register the `SuggestionsApi` service to enable communication with the API:

   ```
   builder.Services.AddTransient<SuggestionsApi>();
   ```

2. Enhance the `IntroduceYourself` component with the implementation of the `IDisposable` interface using the `@implements` directive, below the `@rendermode` directive:

   ```
   @rendermode InteractiveWebAssembly
   @implements IDisposable
   ```

3. Inside the `@code` block of the `IntroduceYourself` component, declare the `Timer` variable and two `TimeSpan` variables – for throttling and overall timeout:

   ```
   private Timer _debounceTimer;
   private readonly TimeSpan
       _throttle = TimeSpan.FromMilliseconds(500),
       _timeout = TimeSpan.FromMinutes(1);
   ```

4. Still within the `@code` block, implement an `OnUserInput()` method with a proxy logic that uses the `Timer` and `TimeSpan` variables to throttle the API requests encapsulated inside the `AutocompleteAsync()` method:

   ```
   private void OnUserInput()
   {
       _debounceTimer?.Dispose();
       _debounceTimer = new Timer(
           _ => InvokeAsync(AutocompleteAsync),
           null, _throttle, _timeout);
   }
   ```

5. To complete the `@code` block, implement the `Dispose()` lifecycle method, required by the `IDisposable` interface, and explicitly dispose of the `_debounceTimer` instance:

   ```
   public void Dispose() => _debounceTimer?.Dispose();
   ```

6. In the `IntroduceYourself` markup, update the `@bind:after` directive to invoke the `OnUserInput()` method, where we've added the throttling logic:

   ```
   <input class="form-control w-50" @bind=@User
          @bind:event="oninput"
          @bind:after="@OnUserInput" />
   ```

How it works...

In *step 1*, we register the SuggestionsApi service in the application's dependency injection container. If you're following along with the entire chapter, you might already have SuggestionsApi there.

In *step 2*, with the help of the @implements directive, we enhance the IntroduceYourself component with an IDisposable pattern. In Blazor, the IDisposable interface is used to release unmanaged resources or detach event handlers when disposing of a component. IDisposable requires the implementation of a Dispose() method, which Blazor will then automatically invoke when a component is removed from the UI, ensuring proper cleanup and preventing memory leaks. Without the Dispose() method in place, your IDE will highlight compilation errors. We will address that in subsequent steps.

In *step 3*, we lay the groundwork for throttling logic. In the @code block of the IntroduceYourself component, we initialize two key variables: _throttle, which defines the idle time (500 milliseconds in our example) between user interactions and API calls, and _timeout, which sets an overall timeout for the external communication. We also declare a _debounceTimer variable of type Timer, which is the backbone of managing the frequency of API calls. The Timer class wraps a scheduler that delays the execution of a method for a specified time, making it ideal for throttling. In *step 4*, still within the @code block, we implement an OnUserInput() method with throttling proxy logic. First, we stop the currently scheduled operation, by disposing of the _debounceTimer instance, to avoid any overlapping executions. Next, we instantiate a new Timer object, wrapping the existing AutocompleteAsync() method within the InvokeAsync() method for thread safety. As we don't need to maintain any state between timer invocations, we pass null for the state object and complete the _debounceTimer initialization with the _throttle and _timeout variables. In *step 5*, we complete the @code block by implementing the missing Dispose() method to gracefully dispose of the _debounceTimer instance. The compilation errors should now be gone.

Lastly, in *step 6*, we slightly update the input field in the IntroduceYourself markup. Rather than invoking AutocompleteAsync() after the binding completes, we update the @bind:after attribute to invoke the OnUserInput() method, containing our throttling logic. Now, every keystroke goes through the throttling mechanism, optimizing application responsiveness and reducing the load on the external API.

3

Taking Control of Event Handling

In this chapter, we'll dive into the world of event handling within Blazor applications. An **event** is a fundamental building block that signifies an action within the browser, such as clicks, inputs, or page loads. Events allow developers to execute specific code upon user interactions – creating an interactive and dynamic user experience.

We'll start by exploring how to hook into event delegates, laying the foundation for event management. Next, we'll discuss delegating responsibilities using `EventCallback` and lambda expressions that increase flexibility in event handling.

We'll also cover essential strategies for controlling event propagation and preventing the triggering of default events. These skills are vital for creating intuitive user interfaces where you have complete control over user interactions. Furthermore, we introduce the concept of custom events, expanding the possibilities for an **event-driven** application design.

A key focus will be on understanding how events trigger rendering in Blazor. This understanding is crucial for optimizing application performance and ensuring a seamless user experience. By the end of this chapter, you'll have a thorough understanding of event handling in Blazor and have gained the practical skills to apply these concepts effectively in your web development projects.

Here's the list of recipes we'll cover in this chapter:

- Hooking into event delegates
- Delegating with lambda expressions
- Delegating with `EventCallback`
- Preventing default event actions
- Controlling event propagation
- Introducing custom events
- Handling long-running events

Technical requirements

The aim of this chapter is to keep the examples straightforward and focus on the principles of event handling in Blazor. With that said, you won't need any additional tools, just these basics:

- A modern IDE (that supports Blazor development)
- .NET 9 installed on your development machine
- A modern web browser (that supports WebAssembly)
- A Blazor project (where you'll write code as you go along)

All the code examples (and data samples) that you'll see can be found in a dedicated GitHub repository at: `https://github.com/PacktPublishing/Blazor-Web-Development-Cookbook/tree/main/BlazorCookbook.App.Client/Chapters/Chapter03`. In each recipe that needs any samples, I will also point you to the directory where you can find them.

Hooking into event delegates

UI events are the cornerstone of user interaction on the web – signaling every click, scroll, or keyboard press and enabling you to craft an interactive application. An event delegate acts as a bridge between the browser and your code. Each user interaction triggers a designated handler that executes a predefined action. In this recipe, we will dive into the mechanics of event delegates, illustrating how they are detected and managed within a Blazor application.

Let's create a page, where users can display and hide a list of tickets by clicking a button.

Getting ready

Before you implement a clickable button, do the following:

- Create a `Chapter03/Recipe01` directory – this will be your working directory
- Copy `Ticket` and `Tickets` sample files from the `Chapter03/Data` directory in the GitHub repository

How to do it...

Follow these steps to implement a basic event delegate hook:

1. Create a new routable `TicketManager` component that renders in `InteractiveWebAssembly` mode:

```
@page "/ch03r01"
@rendermode InteractiveWebAssembly
```

2. Add the `@code` section to your `TicketManager` component. Declare a `ShowTickets` property of type `bool` that will determine the visibility of the ticket list:

```
@code {
    protected bool ShowTickets { get; set; }
}
```

3. Additionally, still inside the `@code` block, implement a method to toggle the `ShowTickets` property to change the ticket list's visibility:

```
private void ToggleTickets()
    => ShowTickets = !ShowTickets;
```

4. In the markup area of the `TicketManager` component, introduce a button that leverages the `ToggleTickets()` method and allows the user to update the UI accordingly:

```
<button class="btn btn-sm btn-success"
    @onclick="@ToggleTickets">
    Toggle Tickets
</button>
```

5. Below the button, based on the current value of the `ShowTickets` property, conditionally skip displaying the list of tickets or render the horizontal separator, indicating where the tickets area starts:

```
@if (!ShowTickets) return;
<hr />
```

6. Under the horizontal separator, render the list of tickets, utilizing the `Tickets.All` collection, from the copied sample data, as your data source:

```
@foreach (var ticket in Tickets.All)
{
    <div class="d-flex justify-content-between mb-1"
        id="ticket-@ticket.Id">

        <div>@ticket.Title</div>

    </div>
}
```

How it works...

We begin the implementation by creating a routable `TicketManager` component, as outlined in *step 1*. We declare the navigable path with the `@page` directive. We also declare an interactive render mode as we will need our button to be actionable. Next, in *step 2*, we introduce a backing `ShowTickets` property. This property serves as a flag indicating the current visibility state of the ticket list – either displayed or hidden. Then, in *step 3*, we introduce a `ToggleTickets()` method designed to toggle the `ShowTickets` property.

We implement the core of interactivity in *step 4* by hooking into the event callback mechanism of Blazor. We add a button in the component's markup to give users the power to control the display state of the ticket list. With `@onclick`, we can trigger our `ToggleTickets()` method when an `onclick` event occurs.

In *step 5*, we check the value of the `ShowTickets` property and decide whether to skip rendering the ticket list entirely. For cases when we render the list, we add a `<hr />` tag to clearly indicate where the tickets area starts. In *step 6*, we iterate over the `Tickets.All` sample collection and render all available ticket titles in a flexible `div` container. With this setup, `TicketManager` reacts to user interactions and either renders or hides the ticket list, as dictated by the current value of the `ShowTickets` property.

There's more...

Blazor offers seamless integration with `onclick`, `ondrag`, `oncopy`, and other HTML events you're already familiar with, allowing for dynamic and interactive web application development. By prefixing the event name with the @ symbol, you signal to Blazor that you're employing a Blazor-specific event rather than a standard HTML event. This distinction is crucial for harnessing the full power of Blazor's event system.

One of the key advantages of using Blazor events is their ability to update the DOM in real time. Blazor employs a native **diffing algorithm**, which calculates precisely which parts of the DOM have changed and updates only those parts. This results in a significantly smaller payload when communicating with the server and faster rendering times regardless of the selected render mode.

It's important to note that Blazor rendering is typically triggered only upon the initial render of a component or when you explicitly invoke the `StateHasChanged()` lifecycle method. If we explore deeper, HTML event counterparts in Blazor are actually instances of `EventCallback<T>` (complete with event arguments). A closer look at the `EventCallback` implementation reveals that it invokes the `HandleEventAsync()` method of the `Receiver` object:

```
public Task InvokeAsync(object? arg)
{
    if (Receiver == null)
    {
```

```
        return EventCallbackWorkItem
            .InvokeAsync<object?>(Delegate, arg);
    }
    return Receiver
        .HandleEventAsync(
            EventCallbackWorkItem(Delegate),arg);
}
```

In most cases, our receiver inherits from ComponentBase. Intriguingly, the ComponentBase. HandleEventAsync() method automatically invokes StateHasChanged(). As a result, the component's state updates without requiring manual intervention:

```
Task IHandleEvent.HandleEventAsync(
    EventCallbackWorkItem callback, object? arg)
{
    // ...
    StateHasChanged();
    // ...
}
```

Delegating with lambda expressions

In this recipe, we will explore the power of **lambda expressions** in .NET and their pivotal role in Blazor event handling. In the simplest terms, a lambda expression is an anonymous method that follows a specific syntax. These expressions are a cornerstone of functional programming in .NET and offer a streamlined approach to writing inline delegate implementations. When it comes to Blazor, delegating with lambda expressions becomes particularly advantageous. They come in handy for defining event handlers and callbacks directly within the markup. They also enable you to intercept incoming parameters and a current operational context.

Let's leverage lambda expressions and add a few more actions to the tickets list, allowing us to modify the state of a given ticket.

Getting ready

Before you dive into delegating with lambda expressions, do the following:

- Create a Chapter03/Recipe02 directory – this will be your working directory
- Copy the TicketManager component from the *Hooking into event delegates* recipe or from the Chapter03/Recipe01 directory in the GitHub repository
- Copy Ticket and Tickets sample files from the Chapter03/Data directory in the GitHub repository

How to do it...

Follow these steps to see the power of delegating with lambda expressions:

1. Navigate to the @code block of TicketManager and, below the existing code, initialize an object of type Ticket to store the details of the currently selected ticket:

    ```
    protected Ticket SelectedTicket;
    ```

2. Below, still within the @code block, implement a Show() method that enables setting the value of the currently selected ticket:

    ```
    private void Show(Ticket ticket)
        => SelectedTicket = ticket;
    ```

3. Jump to the TicketManager markup and extend the rendering of ticket details by adding two action buttons below the Title section and attaching their actions with lambda expressions:

    ```
    <div>@ticket.Title</div>
    <div>
        <button class="btn btn-sm btn-success"
                @onclick=@(() => Show(ticket))>
            Show details
        </button>
        <button class="btn btn-sm btn-success"
                @onclick=@(() => ticket.Stock += 5)>
            Top up
        </button>
    </div>
    ```

4. Below the loop rendering ticket details, check whether the user has already set the SelectedTicket value and conditionally skip the specific ticket details rendering:

    ```
    @if (SelectedTicket is null) return;
    <hr />
    ```

5. For the case where the SelectedTicket variable has a value, render the ticket title, price, and availability. Ensure that this section only becomes visible when the value of SelectedTicket is available:

    ```
    <div>Title: @SelectedTicket.Title</div>
    <div>Price: @SelectedTicket.Price</div>
    <div>Stock: @SelectedTicket.Stock</div>
    ```

How it works...

In *step 1*, we navigate to the @code block of TicketManager and initialize a SelectedTicket variable that will hold a reference to the currently selected ticket. Next, in *step 2*, we implement a Show() method, which accepts Ticket as a parameter. The singular responsibility of the Show() method is to update the SelectedTicket reference.

In *step 3*, we shift to the TicketManager markup where we iterate over the Tickets.All collection from the sample and render each ticket title. Below the section with Title, we add two buttons enabling administrative actions, leveraging the delegation with lambda expressions. With the first button, we allow a user to display a given ticket's details by attaching the Show() method to the button's @onclick event and passing over a reference to the currently iterated ticket object. Here, the use of lambda expressions allows implementing precise and context-aware actions. The second button enables the user to top up the ticket stock. This time, we use an **anonymous lambda expression** – a lambda expression that encapsulates the operation itself rather than delegating to an existing method. We access the Stock property of each ticket as we iterate over the Tickets.All sample collection and increment the Stock value by 5 directly within the markup.

However, with the flexibility and power of lambda expressions comes great responsibility. Minimizing the amount of C# code within the markup is good practice. Use a strongly typed method to encapsulate complex and lengthy lambda expressions and maintain the clarity of your code.

In *step 4*, we extend the TicketManager markup further. Similar to checking the ShowTickets value and conditionally displaying the list of tickets (that we implemented in the *Hooking into event delegates* recipe), we check whether the user set the value of SelectedTicket and conditionally skip the rendering of the specific ticket details. We conclude the implementation in *step 5* by adding a simple markup to render the Title, Price, and Stock properties of the ticket that the user selects. As Blazor converts the lambda expression to an EventCallback object, users will see updates of the Stock property value immediately after each **Top Up** button click.

See also

If you're interested in learning more about the roles and capabilities of lambda expressions, visit the Microsoft Learn section:

```
https://learn.microsoft.com/en-us/dotnet/csharp/language-reference/
operators/lambda-expressions
```

Delegating with EventCallback

In this recipe, we explore event delegation with the help of EventCallback. EventCallback in Blazor is a mechanism that enables components to listen for and react to user-generated events or interactions, tying closely with the framework's architectural design. This Blazor-native feature empowers developers to write cleaner, more efficient code by seamlessly integrating with the component lifecycle and the overall application state. The primary benefit of event callbacks is their ability to automatically manage UI updates through the `StateHasChanged()` method, ensuring that the user interface remains in sync with the application's state. `EventCallback` is also a null-safe object – when it's not assigned but invoked, it safely skips rather than throwing `NullReferenceException`. You will see `EventCallback` in all the recipes in this chapter, as it's a building block of most interactivity in Blazor.

Let's implement a component where we encapsulate administrative ticket actions with the help of `EventCallback` parameters. With that component, we will also simplify the markup of the ticket list.

Getting ready

Before we implement delegation with `EventCallback`, do the following:

- Create a `Chapter03/Recipe03` directory – this will be your working directory
- Copy the `TicketManager` component from the *Delegating with lambda expressions* recipe or from the `Chapter03/Recipe02` directory in the GitHub repository
- Copy the `Ticket` and `Tickets` sample files from the `Chapter03/Data` directory in the GitHub repository

How to do it...

Follow these steps to implement an article management system using `EventCallback` delegates:

1. Create a new `TicketOptions` component.
2. Initialize the `@code` block in `TicketOptions` and declare three required parameters, each of type `EventCallback`, corresponding to the different administrative actions:

```
@code {
    [Parameter, EditorRequired]
    public EventCallback OnShow { get; set; }
    [Parameter, EditorRequired]
    public EventCallback OnTopUp { get; set; }
    [Parameter, EditorRequired]
    public EventCallback OnRemove { get; set; }
}
```

3. Jump to the `TicketOptions` markup and construct buttons allowing a user to invoke `OnShow`, `OnTopUp`, and `OnRemove` actions:

```
<button class="btn btn-sm btn-success"
        @onclick="@OnShow">
    Show
```

```
    </button>
    <button class="btn btn-sm btn-info"
            @onclick="@OnTopUp ">
        Top up
    </button>
    <button class="btn btn-sm btn-danger"
            @onclick="@OnRemove">
        Remove
    </button>
```

4. Navigate to the `TicketManager` component.

5. Within the `@code` block of `TicketManager`, implement two new methods allowing you to remove and top up the stock of a `Ticket` object:

```
private void TopUp(Ticket ticket)
    => ticket.Stock += 5;
private void Remove(Ticket ticket)
    => Tickets.All.Remove(ticket);
```

6. In the `TicketManager` markup, replace the existing action buttons in the ticket details with the `TicketOptions` instance:

```
<div>@ticket.Title</div>
<div>
    <TicketOptions
        OnShow="@(() => Show(ticket))"
        OnTopUp="@(() => TopUp(ticket))"
        OnRemove="@(() => Remove(ticket))" />
</div>
```

How it works...

In *step 1*, we create a new `TicketOptions` component. In *step 2*, we initialize the `@code` block in `TicketOptions` and declare three required `EventCallback` parameters that will carry the action delegates necessary for triggering administrative ticket actions. Next, in *step 3*, we construct the `TicketOptions` markup with three buttons, each invoking `OnShow`, `OnTopUp`, or `OnRemove` parameters when users click them. Notice that we attach the `EventCallback` parameters directly to the `@onclick` event of each button. We don't need to add additional methods that will act as proxies. Blazor will seamlessly link UI interactions with our predefined actions.

In *step 4*, we navigate to the `TicketManager` component. In *step 5*, we extend the `@code` block of `TicketManager` with two additional methods. First, we implement a `TopUp()` method, that increments the current ticket `Stock` property value by 5. Next, we implement a `Remove()` method that simply removes a given ticket from the `Tickets.All` collection. In *step 6*, we locate the `TicketManager` markup area where we render primitive action buttons for each ticket. We replace those buttons with the `TicketOptions` markup and attach respective actions to each of the required `EventCallback` parameters.

There's more...

With the `TicketOptions` component in place, we've significantly simplified the `TicketsManager` markup code. We've refactored ticket-related actions in a more organized and readable manner, making the overall code base cleaner and easier to maintain.

But, since `TicketOptions` acts only as an action proxy and is not based on a `Ticket` reference, we effectively create new delegate instances, wrapping the actionable method inside, every time we render the `TicketOptions` component. This operation might come with a performance penalty even with all the C# optimization magic. In simple applications, the performance impact will likely be negligible. However, you must keep this in mind when working with data-heavy or highly reactive systems.

Preventing default event actions

In this recipe, we explore the mechanics of browsers automatically executing specific actions in response to user events. Default event actions can include form submission when the return key is pressed or navigating to a link's URL when it's clicked. However, there are scenarios in Blazor applications where you might need to intercept these automatic behaviors to control the user experience. Whether to manage form validation, confirm user intentions, or manage dynamic content updates without refreshing the page, preventing default actions becomes essential. I will guide you through stopping these default behaviors programmatically within your application.

Let's implement a fast ticket creation feature, where we will intercept and apply custom logic with each key store a user makes.

Getting ready

Before exploring how to intercept and prevent default event actions, do the following:

- Create a `Chapter03/Recipe04` directory – this will be your working directory
- Copy `TicketManager` and `TicketOptions` from the *Delegating with event callbacks* recipe or from the `Chapter03/Recipe03` directory in the GitHub repository
- Copy `Ticket`, `Tickets`, and `Extensions` files from the `Chapter03/Data` directory in the GitHub repository

How to do it...

Go through the process of preventing default event actions by following these steps:

1. Navigate to the @code block of TicketManager and initialize a new Creator variable below the existing code:

```
internal string Creator = string.Empty;
```

2. Below the Creator variable, still in the @code block, implement a MonitorCreation() method that intercepts a KeyboardEventArgs parameter, resolves its payload, and creates a new ticket instance when the user hits the + symbol on the keyboard:

```
private void MonitorCreation(KeyboardEventArgs args)
{
    if (args.Key == "+")
    {
        Tickets.All.Add(new() { Title = Creator });
        Creator = string.Empty;
        return;
    }
    if (args.IsBackspace() && Creator.Length > 0)
    {
        Creator = Creator[..^1];
        return;
    }
    if (args.IsLetter())
    {
        Creator += args.Key;
        return;
    }
}
```

3. Jump over to the TicketManager markup. Below the render mode declaration at the top, construct a ticket creation area by adding a section header and an input with the MonitorCreation() method attached to its @onkeydown event, preventing the default @onkeydown behavior:

```
<h5>Quick creation</h5>
<p>
    <input value="@Creator"
           @onkeydown="MonitorCreation"
           @onkeydown:preventDefault />
</p>
```

How it works...

In *step 1*, we navigate to the @code block of TicketManager and initialize a Creator variable that will hold the current text that the user inputs in the fast ticket creation field. We will construct the creation field itself in a moment.

In *step 2*, next to the Creator variable, we implement a MonitorCreation() method, where we will put the custom @onkeydown logic for Blazor to execute instead of the default one. The MonitorCreation() method receives a KeyboardEventArgs object, having a Key property that we need for our custom creation logic. First, we check whether the clicked symbol matches the + key and add a new Ticket object to the Tickets.All collection. Next, we leverage the IsBackspace() extension method from the Extensions file provided with data samples. If the user clicks the backspace button and the Creator length indicates there are characters to remove, we remove the last character from the Creator value using the **range operator**. Lastly, we leverage another custom extension method from the Extensions file – IsLetter() – to check whether what the user pressed on their keyboard is in fact a letter and append it at the end of the current Creator value. With that implementation, we ignore all other keyboard actions. I strongly encourage you to experiment and add numbers support on your own!

In *step 3*, we jump to the TicketManager markup and build a section where users can fast-create new tickets. We add a **Quick creation** header, so it's obvious what the intention of the input below is. And finally, we construct the input field where all the event-preventing happens. We set the input value to reflect the value of Creator. Notice, that we don't leverage any binding here (more about binding in *Chapter 2*). Next, we attach the MonitorCreation() method to the @onkeydown event of the input so Blazor seamlessly triggers our custom logic. But @onkeydown has browser-default logic, conflicting with what we just attached. Here, we employ @onkeydown:preventDefault, instructing Blazor to bypass any default key-down behavior.

There's more...

All the events in Blazor behave virtually the same, regardless of the render mode you use. However, some events, like @onkeydown, are inherently client-side in their expected result – responding immediately to user input. When using @onkeydown in InteractiveServer mode, you must consider that each event trigger will travel to the server and back before it's reflected on the UI. In higher-latency scenarios, this round-trip can result in flaky and unstable behavior of the UI. Always consider the nature of the events you're choosing and the appropriate render mode to ensure that your application remains user-friendly.

When building an internationally available application, you may need to support special local characters that require specific key combinations, such as using *Alt* + *a* to produce the letter ą in Polish. To handle these cases effectively, Blazor provides the ability to manage keyboard composition events.

```
private void MonitorCreation(KeyboardEventArgs args)
{
    if (args.IsComposing) return;
```

```
        //rest of the processing logic obscured for simplicity
}
```

You can track the composition state of the input using the `IsComposing` property in `KeyboardEventArgs`. When `IsComposing` is set to `true`, it indicates that the user is entering a composite character. You should delay processing the input until `IsComposing` returns to `false`.

Controlling event propagation

In this recipe, we explore the process of controlling how events travel through the **Document Object Model (DOM)** within Blazor applications. Stopping default event propagation becomes crucial when we work with nested components or elements. You can ensure events such as clicks, hovers, or keyboard inputs have localized effects – thereby avoiding unintended ripple effects or behaviors in the UI. By mastering the control of event propagation, you can fine-tune interaction patterns within your application, leading to a smoother and more intuitive user experience.

Let's allow users to click anywhere on the ticket record to display its details while ensuring that clicking on any of the nested administrative actions won't propagate uncontrollably.

Getting ready

Before diving into controlling events propagation, do the following:

- Create a `Chapter03/Recipe05` directory – this will be your working directory
- Copy `TicketManager` and `TicketOptions` from the *Preventing default event actions* recipe or from the `Chapter03/Recipe04` directory in the GitHub repository
- Copy the `Ticket`, `Tickets`, and `Extensions` files from the `Chapter03/Data` directory in the GitHub repository

How to do it...

To control event propagation and see the `stopPropagation` attribute in action, follow these steps:

1. Navigate to the `TicketManager` markup and locate the container markup that we render for each ticket. Next to the assignment of the `id` attribute, attach the `Show()` method to the container's `@onclick` event:

```
<div class="d-flex justify-content-between mb-1"
     id="ticket-@ticket.Id"
     @onclick="() => Show(ticket)">
    @* here's still the ticket container body *@
</div>
```

2. Navigate to the `TicketOptions` markup and attach the `stopPropagation` attribute to the `@onclick` event of each of the administrative action buttons:

```
<button class="btn btn-sm btn-success"
        @onclick="@OnShow"
        @onclick:stopPropagation>
    Show
</button>
<button class="btn btn-sm btn-info"
        @onclick="@OnTopUp"
        @onclick:stopPropagation>
    Top up
</button>
<button class="btn btn-sm btn-danger"
        @onclick="@OnRemove"
        @onclick:stopPropagation>
    Remove
</button>
```

How it works...

In *step 1*, we navigate to the `TicketManager` markup, where we render each ticket's details in a dedicated container. You'll find the container markup inside the `foreach` loop, with the `id` attribute set to correspond to the current ticket ID. In order to allow users to display ticket details by clicking anywhere on the container, next to the `id` attribute, we attached our `Show()` method to the `@onclick` event of the container. Now, whether users click on the **Show** button or anywhere inside the ticket container, Blazor will trigger the same action and render details of a given ticket.

Now, here is the catch. Inside the ticket container, we have also nested the **Top Up** and **Remove** buttons – all reacting differently to the `@onclick` event. However, nested `@onclick` events within the same area would trigger simultaneously by default. In our example, when the user clicks on the **Top Up** button, they will both increase that ticket stock and render its details. With the **Remove** button, it gets even more confusing, as users can remove a ticket and display its details at the same time. That's where we need the `stopPropagation` attribute. Attaching `stopPropagation` to a desired event, we instruct Blazor to prevent event propagation to the parent DOM element.

In *step 2*, we navigate to the `TicketOptions` markup, where we have all the administrative action buttons. Next to the `@onclick` attribute of each of the three buttons, we append the `@onclick:stopPropagation` attribute. That's all it takes to ensure that users can safely increase the stock of the ticket or remove it entirely without experiencing unwanted rendering of the ticket details display.

There's more...

While the `stopPropagation` attribute is a powerful tool within Blazor applications for managing event flow, it's essential to understand its scope and limitations. This attribute is specifically designed to work with Blazor events and does not directly influence the behavior of standard HTML events. HTML events must first be allowed to execute normally; only then can Blazor intercept these events and make decisions regarding event propagation from child components to their parents.

In our implementation, we focused on controlling the `@onclick` event, but when dealing with complex interfaces where you need to control multiple events, `stopPropagation` must be explicit for each event.

Additionally, when incorporating components from external libraries into your Blazor applications, you might encounter situations where direct control over event propagation is not straightforward. In such cases, a practical workaround is to wrap the external component within a neutral HTML element, for example, a `span` element. By applying `stopPropagation` to events on `span`, you effectively create a barrier for event propagation, with `span` acting as the nearest parent. This method allows you to manage event flow even in complex component hierarchies, ensuring intended behavior without unintended side effects from external components.

Introducing custom events

In this recipe, we explore the possibility of enriching our Blazor application with custom events, diving into slightly more advanced territory where **JavaScript** interplays with Blazor. Alongside custom events, the concept of custom event arguments arises, allowing for the passage of tailored data that goes beyond the standard event payloads. Custom events and their corresponding arguments become invaluable when predefined events fall short, offering the flexibility to capture and respond to specific user actions or external system triggers with precision.

Let's implement a component that overwrites the data that a user tries to copy from the area that this component protects.

Getting ready

Before we explore the implementation of custom events, do the following:

- Create a `Chapter03/Recipe06` directory – this will be your working directory
- Copy `TicketManager` and `TicketOptions` from the *Controlling event propagation* recipe or from the `Chapter03/Recipe05` directory in the GitHub repository
- Copy the `Ticket`, `Tickets`, and `Extensions` files from the `Chapter03/Data` directory in the GitHub repository

How to do it...

Follow these steps to implement custom logic for a copy event:

1. Add a new JavaScript (.js) file to the application's wwwroot directory. Adhere to the naming convention, {ASSEMBLY NAME}.lib.module.js. This file will contain the functions necessary for our custom events.

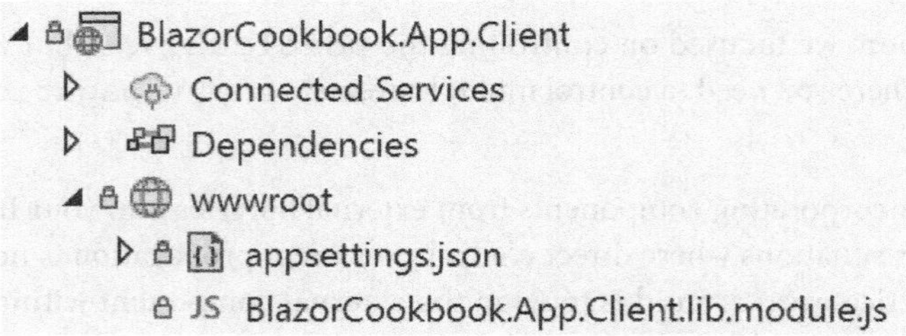

Figure 3.1: Adding a BlazorCookbook.App.Client.lib.module.js file with JavaScript functions

2. Inside your newly created .js file, declare an afterWebStarted() function. Use the registerCustomEventType API to declare a new preventcopy event. Implement custom logic within this event to overwrite the current clipboard data:

```
export function afterWebStarted(blazor) {
    blazor.registerCustomEventType('preventcopy', {
        browserEventName: 'copy',
        createEventArgs: event => {
            event.clipboardData.setData('text/plain',
                '--------');
            event.preventDefault();
            return {
                stamp: new Date()
            };
        }
    });
}
```

3. Create a new CustomEvents.cs file that will serve as a central repository for all details related to custom events.

4. In CustomEvents.cs, add a class named PreventedCopyEventArgs that extends EventArgs. Include a Stamp property to persist when Blazor prevents the copy action:

```
public class PreventedCopyEventArgs : EventArgs
{
    public DateTime Stamp { get; init; }
}
```

5. Still within `CustomEvents.cs`, declare a `public` and `static` class named `EventHandlers`. Add a custom `EventHandler` attribute to this class and define an `onpreventcopy` event that returns `PreventedCopyEventArgs`.

```
[EventHandler("onpreventcopy",
    typeof(PreventedCopyEventArgs))]
public static class EventHandlers { }
```

6. Add a new `PreventCopy` component responsible for invoking the custom event logic you've defined.

7. In the `@code` section of the `PreventCopy` component, declare a required `ChildContent` parameter of type `RenderFragment`. Also, implement a `Log()` method to intercept and log the timestamp that `PreventedCopyEventArgs` carries:

```
@code {
    [Parameter, EditorRequired]
    public RenderFragment ChildContent { get; set; }

    private void Log(PreventedCopyEventArgs args)
        => Console.WriteLine(
            $"Prevented data leak at {args.Stamp}
                UTC.");
}
```

8. Within the `PreventCopy` markup, construct a wrapping container, where you intercept the custom `@onpreventcopy` event and delegate it to the `Log()` method, while rendering `ChildContent` inside:

```
<div @onpreventcopy="@Log">
    @ChildContent
</div>
```

9. Navigate to the `TicketManager` markup, locate the area where we render the `SelectedTicket` details, and wrap it with the `PreventCopy` tags:

```
<PreventCopy>
    <div>Title: @SelectedTicket.Title</div>
    <div>Price: @SelectedTicket.Price</div>
    <div>Stock: @SelectedTicket.Stock</div>
</PreventCopy>
```

How it works...

We kick off the integration of a custom event by establishing a bridge between Blazor and JavaScript. In *step 1*, we add a `.js` file within the `wwwroot` directory, adhering to a specific naming convention (`{ASSEMBLY NAME}.lib.module.js` or `{PACKAGE ID}.lib.module.js`). This convention is crucial as Blazor automatically searches for these files to support custom events defined within the application. In *step 2*, we define an `afterWebStarted()` function, which takes a `blazor` argument (intentionally lowercase to differentiate from the globally available `Blazor` object) and which Blazor compilers expect. Using the `registerCustomEventType` API, we declare our `preventcopy` event, designed to intercept the browser's `copy` event and overwrite clipboard data. While at it, we must also cancel the browser's default copy behavior using the `preventDefault()` method. We return a timestamp marking the event trigger that we will utilize later.

Transitioning to Blazor in *step 3*, we introduce the `CustomEvents.cs` file to define our Blazor-side custom event handling. We implement the `PreventedCopyEventArgs` class in *step 4*, inheriting from `EventArgs` and reflecting our JavaScript function's structure, including a `Stamp` property. In *step 5*, we register a Blazor custom event using the Razor compiler's capabilities. Following the code generators convention, we declare `public static class EventHandlers` and leverage the `[EventHandler]` attribute to inform the Razor compiler of our custom `onpreventcopy` event. The Razor compiler will automatically align `onpreventcopy` with its JavaScript counterpart – `preventcopy`.

Next, in *step 6*, we add a `PreventCopy` component as a wrapper preventing copy operations within specified content. In *step 7*, in the `@code` block of `PreventCopy`, we declare a `ChildContent` parameter, where we can provide content to be protected and a primitive `Log()` method to log the timestamp of a prevented copy attempt. In *step 8*, we construct the `PreventCopy` markup. We add a container and intercept the `@onpreventcopy` event while also invoking the `Log()` method every time it's triggered. Inside the container, we render the provided `ChildContent` markup. Now, Blazor will effectively prevent data leakage while maintaining an audit trail of any data copy attempts.

There's more...

While the `afterWebStarted()` function is crucial in integrating custom events within a **Blazor Web App**, it's important to note that it's designed specifically for this environment. When working outside the Blazor Web App context, an analogous approach is required but with a slight adjustment in the function naming. For plain server or WebAssembly projects, you must implement the `afterStarted()` function. This naming distinction allows us to clearly define when Blazor registers custom events and ensures clarity in the application's lifecycle.

Handling long-running events

In this recipe, we tackle a critical aspect of **single-page application** (**SPA**) development – ensuring users are aware of operations occurring in the background. Unlike traditional web applications, SPAs do not naturally indicate when a process is executing behind the scenes. This lack of feedback can leave users staring at what appears to be a stale or unresponsive page, leading to frustration and confusion. It's essential that you incorporate visual action indicators such as preloaders, loading spinners, or progress bars. These elements serve as visual cues that inform the user something is happening, enhancing the user experience by providing a sense of activity and progress. I will guide you through implementing these indicators in your SPA, ensuring that during long-running requests or operations, your users are kept in the loop, maintaining engagement and satisfaction with your application.

Let's implement two kinds of action indicators – a simple loading indicator and a primitive progress indicator.

Getting ready

Before starting the implementation of user-friendly status indicators, do the following:

- Create a `Chapter03/Recipe07` directory – this will be your working directory
- Copy `TicketManager`, `TicketOptions`, `PreventCopy`, and `CustomEvents` from the *Introducing custom events* recipe or from the `Chapter03/Recipe07` directory in the GitHub repository
- Copy the `Ticket`, `Tickets`, and `Extensions` files from the `Chapter03/Data` directory in the GitHub repository

How to do it...

To build loading and progress indicators that improve the user experience of your app, follow these steps:

1. Create a new `LoadingIndicator` component that will visually communicate to users when an operation is loading.

2. In the `@code` block of `LoadingIndicator`, declare a `Job` parameter – representing the task to display the loading state for, and a `ChildContent` parameter to allow passing the content to render when loading is complete:

```
@code {
    [Parameter, EditorRequired]
    public Func<Task> Job { get; set; }
    [Parameter, EditorRequired]
    public RenderFragment ChildContent { get; set; }
}
```

3. Below the parameter declaration, still within the @code block, initialize an IsLoading state variable and implement a RunAsync() method, which encapsulates the logic for managing the loading state while executing the Job delegate:

```
internal bool IsLoading;
private async Task RunAsync()
{
    IsLoading = true;
    StateHasChanged();

    await Job.Invoke();
    IsLoading = false;
}
```

4. In the LoadingIndicator markup, add a button for users to initiate the loading process by attaching the RunAsync() method to the button's @onclick event and conditionally disabling it while loading is in progress:

```
<button class="btn btn-sm btn-success"
        @onclick="@RunAsync"
        disabled="@IsLoading">
    Load
</button>
```

5. Below the loading button, construct two areas – for when the loading is in progress and when it completes, based on the value of the IsLoading state variable:

```
@if (IsLoading)
{
    <hr />
    <p>Loading...</p>
}
else
{
    @ChildContent
}
```

6. Create another component – ProgressIndicator – that will visually communicate to users the progress of the operation they request.

7. Within the @code block of ProgressIndicator, declare two required parameters: a Job parameter – representing an abstract operation the progress indicator should monitor, and a Total parameter – to provide the number of elements the operation should run for:

```
@code {
    [Parameter, EditorRequired]
```

```
        public Func<int, Task> Job { get; set; }
        [Parameter, EditorRequired]
        public int Total { get; set; }
    }
```

8. Below the parameter declaration, initialize a `Progress` state variable to reflect the operation's progress:

```
    internal double Progress = 0;
```

9. Still within the @code block, implement an expression-bodied `Label` property, where based on the `Progress` value, you construct a label for the action button (which we will add shortly):

```
    private string Label
        => Progress > 0 ? $"Processing {Progress:0%}"
                        : "Process";
```

10. Complete the @code block by implementing a `RunAsync()` method to loop through the total amount of elements and execute the job for each index:

```
    private async Task RunAsync()
    {
        for (int i = 0; i < Total; i++)
        {
            Progress = 1.0 * (1 + i) / Total;
            StateHasChanged();
            await Job.Invoke(i);
        }
        Progress = 0;
    }
```

11. In the `ProgressIndicator` markup, construct a button for users to invoke the processing through the `RunAsync()` method. Check the current value of the `Progress` variable to conditionally disable the action button and leverage the `Label` property to generate the button label dynamically:

```
    <button class="btn btn-sm btn-success"
            @onclick="@RunAsync"
            disabled="@(Progress > 0)">
        @Label
    </button>
```

12. Navigate to the `TicketManager` component, to its `@code` block, and implement a simple `SaveAsync()` method, leveraging `Tickets.SaveAsync()` provided with data samples:

```
public Task SaveAsync(int index)
    => Tickets.SaveAsync(Tickets.All[index]);
```

13. In the `TicketManager` markup, below the render mode declaration, embed `ProgressIndicator` with `SaveAsync()` and `Tickets.All.Count` attached to the `Job` and `Total` parameters respectively:

```
<ProgressIndicator Job="SaveAsync" Total="@Tickets.All.Count" />
```

14. Still in the `TicketManager` markup, remove the button allowing to toggle tickets and the `ShowTickets` check.

15. Now, in the `TicketManager` markup, find the `foreach` loop, where you render each ticket container, and wrap it inside the `LoadingIndicator` component. Attach the `Tickets.GetAsync()` method to the `Job` parameter that `LoadingIndicator` requires:

```
<LoadingIndicator Job="@(() => Tickets.GetAsync())">
    <hr />
    @foreach (var ticket in Tickets.All)
    {
        @* here's still the ticket container markup *@
    }
</LoadingIndicator>
```

How it works...

In *step 1*, we create a new `LoadingIndicator` component. In *step 2*, we initialize the `@code` block of the `LoadingIndicator` component and declare two key parameters: `Func<Task> Job` to reference the asynchronous operation we intend to monitor, and `ChildContent` to allow passing the content to display when loading completes. Both parameters are designed to be operation-agnostic, making the component versatile and adaptable to various use cases. In *step 3*, we initialize an `IsLoading` state variable and implement the core functionality in the `RunAsync()` method. `RunAsync()` updates the `IsLoading` value to reflect the operation's start, executes the declared `Job` delegate, and then resets `IsLoading` upon completion, seamlessly transitioning to display `ChildContent`. Notice that we've invoked the `StateHasChanged()` lifecycle method, before starting the `Job` operation. With that implementation, the moment Blazor reaches an asynchronous operation, and frees up the UI thread, it will re-render the component markup, reflecting the state changes based on the `IsLoading` value. In *step 4*, we build the `LoadingIndicator` markup. First, we construct an action button for initiating the load process with the help of `RunAsync()`. We also attach the `disabled` button's attribute to the value of the `IsLoading` state variable. Now, whenever loading is in progress, Blazor will disable the action button, effectively preventing users from requeuing the already running operation. In *step 5*, we add the visual loading indicator. During operation execution, we render a simple **Loading...** message, which you can enhance with CSS for a modern look, such as incorporating a spinner. When loading completes, we render the markup provided with the `ChildContent` parameter.

In *step 6*, we create a component with a different type of indicator – `ProgressIndicator`. In *step 7*, we initialize the `@code` block and define a `Job` parameter – allowing us to define an operation to run – and a `Total` parameter – representing the number of iterations the operation must go through. The `Job` signature effectively abstracts any asynchronous operation but also ensures that the operation accepts an `int` parameter, representing the index of the current execution iteration. In *step 8*, we initialize a `Progress` variable that we'll use to monitor the actual execution progress from 0% to 100%. In *step 9*, we implement a `Label` property. With simple logic, based on the current `Progress` value, we generate either a **Process** call to action or actual processing progress. In *step 10*, we complete the `@code` block by implementing the core `RunAsync()` method. In `RunAsync()`, we loop from 0 to `Total` and invoke the `Job` delegate for each index while continuously updating the `Progress` value. When the processing is done, we reset the `Progress` value to a neutral 0. In *step 11*, we build the `ProgressIndicator` markup. We construct a button allowing us to start the processing by triggering `RunAsync()` on the `@onclick` event. We also prevent the requeuing of the running operation by disabling the action button based on the `Progress` value, similar to the action button in the `LoadingIndicator` component. Lastly, to provide real-time progress feedback, we leverage the `Label` property to render the text on the button. Now, when the operation is running, Blazor will not only disable the button but also render the current progress on it.

In *step 12*, we navigate to the `@code` block of the `TicketManager` component and implement a `SaveAsync()` method. The `SaveAsync()` method is just a proxy method that allows intercepting the current iteration index, finding the related ticket object in the `Tickets.All` collection, and passing it over for saving. In *step 13*, we jump to the `TicketManager` markup and, at the very top, we embed `ProgressIndicator`. Having the `SaveAsync()` method in place, we can attach it to the `ProgressIndicator` component required `Job` parameter. For the other required parameter – `Total` – we count the number of objects in the `Tickets.All` collection. With that setup, `ProgressIndicator` allows users to trigger the saving of each ticket and see the operation progress as it's running. In *step 14*, we remove the button allowing to toggle tickets and the related `ShowTickets` check. We will no longer need them, as we will delegate the control over displaying the `Tickets.All` collection to `LoadingIndicator`. In *step 15*, we locate the loop in which we render ticket containers. We wrap that entire area inside the `LoadingIndicator` component. As `LoadingIndicator` requires a `Job` delegate, we leverage a lambda expression and attach the `Tickets.GetAsync()` method. Now, when users request to load data, `LoadingIndicator` renders the **Loading...** message and triggers `Tickets.GetAsync()` seamlessly. When loading completes, the `LoadingIndicator` component updates the UI with a fresh set of ticket containers.

There's more…

You might have already realized which scenarios the loading and progress indicators fit but let me give you a simple rule of thumb.

Any loading indicators are ideally suited for operations with unpredictable completion times, such as fetching data from an API, where the number of results and their arrival time are unknown.

Progress indicators, such as a progress bar, are ideal for operations with known results, such as submitting data changes or sending notifications.

4
Enhancing Data Display with Grids

In this chapter, we'll dive into data presentation within Blazor applications through the implementation of advanced grid functionalities. Starting with the essential task of refactoring traditional tables into more dynamic grid components, we'll explore the significance of attaching interactive actions to various parts of a grid, such as buttons or links within cells, enhancing user engagement and operational efficiency.

We'll also cover pagination techniques to manage large datasets effectively and explore infinite scrolling as a modern alternative to traditional pagination. Additionally, we'll walk through creating a customizable grid, offering flexibility in adapting the grid to specific application needs. Lastly, we will discuss **QuickGrid** – a ready-to-use Blazor grid component with a predefined feature set and the quickest and simplest data-grid option you can leverage.

By the end of this chapter, you will be equipped with the knowledge to enhance data display in your Blazor applications, improving the aesthetics and functionality of data presentation through the effective use of grids.

Here are the recipes we will follow in this chapter:

- Refactoring a table to a grid component
- Attaching actions to parts of a grid
- Implementing pagination
- Implementing sorting
- Implementing infinite scrolling
- Utilizing QuickGrid

Technical requirements

We will maintain simplicity across all examples to facilitate understanding and learning. We will use the same dataset for all recipes, so you can see the impact of different technical aspects of working with grid components. No external tools will be required but the following basics:

- A modern IDE (that supports Blazor development)
- .NET 9 installed on your development machine
- A modern web browser (that supports WebAssembly)
- A Blazor project (where you'll write code as you go along)

All the code examples (and data samples) that you'll see can be found in a dedicated GitHub repository at: `https://github.com/PacktPublishing/Blazor-Web-Development-Cookbook/tree/main/BlazorCookbook.App.Client/Chapters/Chapter04`. In each recipe that needs any samples, I will also point you to the directory where you can find them.

Refactoring a table to a grid component

In this recipe, we'll explore the fundamentals of developing a reusable grid component. Grids are a cornerstone in designing intuitive and organized user interfaces, enabling structured data display. Transitioning from using basic tables to implementing a reusable grid component is a strategic move toward achieving modular, maintainable, and scalable frontend architecture. Such a component can be adapted across different parts of an application, ensuring consistency and reducing redundancy in code.

Let's start from the basics and refactor an existing, standard HTML table to a componentized grid.

Getting ready

Before we dive into exploring grid and refactoring markup, let's get the stage ready:

- Create a `Chapter04/Recipe01` directory – this will be your working directory
- Copy the `Samples` and `HtmlGrid` files from the `Chapter04/Data` directory of the GitHub repository

How to do it...

Follow these steps to rebuild the standard HTML markup into a modular grid component:

1. Locate the `HtmlGrid` component. Rename `HtmlGrid` to `Grid` and convert it to a generic version by adding the `@typeparam` attribute at the top of the file:

    ```
    @typeparam T
    ```

2. Add a @code section within the Grid component. Declare three critical parameters: Header and the generic Data and Row, allowing for dynamic content rendering:

```
@code {
    [Parameter, EditorRequired]
    public List<T> Data { get; set; }
    [Parameter, EditorRequired]
    public RenderFragment Header { get; set; }
    [Parameter, EditorRequired]
    public RenderFragment<T> Row { get; set; }
}
```

3. Modify the table header cell markup to utilize the Header parameter, representing a flexible template:

```
<thead>
    @Header
</thead>
```

4. Revise the loop responsible for rendering the table body. Instead of a fixed dataset, iterate over the Data collection provided through the parameter. Similarly, replace static row cells with the Row template parameter:

```
<tbody>
    @foreach (var element in Data)
    {
        @Row(element)
    }
</tbody>
```

5. Create a new routable TicketManager component and embed the newly modularized Grid component in the markup area. Leverage the provided Tickets.All sample data for the Grid data source:

```
@page "/ch04r01"
<Grid Data="@Tickets.All">
    @* we will construct the grid body next @*
</Grid>
```

6. Declare the Header markup for the embedded grid by extracting the header area from the original raw table:

```
<Header>
    <tr>
        <td>Tariff</td>
        <td>Price</td>
```

```
        </tr>
    </Header>
```

7. Construct the `Row` markup for the embedded grid by extracting the row markup from the original raw table:

```
<Row>
    <tr>
        <td>@context.Tariff</td>
        <td>@context.Price</td>
    </tr>
</Row>
```

How it works...

In *step 1*, we begin implementing a modular grid by renaming `HtmlGrid` to `Grid`. Then, we convert the `Grid` component into a generic component by adding the `@typeparam T` attribute at the top. If you haven't seen generic components before, we already explored that topic in *Chapter 1*, in the *Making components generic* recipe. In *step 2*, we declare three required parameters. With a generic `Data` collection and a generic `Row` template, we enable the dynamic rendering of any objects as table rows. With `Header`, we can dynamically provide a table header setup without depending on any fixed layout. In *step 3*, we utilize the `Header` parameter to modularize the table's `thead` content, effectively making the table header fully customizable. In *step 4*, we configure table body rendering. We iterate over the `Data` collection and leverage the type-aware `Row` template to render table rows dynamically with the provided template.

In *step 5*, we add a new routable `TicketManager` component. We showcase the new modularized `Grid` component, thereby embedding it into the `TicketManager` markup area. We utilize the `Tickets.All` dataset sample as the data source for the `Grid` instance. In *step 6*, we construct the `Header` markup by repurposing the original table header. In *step 7*, we do the same for the `Row` markup. However, with `Row`, there's no need to implement a loop here – the `Grid` component already iterates over the provided dataset.

Such a modularized approach not only simplifies the implementation but also ensures that the grid remains highly customizable and adaptable to various data types. We've effectively only simplified the loop mechanism to render grid rows, but it was important to showcase the thought process behind breaking the HTML table into modular pieces. Understanding that allows us to take the grid concept further in the following recipes.

There's more...

While modularizing grids in Blazor applications enhances flexibility and reusability, you must consider the potential rendering overhead this introduces, especially with interactive grids. Every user interaction could activate the diffing algorithm (we touched upon diffing in *Chapter 3*) and trigger re-rendering, which, depending on the complexity of your logic, might significantly affect performance. It's essential that you find a balance in componentizing your grid – implement enough modularity to maintain flexibility without overcomplicating your components. Strategic API call placement and the judicious use of static `RenderFragment` instances can help manage performance impacts.

An effective strategy to improve grid performance is leveraging the `@key` Blazor attribute. This attribute helps Blazor's diffing algorithm to identify elements more efficiently, reducing unnecessary DOM updates by associating each grid row or component with a unique identifier. If we were to assume that we expect only row-level changes in our grid, then we could leverage the `Id` property of the `Ticket` object and attach `@key` in the following way:

```
<Grid Tickets="@Tickets.All">
    @* ... *@
    <Row>
        <tr @key="context.Id">
            <td>@context.Tariff</td>
            <td>@context.Price</td>
        </tr>
    </Row>
</Grid>
```

When Blazor can correlate DOM elements with backing data objects, it can smartly decide when re-rendering is actually necessary and when it can skip updating certain parts of the DOM. By using the `@key` attribute, you not only enhance the rendering performance of your grids but also ensure a smoother user experience, particularly in data-intensive scenarios where the grid's contents change frequently.

Attaching actions to parts of a grid

Interactive grids play a pivotal role in enhancing the user experience within frontend applications, allowing users to interact with and manipulate data in intuitive and efficient ways. By attaching actions to parts of a grid, you can significantly improve the grid's functionality, paving the way for advanced features such as sorting, filtering, and dynamic data management. We explored how actions and events correlate in Blazor in *Chapter 3*. In this recipe, you'll learn about the techniques and best practices for integrating actionable elements within your grid components. Attaching actions effectively to grid parts not only enriches the user interface but also provides a seamless experience for users as they interact with your application.

Let's implement a table that allows you to attach an action to its columns that Blazor will execute when the user clicks on them and refactor the grid so it's more flexible.

Getting ready

Before you dive into making columns and rows interactive, do the following:

- Create a `Chapter04/Recipe02` directory – this will be your working directory
- Copy `Grid` and `TicketManager` from the *Refactoring a table to a grid component* recipe or from the `Chapter04/Recipe01` directory in the GitHub repository
- Copy `Samples` from the `Chapter04/Data` directory in the GitHub repository

How to do it...

To implement interactive table columns and rows, follow these steps:

1. Create a new, generic `ColumnViewModel` class with `Label`, `Template`, and `OnSort` properties:

```
public class ColumnViewModel<T>
{
    public string Label { get; init; }
    public RenderFragment<T> Template { get; init; }
    public EventCallback OnSort { get; init; }
}
```

2. Navigate to the `Grid` component and, below the `@typeparam` directive, add an attribute indicating that the generic type of the `Grid` component should cascade to descendant components:

```
@typeparam T
@attribute [CascadingTypeParameter(nameof(T))]
```

3. In the `@code` block of the `Grid` component, remove the `Row` parameter and rename the `Header` parameter to `ChildContent`. You already have the `Data` collection that you will also need:

```
@code {
    [Parameter, EditorRequired]
    public List<T> Data { get; set; }
    [Parameter, EditorRequired]
    public RenderFragment ChildContent { get; set; }
}
```

4. Below the parameters, initialize a `Columns` collection, with objects of type `ColumnViewModel`, and implement an `AddColumn()` method, allowing you to add a new column to the internal collection:

```
protected List<ColumnViewModel<T>> Columns = [];
public void AddColumn(ColumnViewModel<T> column)
    => Columns.Add(column);
```

5. Lastly, at the end of the `@code` block, override the `OnAfterRender()` lifecycle method to ensure Blazor re-renders `Grid` when the rendering of all the nested components completes:

```
protected override void OnAfterRender(
    bool firstRender)
{
    if (firstRender) StateHasChanged();
}
```

6. Move to the `Grid` markup and replace the existing table header with a loop constructing column headers based on the objects in the `Columns` collection:

```
<thead>
    <tr>
        @foreach (var column in Columns)
        {
            <th @onclick="@column.OnSort">
                @column.Label
            </th>
        }
    </tr>
</thead>
```

7. Still within the `Grid` markup, in the table body area, nest another `foreach` loop where you render each column template for all elements in the `Data` collection:

```
<tbody>
    @foreach (var element in Data)
    {
        <tr>
            @foreach (var column in Columns)
            {
                <td>@column.Template(element)</td>
            }
        </tr>
    }
</tbody>
```

8. To complete the markup, add a `CascadingValue` markup to share the current `Grid` instance with all the nested components it might contain:

```
<CascadingValue Value="this">
    @ChildContent
</CascadingValue>
```

9. Create a new, generic `Column` component, with a `@code` block where you intercept a cascading reference to the `Grid` instance and allow passing `Label`, `ChildContent`, and `OnSort` parameters:

```
@typeparam T
@code {
    [CascadingParameter]
    public Grid<T> Grid { get; set; }

    [Parameter, EditorRequired]
    public string Label { get; set; }
    [Parameter, EditorRequired]
    public RenderFragment<T> ChildContent { get; set; }
    [Parameter]
    public EventCallback OnSort { get; set; }
}
```

10. Still in the `@code` block of the `Column` component, override the `OnInitialized()` lifecycle method to convert `Column` parameters to `ColumnViewModel` and pass the `model` instance to the parent `Grid` component:

```
protected override void OnInitialized()
{
    var model = new ColumnViewModel<T>
    {
        Label = Label,
        Template = ChildContent,
        OnSort = OnSort
    };
    Grid.AddColumn(model);
}
```

11. Navigate to the `TicketManager` component and initialize an `@code` block to implement a `Sort()` placeholder method, where you just log the intention:

```
@code {
    private void Sort(string prop)
        => Console.WriteLine($"Sorted by {prop}!");
}
```

12. In the `TicketManager` markup, replace the no longer compatible `Grid` content with columns rendered with the help of the `Column` component:

```
<Column OnSort="@(() => Sort(nameof(Ticket.Tariff)))"
        Label="Tariff">
    @context.Tariff
</Column>
<Column OnSort="@(() => Sort(nameof(Ticket.Price)))"
        Label="Price">
    @context.Price
</Column>
```

13. Lastly, enhance the `TicketManager` component to render in `InteractiveWebAssembly` mode:

```
@rendermode InteractiveWebAssembly
```

How it works...

In *step 1*, we create a generic `ColumnViewModel` class. `ColumnViewModel` contains three properties: `Label`, representing the title of the column; `Template`, representing the markup to be rendered for each data point in the column; and `OnSort`, a callback to trigger sorting when a user clicks on the column header. Using `ColumnViewModel`, you can simplify the definition of a column in the grid without passing all the column properties explicitly.

In *step 2*, we navigate to the `Grid` component and perform some refactoring to make its construction more dynamic. While the `Grid` component is already generic, we will work with cascading values next and want Blazor to automatically propagate these values type down the component tree. To achieve this descendant sharing, we leverage the `CascadingTypeParameter` attribute. `CascadingTypeParameter` allows a generic type to be shared across the component tree. Instead of passing the generic type `"T"` as a string, we use the `nameof()` method, achieving the same result while maintaining compile-time validation.

In *step 3*, we change the parameters required by `Grid`. We remove the `Row` parameter, as we will move the data point template into `ColumnViewModel`. With the `Grid` component now requiring only one `RenderFragment` parameter, we rename `Header` to `ChildContent` to simplify the grid's construction later.

In *step 4*, we add a `Columns` collection that will serve as a container for the grid columns we will render. To populate that collection, we expose an `AddColumn()` method, which accepts a `ColumnViewModel` object and adds it to `Columns`.

In *step 5*, we override the `OnAfterRender()` lifecycle method of the `Grid` component. This instructs Blazor to re-render the `Grid` component immediately after the initial render completes. This might seem counter-intuitive now, but it will make more sense when we implement the `Column` component later.

In *step 6*, we adjust the `Grid` markup to comply with the changes in the `@code` block. As we've removed the `Header` parameter, we rebuild the table header area. We reconstruct the `thead` content by explicitly embedding `tr` tags and rendering the `Label` properties of columns from the `Columns` collection. We also attach the declared sorting action of each column to the `@onclick` event of each `th` element. You attach actions to grid elements the same as any other HTML element.

In *step 7*, we reconstruct the table body. We replace the `Row` reference (which we've removed) with explicit `tr` tags inside the loop iterating over the `Data` collection. Inside each `tr`, we nest another loop, instructing Blazor to render each `Data` element using the template from the `Template` property of the current column.

In *step 8*, we complete the `Grid` markup by constructing a `CascadingValue` area, where we share the current grid instance with nested components. We will also need the `Column` component to understand this part, so we will implement it next.

In *step 9*, we create a generic `Column` component, which will be the primary construction element for the grid. The `Column` component intercepts the `Grid` instance where it is rendered and requires `Label` and `ChildContent` parameters. The `Label` parameter defines the column title, while `ChildContent` represents a template for the data point belonging to that column. This markup will be rendered for each element of the `Data` collection in the grid. We also declare one optional parameter, `OnSort`, allowing the attachment of sorting behavior triggered by clicking the column header.

In *step 10*, we complete the `Column` implementation by overriding the `OnInitialized()` lifecycle method, where we convert the incoming parameters into a `ColumnViewModel` object that we then register in the `Grid` component using the previously implemented `AddColumn()` method. The `Column` component is markupless by design – it doesn't render any markup explicitly. Instead, it registers the row template and column definition directly in the `Grid` instance, which knows how to construct the table markup from those details.

In *step 11*, we navigate to the `TicketManager` component. First, we initialize a `@code` block where we implement a `Sort()` method – a behavior placeholder that only logs an operation intention (we will implement the sorting in a separate step).

In *step 12*, we reconstruct the grid content, leveraging the `Column` component. As all grid elements are generic and the `Grid` component cascades the generic parameter type downwards, we can access the `Ticket` properties with a `context` reference. Knowing this, we build the first column with a `Tariff` title and declare that for each data point, we want to render the value of the `Tariff` property of the current element. We also declare that the `OnSort` callback exposed by `Column` will trigger the `Sort()` method on the `Tariff` property. For the second column, we duplicate these steps for the `Price` property.

In *step 13*, since we expect the grid to be interactive, we declare that the `TicketManager` component will render in `InteractiveWebAssembly` mode.

Now, with the entire implementation in place, it will be easier to understand the rendering of the enhanced `Grid` component. As you can see, the `Column` component we use to construct the grid doesn't carry any markup, so it will be fully transparent in the DOM. However, `Column` still requires cascading access to the `Grid` instance, which is why we put all the customizable `Grid` content in the `CascadingValue` tags in *step 8*. With that, each `Column` instance can register the render template it carries directly within the `Grid` instance, so it is rendered together with the `Grid` markup. This is also why we've overridden the `OnAfterRender()` lifecycle method of the `Grid` component in *step 5*. We must re-render the table markup after the initial render of the grid and after all the `Column` instances register their payload within the `Grid` instance.

There's more...

In some scenarios, you might need to attach actions to entire grid rows and specific grid cells. When a row overlaps a cell, you will face **event bubbling**. When an event, such as a mouse click or key press, occurs in the browser, it propagates (or bubbles) from the target element through its ancestors, resulting in unwanted behavior in parent elements listening for the same event. With Blazor's `@onEvent:stopPropagation` attribute, you can prevent this propagation, ensuring that only the intended event handler executes:

```
<tr @onclick="@ShowTicketDetails">
    <td>@ticket.Tariff</td>
    <td @onclick="@AddToCart"
        @onclick:stopPropagation>
        @ticket.Price
    </td>
</tr>
```

In this code snippet, we allow users to display ticket details when they click on a table row and add a ticket to the cart when they click on the cell with the price. We've attached the desired event handlers to the `tr` and `td` elements. Additionally, we've attached the `@onclick:stopPropagation` attribute to `td` with a price. Now, we prevent the click event from propagating to the parent row. As a result, when the user clicks the cell, Blazor executes only the `AddToCart()` handler and omits the `ShowTicketDetails()` handler. With `@onclick:stopPropagation`, we ensure that the click event is handled solely by the cell and does not affect the surrounding row element.

Implementing pagination

Pagination refers to dividing content into separate pages, which is particularly crucial for tables and grids displaying large datasets. This approach improves the readability and navigability of data and significantly enhances performance by reducing the volume of data loaded and rendered at any given time. Pagination is often required in tables and grids to manage large amounts of data efficiently, preventing overwhelming users with too much information at once and ensuring that the application remains responsive.

Let's add a simple pagination to the grid.

Getting ready

Before we dive in, ensure that you do the following:

- Create a `Chapter04/Recipe03` directory – this will be your working directory
- Copy `Column`, `ColumnViewModel`, `Grid`, and `TicketManager` from the *Attaching actions to parts of a grid* recipe or the `Chapter04/Recipe02` directory in the GitHub repository
- Copy `Samples` from the `Chapter04/Data` directory in the GitHub repository

How to do it...

To add pagination to your `Grid` component, follow these steps:

1. Create a new `PaginateEventArgs` record with `Page` and `Size` properties:

   ```
   public record PaginateEventArgs(int Page, int Size);
   ```

2. Add a new `Paginator` component and initialize a @code block with two required parameters: a `Paginate` callback with `PaginateEventArgs` and `DataSize`:

   ```
   [Parameter, EditorRequired]
   public EventCallback<PaginateEventArgs>
       Paginate { get; set; }
   [Parameter, EditorRequired]
   public int DataSize { get; set; }
   ```

3. Below the parameters, initialize variables defining the pagination state: `TotalPages`, `CurrentPage`, and `PageSize` with default initial values:

   ```
   protected int TotalPages,
       CurrentPage = 1, PageSize = 5;
   ```

4. Next to the state variables, override the `OnInitialized()` lifecycle method and calculate the `TotalPages` value:

```
protected override void OnInitialized()
    => TotalPages =
        (DataSize + PageSize - 1)
        / PageSize;
```

5. Still within the @code block, implement a `LoadAsync()` method, invoking the `Paginate` callback with the current pagination state:

```
private Task LoadAsync()
{
    var state = new PaginateEventArgs(
        CurrentPage,
        PageSize
    );
    return Paginate.InvokeAsync(state);
}
```

6. Below the loading method, define a `NextAsync()` method to enable the forward navigation of data pages:

```
private async Task NextAsync()
{
    if (CurrentPage == TotalPages) return;
    CurrentPage++;
    await LoadAsync();
}
```

7. Similarly, next to the forward navigation, implement a `PreviousAsync()` method to handle backward navigation of data pages:

```
private async Task PreviousAsync()
{
    if (CurrentPage == 1) return;
    CurrentPage--;
    await LoadAsync();
}
```

8. Complete the @code block by overriding the `OnAfterRenderAsync()` lifecycle method and load the initial data page, after the first render:

```
protected override async Task
    OnAfterRenderAsync(bool firstRender)
{
```

```
        if (firstRender) await LoadAsync();
    }
```

9. Move to the `Paginator` markup area and construct a container with two `button` elements for page navigation and an `input` field to display the `CurrentPage` value:

```
<div class="d-flex">
    <button @onclick="@PreviousAsync">
        Previous
    </button>
    <input disabled
            class="text-center"
            value="@CurrentPage" />
    <button @onclick="@NextAsync">
        Next
    </button>
</div>
```

10. Navigate to the `Grid` component and, within the `@code` block, initialize a generic `Set` collection to persist currently displayed data:

```
protected IEnumerable<T> Set = [];
```

11. Next to the `Set` initialization, implement a `LoadAsync()` method, accepting a `PaginationEventArgs` parameter, that takes a slice of data from the `Data` collection based on the incoming pagination state details:

```
public Task LoadAsync(PaginateEventArgs args)
{
    Set = Data
        .Skip((args.Page - 1) * args.Size)
        .Take(args.Size);
    return Task.CompletedTask;
}
```

12. Jump to the `Grid` component markup and update the loop generating table rows to iterate over the `Set` collection:

```
<tbody>
    @foreach (var element in Set)
    {
        @* nested loop through Columns *@
    }
</tbody>
```

13. Still within the Grid markup, under the table, embed the Paginator component, attaching the LoadAsync() method to its Paginate callback and passing the size of the Data collection as the DataSize parameter:

```
<hr />
<Paginator Paginate="@LoadAsync"
           DataSize="@Data.Count"/>
```

How it works...

In *step 1*, we create a PaginateEventArgs record with Page and Size properties representing the currently visible page and the size of each page a user is viewing. Having these details allows us to fetch data in expected batches effectively. As we expect PaginateEventArgs to represent a pagination event, it makes sense to make the object immutable, so we declare it as a record object. To simplify the PaginateEventArgs initialization, we also leverage the primary constructor rather than the legacy one and explicit property declaration.

In *step 2*, we introduce a Paginator component to encapsulate the grid pagination logic. First, we initialize a @code block within Paginator. We declare a Paginate callback that returns PaginateEventArgs to communicate page navigation changes. We also declare a DataSize parameter. Knowing the amount of data to paginate allows us to improve the pagination experience by setting the maximum page a user can reach.

In *step 3*, we initialize three state properties: TotalPages, indicating where the pagination navigator should stop; CurrentPage, indicating the current page a user is viewing; and PageSize, defining how many elements we allow to load per page. For CurrentPage, we set the initial value to 1 since we naturally start from the first page. We also fix PageSize to 5, allowing us to focus on the pagination behavior.

In *step 4*, we override the OnInitialized() lifecycle method of Paginator to calculate the TotalPages value based on the incoming DataSize parameter and the PageSize variable. We implement the simplest arithmetic calculation that always rounds up to the next whole number, whenever the division of DataSize and PageSize is an odd number, indicating that the last page is not full.

In *step 5*, we implement a LoadAsync() method, which is central to the pagination request communication. Every time Blazor invokes LoadAsync(), we create a PaginationEventArgs instance from the current value of CurrentPage and PageSize variables and asynchronously pass it to the Paginate callback for the callback consumer to interpret.

In *step 6*, we construct the first part of the Paginator navigation capabilities by implementing a NextAsync() method. NextAsync() allows the user to fetch the next page of data – we check whether the user is already on the last available page to prevent further navigation; if not, we increment CurrentPage and invoke the LoadAsync() method.

In *step 7*, we construct the `NextAsync()` counterpart, `PreviousAsync()`. The `PreviousAsync()` method allows the user to navigate backward and fetch the previous dataset. To prevent the user from navigating too far back, we check whether `CurrentPage` is already the first available page. If not, we decrease `CurrentPage` and invoke `LoadAsync()`.

The last thing we must cover is the initial loading of data. In *step 8*, we override the `OnAfterRenderAsync()` lifecycle method of `Paginator`. After the first render, we invoke `LoadAsync()` to instruct Blazor to load the defined initial page with the specified number of elements.

In *step 9*, we build the `Paginator` markup. We construct a primitive bar with two buttons allowing navigation back and forth using `PreviousAsync()` and `NextAsync()` respectively. We also add a disabled input field displaying the current page based on the `CurrentPage` variable.

In *step 10*, we move to the `Grid` component and enhance it to comply with `Paginator` and pagination. First, we focus on the `@code` block and declare a generic `Set` collection to store the currently fetched dataset.

In *step 11*, we implement a `LoadAsync()` method that consumes `PaginateEventArgs` and reacts to the `Paginator` callback. Inside `LoadAsync()`, we use **LINQ methods** to load only the required elements from `Data`. We use the `Skip()` method to skip elements the user has already seen. Since the `Paginator` component starts the page count from 1 while collection indexing starts from 0, we reduce the `args.Page` value by 1 and then multiply it by `args.Size` to get the number of elements to omit from the start of the `Data` collection. Then, we use a `Take()` method to fetch the desired amount of elements.

In *step 12*, we jump to the `Grid` markup, locate the loop where we iterate over `Data` elements, and update the loop to work with `Set`.

Lastly, in *step 13*, we embed the `Paginator` component into the `Grid` markup. We attach the `LoadAsync()` method to the `Paginate` callback and count the `Data` elements to provide the required `DataSize` parameter.

With very little code, we have arrived at a fully functional and generic pagination feature.

Tariff	Price
Adult	70.10
Adult	86.99
Elderly	82.39
Elderly	66.64
Elderly	5.52

Previous   1   Next

Figure 4.1: Grid loading with a functional pagination bar

There's more...

In the pagination implementation, we have some methods returning `Task` that we didn't declare as `async` but rather returned the `Task.CompletedTask` object. This approach is beneficial when we don't perform asynchronous operations inside the method but must adhere to an asynchronous method signature. Returning `Task.CompletedTask` is more efficient in such scenarios because we avoid the overhead of the async state machine that the compiler generates for `async` methods. By not awaiting `Task` and simply returning `Task.CompletedTask`, we minimize unnecessary performance costs associated with task scheduling and context switching.

See also

In this recipe, we also saw the LINQ methods in action. LINQ methods could fill a book on their own, so if you'd like to explore that topic, head over to `https://learn.microsoft.com/en-us/dotnet/csharp/linq/`.

Implementing sorting

In this recipe, we dive into organizing data within grids by arranging rows based on column values. Sorting allows users to easily navigate and analyze data by prioritizing it according to relevant criteria, such as alphabetical order, numerical values, dates, or custom parameters. This capability becomes increasingly important in applications dealing with extensive datasets, where locating specific information or understanding data trends can become cumbersome without effective sorting mechanisms. By introducing sorting functionalities, developers can significantly improve the user experience, offering intuitive interactions and insights into the data presented.

Let's enhance the grid with sorting functionality that users can trigger by clicking on the grid column headers.

Getting ready

Before we explore sorting in a grid, do the following:

- Create a `Chapter04/Recipe04` directory – this will be your working directory
- Copy `Column`, `ColumnViewModel`, `Grid`, `PaginateEventArgs`, `Paginator`, and `TicketManager` from the *Implementing pagination* recipe or from the `Chapter04/Recipe04` directory in the GitHub repository
- Copy `Samples` from the `Chapter04/Data` directory in the GitHub repository

How to do it...

Follow these steps to add sorting to a grid:

1. Navigate to the `ColumnViewModel` class and replace the `OnSort` callback with a `Property` delegate, encapsulating the logic to select a property from a generic model:

```
public Func<T, object> Property { get; init; }
```

2. Go to the `@code` block of the `Column` component and replace the `OnSort` parameter with a `Property` delegate parameter, allowing you to pass a property selector from a generic model:

```
[Parameter]
public Func<T, object> Property { get; set; }
```

3. Still in the `Column` component, fix the implementation of the overridden `OnInitialized()` method by updating the `ColumnViewModel` construction to utilize the `Property` parameter:

```
var model = new ColumnViewModel<T>
{
    Label = Label,
    Template = ChildContent,
    Property = Property
};
```

4. Move to the `Grid` component. At the end of the `@code` block, declare variables to persist the current sorting column and order:

```
private string _currentSortColumn;
private bool _isAsc;
```

5. Below the sorting state variables, add a `PaginatorRef` variable to allow referencing the `Paginator` component from within the `Grid` code:

```
protected Paginator PaginatorRef;
```

6. Complete the `@code` block of the `Grid` component, by implementing a `SortAsync()` method, allowing you to dynamically sort the `Data` collection based on the `Property` selector set for each `ColumnViewModel` column object:

```
public Task SortAsync(ColumnViewModel<T> column)
{
    if (_currentSortColumn == column.Label)
        _isAsc = !isAsc;
    else
        _isAsc = true;

    Comparison<T> comparer = (left, right) =>
```

```
{
    var result = Comparer<object>.Default
        .Compare(column.Property(left),
            column.Property(right));

    return _isAsc ? result : -result;
};
Data.Sort(comparer);

_currentSortColumn = column.Label;
return PaginatorRef.LoadAsync();
}
```

7. In the `Grid` markup, replace the delegate attached to the table column headers with the newly implemented `SortAsync()`:

```
<th @onclick="@(() => SortAsync(column))">
    @column.Label
</th>
```

8. Still within the `Grid` markup, locate the `Paginator` instance and attach its reference to the `PaginatorRef` variable:

```
<Paginator @ref="@PaginatorRef"
           Paginate="@LoadAsync"
           DataSize="@Data.Count" />
```

9. Navigate to the `TicketManager` component and fix the `Column` instances by passing in the `Property` selector and defining the `Ticket` properties to sort on:

```
<Column Property="@(it => it.Tariff)"
        Label="Tariff">
    @context.Tariff
</Column>
<Column Property="@(it => it.Price)"
        Label="Price">
    @context.Price
</Column>
```

How it works...

In *step 1*, we update the `ColumnViewModel` class and replace the `OnSort` callback with a generic `Func<T, object>`. `Func<T, object>` is a delegate that represents a method returning an object from a given type, `T`. We use `Func<T, object>` as a selector for the property to sort by and name it `Property` intuitively.

In *step 2*, we jump to the `Column` component to update the `Grid` building block with the same logic as we did for `ColumnViewModel`. Inside the `@code` block of `Column`, we replace the `OnSort` callback with the `Func<T, object>` parameter. In *step 3*, we fix the mapping in the overridden `OnInitialized()` method to pass the sorting property selector into the `ColumnViewModel` constructor and consequently into the `Grid` instance.

In *step 4*, we navigate to the `Grid` component and implement the backing logic for the sorting feature. First, we declare two variables representing the current state of the sorting: `_currentSortColumn`, indicating which sorting property is currently selected, and an `_isAsc` flag, implying whether the sorting order is ascending or descending.

In *step 5*, we introduce a `PaginatorRef` variable of type `Paginator`. It might look a bit confusing at first glance. Using a component as a variable in your C# code in Blazor allows you to interact with the component's public API. Furthermore, with the `@ref` attribute, you can capture a reference to the rendered component and leverage its methods and properties. But `@ref` has one major limitation – the reference is only populated after the component rendering completes. Since Blazor's rendering process is asynchronous, any attempt to use the reference immediately after component initialization may fail because the reference might not yet be available. Therefore, you must ensure that you access the `@ref` bound reference only after the component render cycle completes.

In *step 6*, we implement a `SortAsync()` method, the center of our sorting logic. The `SortAsync()` method requires a `ColumnViewModel` object to define the sorting to perform. First, we determine the sorting order by checking whether the current sorting column label matches the one selected by the user. If they match, it indicates the user is trying to invert the sorting order, so we flip the current value of `_isAsc`. Otherwise, we set it to ascending order, as expected for the initial behavior. Next, we leverage a generic `Comparison` C# object. The `Comparison<T>` delegate represents a comparison method that compares two objects of the same type. We build the `comparer` delegate using a lambda expression that compares the `left` and `right` objects in the collection using the default `Comparer`. The `Comparer<T>` class provides a way to compare two objects and returns an integer indicating their relative order. By checking `_isAsc`, we can negate the comparison result to arrive easily at a descending order. With the `comparer` instance in place, we use the `Sort()` LINQ extension method on the `Data` collection to reshuffle the elements according to our logic. Finally, we update the current sorting column reference with the latest `column.Label` value and invoke the `LoadAsync()` method exposed by the `PaginatorRef` object to reload the dataset with the new sorting.

In *step 7*, we jump to the `Grid` markup, locate the table header area where we render each table column header, and attach the `SortAsync()` method to the `@onclick` event handler with the current `column` reference. In *step 8*, we scroll down to where we constructed the `Paginator` instance and, with the help of the `@ref` attribute, attach the `Paginator` instance to the `PaginatorRef` variable we have in the code part of the component.

After all the sorting enhancements, the `TicketManager` component is no longer compatible. In *step 9*, we move to the `TicketManager` markup and update the `Column` instances by declaring the `Property` delegate with a lambda expression for each column we render.

Implementing infinite scrolling

In user experience trends, there's a shift from traditional pagination to a more dynamic and seamless infinite scrolling approach. `Virtualize`, integrated into the Blazor framework, was designed to enhance the user interface by loading content on-demand as users scroll through the page. It smartly manages resources by only rendering items in the viewport and fetching additional content as needed, significantly improving performance and user experience, especially in applications dealing with large datasets. By implementing infinite scrolling with the `Virtualize` component, you can offer a smoother, more engaging interaction pattern, eliminating the need for manual page navigation and making content exploration effortless.

Let's construct a simple grid and implement infinite scrolling, leveraging the `Virtualize` component.

Getting ready

To simplify the grid itself and focus on the infinite scrolling implementation, we will not leverage any grid markup built in prior recipes but rather start from scratch. But before you dive in, do the following:

- Create a `Chapter04/Recipe05` directory – this will be your working directory
- Copy `Samples` from the `Chapter04/Data` directory in the GitHub repository
- Navigate to the `Program` file of your application and register the `TicketsApi` service, from `Samples`, in the application dependency injection container:

```
builder.Services.AddScoped<TicketsApi>();
```

How to do it...

Follow these steps to add infinite scrolling to a grid:

1. Create a generic `Grid` component using the `typeparam` attribute:

```
@typeparam T
```

2. Inside the `@code` block of the `Grid` component, declare three required parameters:

```
[Parameter, EditorRequired]
public Func<int, int, CancellationToken,
    Task<(int, List<T>)>> Provider { get; set; }

[Parameter, EditorRequired]
public RenderFragment Header { get; set; }
[Parameter, EditorRequired]
public RenderFragment<T> Row { get; set; }
```

The three parameters are:

- `Provider` – delegate that encapsulates data fetching
- `Header` – `RenderFragment` for the table header template
- `Row` – generic `RenderFragment` for the table row template

3. Below the parameters, implement a `LoadAsync()` method to handle dynamic data loading; accepting `ItemsProviderRequest` as input and returning a generic `ItemsProviderResult` object:

```
private async ValueTask<ItemsProviderResult<T>>
    LoadAsync(ItemsProviderRequest request)
{
    (var total, var data) = await Provider
        .Invoke(request.StartIndex, request.Count,
                request.CancellationToken);
    return new(data, total);
}
```

4. Move to the `Grid` component's markup area and construct a table: embed the `Header` template within the `<thead>` tags and for the `<tbody>` section, utilize the `Virtualize` component, linking it to the `LoadAsync()` method via its `ItemsProvider` parameter, and pass the `Row` template as its `ChildContent` parameter:

```
<table class="table table-bordered">
    <thead>
        @Header
    </thead>
    <tbody>
        <Virtualize ItemsProvider="@LoadAsync">
            @Row(context)
        </Virtualize>
    </tbody>
</table>
```

5. Create a routable `TicketManager` component. Set `TicketManager` to render in `InteractiveWebAssembly` mode and inject `TicketsApi`:

```
@page "/ch04r05"
@rendermode InteractiveWebAssembly
@inject TicketsApi Tickets
```

6. Within the `TicketManager` markup, incorporate the newly created `Grid` component. Attach the `Tickets.GetAsync()` method to the `Provider` parameter and define the `Header` and `Row` templates for rendering `Ticket` properties within the grid:

```
<Grid Provider="@Service.GetAsync">
    <Header>
        <tr>
            <td>Id</td>
            <td>Tariff</td>
            <td>Price</td>
        </tr>
    </Header>
    <Row>
        <tr>
            <td>@context.Id</td>
            <td>@context.Tariff</td>
            <td>@context.Price</td>
        </tr>
    </Row>
</Grid>
```

How it works...

In *step 1*, we create a generic `Grid` component that serves as the foundation for dynamically displaying data in a tabular format with infinite scrolling capabilities.

In *step 2*, we declare a few required parameters within the `Grid` component. `Header` and `Row`, of type `RenderFragment`, enable the customization of the table's header and facilitate the dynamic rendering of table rows. Additionally, we specify a `Provider` delegate to encapsulate the logic for fetching data. We intentionally designed `Provider` to match the `ItemsProvider` signature required by the `Virtualize` component, ensuring compatibility and seamless integration.

In *step 3*, we implement a `LoadAsync()` method that plays a pivotal role in fetching data in response to the user's scroll actions. It accepts an `ItemsProviderRequest` parameter and returns an `ItemsProviderResult<T>` object to enable the `Virtualize` component continuous population of the grid as users scroll through the content. `ItemsProviderRequest` provides the current state of scrolling, exposing `StartIndex`, which defines from which index the next data batch should start. To construct the `ItemsProviderResult<T>` response, we need a subset of new objects to render and a total number of objects in the collection. The `Virtualize` component uses that total to safely stop data fetching and avoid throwing an indexing exception.

In *step 4*, we set up the `Grid` markup. We add a `<table>` structure where we place the `Header` template within `<thead>` tags and utilize the `Virtualize` component within the `<tbody>` tags. By attaching the `LoadAsync()` method as the `ItemsProvider` parameter and including the `Row` template as the `Virtualize` component `ChildContent`, the grid dynamically renders additional rows of data, creating an infinite scrolling effect.

To demonstrate the usage of the `Grid` component, in *step 5*, we introduce a routable `TicketManager` component. We set `TicketManager` to render in `InteractiveWebAssembly` mode and inject `TicketsApi` as we will need it as the data source. In *step 6*, we integrate the `Grid` component into the `TicketManager` markup, with `Tickets.GetAsync` serving as the data provider and `Header` and `Row` templates specified to display the properties of the `Ticket` objects.

There's more...

Utilizing the `Virtualize` component in your Blazor applications brings forth a multitude of benefits that enhance both performance and user experience:

- Firstly, `Virtualize` dramatically improves performance and reduces memory usage when dealing with large datasets. This efficiency gain comes from its rendering approach, where only a visible subset of items is rendered at any given time, reducing the overall load on the browser.

- Secondly, the simplicity offered by `Virtualize` cannot be overstated. You can implement sophisticated infinite scrolling functionalities with minimal code, as the component abstracts the complexities of item virtualization and automatic event handling.

- Lastly, `Virtualize` provides remarkable flexibility, enabling seamless integration with a wide array of data sources. This flexibility is especially beneficial for applications requiring real-time data fetching, as you can tailor the `ItemsProvider` delegate to suit specific data fetching logic, ensuring that applications remain responsive and up to date with the latest information.

Utilizing QuickGrid

In this recipe, we'll explore a powerful component now embedded directly into the Blazor framework – **QuickGrid**. QuickGrid simplifies the creation and management of dynamic, data-driven grids in Blazor applications, offering out-of-the-box functionalities such as sorting, pagination, and filtering. This component stands out for its ease of implementation and high performance in presenting and manipulating large datasets thanks to the baked-in virtualization. QuickGrid eliminates the need for additional NuGet packages, streamlining development processes and reducing project complexity.

Let's walk through the essentials of QuickGrid and showcase how simple it is to implement.

Getting ready

Before we explore the QuickGrid implementation, do the following:

- Create a `Chapter04/Recipe06` directory – this will be your working directory
- Copy `Samples` from the `Chapter04/Data` directory in the GitHub repository

- Navigate to the `Program` file of your application and register the `TicketsApi` service, from `Samples`, in the application dependency injection container:

```
builder.Services.AddScoped<TicketsApi>();
```

How to do it...

To render a grid utilizing QuickGrid, follow these steps:

1. Navigate to the `.csproj` configuration file of your project and add the `Microsoft.AspNetCore.Components.QuickGrid` package to your project:

```
<ItemGroup>
  <PackageReference
      Include=
           "Microsoft.AspNetCore.Components.QuickGrid"
      Version="8.0.2" />
</ItemGroup>
```

2. Create a new routable `TicketManager` component, with a reference to the `QuickGrid` package, that renders in `InteractiveWebAssembly` mode, and inject the `TicketApi` service:

```
@page "/ch04r06"
@using Microsoft.AspNetCore.Components.QuickGrid
@rendermode InteractiveWebAssembly
@inject TicketsApi Tickets
```

3. In the `@code` block of the `TicketManager` component, introduce a `Pagination` variable of type `PaginationState` to configure data pagination of the `QuickGrid` instance:

```
@code {
    protected PaginationState Pagination = new()
    {
        ItemsPerPage = 5
    };
}
```

4. In the `TicketManager` markup, construct the `QuickGrid` component with nested `PropertyColumn` components to define the data columns and integrate a `Paginator` component to manage data pagination:

```
<QuickGrid Class="w-100 table table-bordered"
          Items="@Tickets.Get()"
          Pagination="@Pagination">
    <PropertyColumn Property="@(x => x.Tariff)"
                   Sortable="true" />
```

```
            <PropertyColumn Property="@(x => x.Price)"
                            Sortable="true" Format="0.00" />
    </QuickGrid>
    <Paginator State="@Pagination" />
```

How it works...

In *step 1*, we navigate to the configuration file of the project (the one with a `.csproj` extension) and add the `Microsoft.AspNetCore.Components.QuickGrid` package into the project. QuickGrid is officially a part of the Blazor ecosystem but isn't included in the Blazor project by default.

In *step 2*, we create a new routable `TicketManager` component, where we will put QuickGrid to the test. As the grid will be interactive, we declare `TicketManager` to render in `InteractiveWebAssembly` mode. We also include a `using` directive, referencing the `QuickGrid` namespace. And lastly, we inject the `TicketsApi` service to have a data source for the grid.

In *step 3*, we initialize the `@code` block of the `TicketManager` component where we construct an instance of a `Pagination` variable and set its `ItemsPerPage` property. `QuickGrid` requires a `PaginationState` object to enable the pagination.

Finally, in *step 4*, we embed `QuickGrid` in the `TicketManager` markup. We attach the `Tickets.Get()` method and the `Pagination` object to QuickGrid's `Items` and `Pagination` parameters respectively. Next, we construct grid columns using `PropertyColumn` components. We specify properties to render with a delegate and enable sorting by setting the `Sortable` parameter accordingly. For the `Price` column, we additionally set the `Format` parameter. The `QuickGrid` component will automatically apply this formatting to all prices in that column. Lastly, we incorporate a `Paginator` component that we link to the same `Pagination` variable as the `QuickGrid` Instance. `Paginator` exposes the pagination UI to the user and executes navigation requests directly on `QuickGrid`.

At the end, we get a fully functional, optimized, and feature-rich grid:

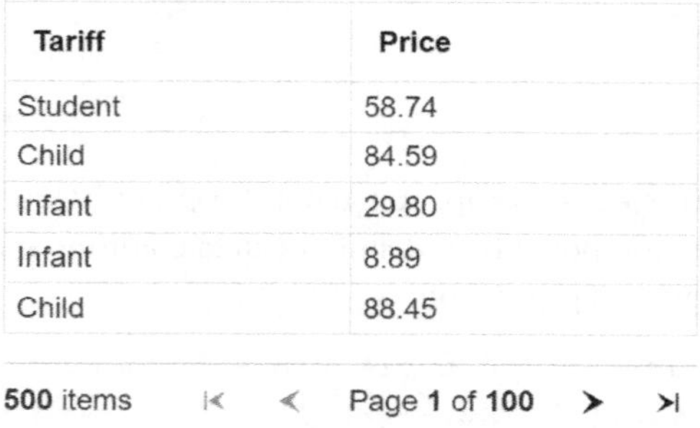

Tariff	Price
Student	58.74
Child	84.59
Infant	29.80
Infant	8.89
Child	88.45

500 items |<   <   Page **1** of **100**   >   >|

Figure 4.2: Grid with sortable columns and pagination rendered with QuickGrid

5

Managing Application State

In this chapter, we will explore the crucial aspect of maintaining and manipulating the state of a Blazor application. An **application state** is the runtime data that dictates the behavior and appearance of an application, reflecting user interactions and decisions.

We will walk through various strategies for state management, from encoding state in the URL for bookmarkable states and easy sharing to implementing in-memory state containers for rapid access. You'll learn how to inject application state as a service, allowing centralized state management across different components, and how to persist state to ensure data continuity across sessions. Furthermore, we will explore techniques to resolve persisted state upon application load, invoking state changes from anywhere within an application, and monitoring these changes with dedicated listening components. We will pay special attention to sharing state across different render mode boundaries.

By the end of this chapter, you'll have a solid foundation in state management practices that will help you build dynamic, responsive, and stateful Blazor applications.

Here are the recipes that will take us there:

- Having a bookmarkable state
- Implementing an in-memory state container
- Injecting application state as a service
- Invoking state changes from anywhere
- Persisting state
- Resolving persisted state
- Sharing state across interactive render mode boundaries

Technical requirements

The barrier of entry to that chapter is not high. You'll need the following tools:

- A modern IDE (that supports Blazor development)
- .NET 9 installed on your development machine
- A modern web browser (one that supports Web Assembly and has DevTools)
- A bare-bone Blazor project (where you'll write your code)

You can find all the examples and data samples referenced in the following recipes in a dedicated GitHub repository at: `https://github.com/PacktPublishing/Blazor-Web-Development-Cookbook/tree/main/BlazorCookbook.App.Client/Chapters/Chapter05`. In each recipe that needs any samples, I will also point you to the directory where you can find them.

Having bookmarkable state

In this recipe, we will introduce the simplest yet powerful pattern of leveraging a URL to maintain and share application state. Unlike more complex state management strategies, embedding state flags directly in the URL doesn't require in-memory persistence. A static URL allows users to bookmark a specific application state and facilitates the easy sharing of that state with others. We will follow the well-known **restful routing** pattern and elegantly map application states to readable and shareable URLs.

Let's create a component that allows us to bookmark and view an entire event list or specific event information.

Getting ready

Before we start implementing a component with bookmarkable state, we need to do the following:

- Create a `Chapter05/Recipe01` directory – this will be our working directory
- Copy the `Api` and `Event` files from the `Chapter05/Data` directory in the GitHub repository

How to do it...

Follow these steps to implement stateful URLs in your application:

1. Navigate to the `Program` file of your application and register the `Api` service, as scoped in the application's dependency injection container:

```
builder.Services.AddScoped<Api>();
```

2. Create a `Store` component with two navigable routes to facilitate user access to different application states through the URL:

```
@page "/ch05r01/events"
@page "/ch05r01/events/{eventId:guid}"
```

3. Inside the `@code` block of the `Store` component, inject the `Api` service and declare an `EventId` parameter that we will use to fetch specific event details:

```
[Inject] private Api Api { get; init; }
[Parameter] public Guid EventId { get; set; }
```

4. Still within the `@code` block, initialize the `Collection` and `Event` variables that will hold the fetched data, based on the application's current state:

```
protected IList<Event> Collection = [];
protected Event Event;
```

5. Override the `OnParametersSetAsync()` life cycle method and implement the logic to update the component's state, based on the parameters passed in the URL:

```
protected override async Task OnParametersSetAsync()
{
    if (EventId != Guid.Empty)
    {
        Event = await Api
            .GetEventAsync(EventId, default);
        return;
    }
    Collection = await Api.GetEventsAsync(default);
}
```

6. In the markup of the `Store` component, add a section to render `Event` details conditionally:

```
@if (Event is not null)
{
    <p>Viewing: @Event.Id</p>
    return;
}
```

7. Add another section to the `Store` markup to render the `Collection` elements:

```
@foreach (var item in Collection)
{
    <div class="w-100">
        <a href="/ch05r01/events/@item.Id">
            @item.Id
```

```
            </a>
        </div>
    }
```

How it works...

In *step 1*, we navigate to the `Program` of the application and register the API service in the application's dependency injection container, so we can inject it later when required.

In *step 2*, we create a routable `Store` component a slightly enhanced routing. We declare two routable paths – `/ch05r01/events` for rendering all available events and `/ch05r01/events/{eventId:guid}` for specific event details. By leveraging path parametrization and path constraints, we specify the `EventId` parameter within the curly braces, setting `Guid` as its expected value type.

In *step 3*, we initialize the `@code` block, where we declare the `EventId` parameter expected by the route. Blazor automatically intercepts and assigns path parameter values based on the name matching. We also inject the `Api` service from the provided sample data, allowing us to fetch event information seamlessly. In *step 4*, we initialize the `Collection` and `Event` variables. These are essential in supporting the dual states of the `Store` component – one for showcasing a list of available events and another for presenting details of a specific, selected event. In *step 5*, we fine-tune the rendering logic by overriding the `OnParametersSetAsync()` life cycle method. We determine whether the `EventId` was correctly resolved and fetch the details of that specific event, using the injected `Api` service. Otherwise, we retrieve the entire collection of available events.

From *step 6*, we implement the `Store` markup that supports two distinct states. To accommodate this, we include two conditional markup sections. If `Event` was fetched, indicating that a specific event's details are ready for display, we render its `Id` and quickly return to skip any further logic. We cover the component's alternative state in *step 7* by iterating over `Collection`. We render links to each event's details, utilizing the `Store` component's parametrized path and providing `item.Id` where the `eventId` parameter goes.

There's more...

You will find parameterized paths most useful in **CRUD (Create, Read, Update, Delete)** scenarios. Assuming we would implement a form within the `Store` component designed to attach to an `Event` object, we could ingeniously treat a `Guid.Empty` value as a trigger to initiate the creation process and initialize a new, empty `Event` model. Conversely, if a valid `Guid` is provided, we would fetch the existing `Event` from the API. We've effectively covered two scenarios with the same form and avoided code duplication.

Specifying the type for a value in a path isn't a strict requirement. By default, Blazor will map parameters as strings, giving you the flexibility to parse them into the required type at a later stage. However, the real power lies in utilizing route constraints effectively. While parsing parameters later provides flexibility, I strongly recommend leveraging route constraints wherever possible. In the `Store` component example, by specifying a parameter type as `Guid`, if the route does not match due to the route constraint, Blazor shows a `NotFound` content – filtering out invalid inputs preemptively and enhancing the robustness and security of your application. We will explore routing and the `NotFound` content in *Chapter 9*.

Implementing an in-memory state container

Efficiently managing interactions with external APIs is absolutely crucial in modern web development. An **in-memory state container** allows you to persist specific objects for an application lifetime unless configured otherwise. When you receive a comprehensive data object from the API upon the initial call, rather than fetching this data anew for every page transition, an in-memory state container facilitates the smooth transfer of the entire object throughout the various stages and pages of the application. Furthermore, an in-memory state container proves invaluable during multi-stage setup processes, allowing the current state of a complex setup object to be persistently carried forward without loss or repeated external calls.

Let's implement a container where we will persist event information and display it after redirecting a user to an event details page.

Getting ready

Before diving into the implementation of an in-memory container, we need to do the following:

- Create a `Chapter05/Recipe02` directory – this will be your working directory
- Copy `Api` and `Event` files from the `Chapter05/Data` directory in the GitHub repository
- Register the `Api` service as scoped in the application's dependency injection container (you can check the *Having a bookmarkable state* recipe to see how)

How to do it...

Implement the in-memory state container with the following steps:

1. Create a generic `StateContainer<T>` class to hold any type of object in memory:

   ```
   public class StateContainer<T> { }
   ```

2. Within `StateContainer<T>`, initialize a backing `_container` as a generic `Dictionary` where you will persist state objects:

   ```
   private readonly Dictionary<Guid, T> _container = [];
   ```

3. Add the `Persist()` and `Resolve()` methods to `StateContainer<T>` that either store or retrieve objects from `_container`, using a `Guid` key:

```
public void Persist(Guid key, T value)
    => _container.TryAdd(key, value);
public T Resolve(Guid key) => _container[key];
```

4. Navigate to the `Program` application root and register the `StateContainer<Event>` in the dependency injection container:

```
builder.Services.AddScoped<StateContainer<Event>>();
```

5. Add a static `Config` class and define a customized `PrerenderDisabled` render mode, based on `InteractiveWebAssembly` but with disabled pre-rendering:

```
internal static class Config
{
    public static readonly IComponentRenderMode
        PrerenderDisabled = new
            InteractiveWebAssemblyRenderMode(
                prerender: false);
}
```

6. Create a routable `Store` component that renders in `PrerenderDisabled` mode:

```
@page "/ch05r02"
@rendermode Config.PrerenderDisabled
```

7. In the `@code` section of `Store`, inject `StateContainer<Event>` to persist `Event` objects, `NavigationManager` to facilitate navigation, and `Api` to seed data from an external source:

```
[Inject]
private StateContainer<Event> Container { get; init; }
[Inject]
private NavigationManager Navigation { get; init; }
[Inject]
private Api Api { get; init; }
```

8. Still inside the `@code` block, initialize a backing `Data` collection and override the `OnInitializedAsync()` life cycle method to fetch `Data` objects from `Api`:

```
protected IList<Event> Data = [];
protected override async Task OnInitializedAsync()
    => Data = await Api.GetEventsAsync(default);
```

9. Lastly, in the `@code` block, implement a `ShowDetails()` method that stores a requested `Event` in the in-memory `StateContainer<Event>` and redirects to a page displaying the event details:

```
public void ShowDetails(Event @event)
{
    Container.Persist(@event.Id, @event);
    Navigation.NavigateTo(
        $"/ch05r02/events/{@event.Id}"
    );
}
```

10. In the `Store` markup, construct a loop where you render navigation buttons to all elements from the `Data` collection:

```
@foreach (var item in Data)
{
    <div class="row w-50 m-1">
        <button @onclick="@(() => ShowDetails(item))">
            @item.Id
        </button>
    </div>
}
```

11. Create an `EventDetails` component with a route matching the one specified in the previous step and rendering in `PrerenderDisabled` mode:

```
@page "/ch05r02/events/{eventId:guid}"
@rendermode Config.PrerenderDisabled
```

12. In the `@code` section of `EventDetails`, inject `StateContainer<Event>` and declare an `EventId` parameter to capture an event identifier from the URL:

```
[Inject]
private StateContainer<Event> Container { get; init; }
[Parameter]
public Guid EventId { get; set; }
```

13. Still within the `@code` block, declare a `Model` variable to maintain the current component state and override the `OnParametersSet()` life cycle method to resolve `Model` from the injected `Container`:

```
protected Event Model;
protected override void OnParametersSet()
    => Model = Container.Resolve(EventId);
```

14. In the `EventDetails` markup, introduce a nullability check for `Model`, and render the current capacity of the underlying event if `Model` is successfully resolved:

```
@if (Model is null) return;
It has @Model.Capacity spots left!
```

How it works...

We start the implementation by laying the foundation of in-memory state persistence. In *step 1*, we add a generic class, `StateContainer<T>`. In *step 2*, we initialize a backing collection within `StateContainer<T>` to persist state objects. We opt for `Dictionary<Guid, T>`, as we will exploit its straightforward key-value API, but any alternative collection type would also work. In *step 3*, we implement the `Persist()` and `Resolve()` methods. The `Persist()` method, accepting `key` and `value`, allows us to add objects to our in-memory container. Concurrently, the `Resolve()` method allows to retrieve these objects using their keys. In *step 4*, we add our in-memory state container to the application's dependency injection container. As we will be working with `Event` objects, we register `StateContainer<Event>`. We give it a `Scoped` lifetime to ensure that `Event` objects are available throughout the user session.

In *step 5*, we introduce a custom render mode – `PrerenderDisabled`. We place `PrerenderDisabled` in a new, static `Config` class so that it's easily reusable. Why do we need a custom render mode? When you declare interactivity mode per component, Blazor serves pre-rendered content by default and hydrates the component state subsequently. In our case, this would raise exceptions, as the in-memory state container remains inaccessible during the initial component render. Our `PrerenderDisabled` mode, based on `InteractiveWebAssembly`, solves that challenge.

In *step 6*, we create a routable `Store` component, referencing the sample data assembly, and we leverage `PrerenderDisabled` mode, defined in `Config`. In *step 7*, we inject the required services – `StateContainer<Event>` for object state persistence, `Navigation` for user-directed navigation, and `Api` for fetching events from an external data source. In *step 8*, we initialize the `Data` collection within the `Store` component and populate it by invoking `Api` in the `OnInitializedAsync()` life cycle method. In *step 9*, we define a `ShowDetails()` method that adds the selected `Event` object to the in-memory state container and redirects the user to an event details page. In *step 10*, we jump to the `Store` markup and render buttons, allowing us to navigate to the details of any element from the `Data` collection.

Now, we also need to add the event details page. In *step 11*, we create an `EventDetails` component with a route matching the one chosen in *step 9*. We also declare its render mode to `PrerenderDisabled`- in line with the `Store` component. In *step 12*, we inject the `StateContainer<Event>` and declare `EventId`, allowing Blazor to intercept the event identifier directly from the page URL. In *step 13*, we declare `Model` for the `EventDetails` component and override the `OnParametersSet()` life cycle method, where we resolve the `Model` value using the intercepted `EventId`. Note that we leverage our `StateContainer<Event>` to fetch the `Model` details and avoid additional fetching from external sources. As we wrap up the implementation, in *step 14*, we complete the `EventDetails` component with a markup that checks for the Model state and displays information about the event's current capacity.

There's more...

Interestingly, the in-memory state container isn't just for holding onto data. It's also handy when managing multi-step forms or complex configuration processes, as you can save and retrieve the progress efficiently.

A critical aspect we've deliberately omitted is the mechanism for cleaning up the state container. Depending on your application's requirements, you may need to persist state for different durations. By following our implementation above, simply registering StateContainer<T> as Scoped ensures that the state lives as long as the user session. However, you might face scenarios where you need more control over the life cycle of state objects. Should you need to clear the state when the user navigates away from a specific component or completes a set of steps, implementing IDisposable or utilizing OwningComponentBase for scoped disposal are more effective strategies.

A word of caution before we end this recipe – you must strategically assess the feasibility of in-memory state containers in your scenarios. The complexity of the persisted objects and the duration of their persistence might put an unnecessary strain on application memory and lead to performance issues.

Injecting application state as a service

In this recipe, we will showcase a design pattern to streamline state management across your application by introducing an application state service and leveraging dependency injection. This method simplifies how components interact with each other, enabling them to seamlessly listen to or communicate changes in the application's state. Leveraging dependency injection, you enhance the responsiveness of your application and maintain a clean architecture by avoiding tight coupling between components. With an application state service, your application remains agile, maintainable, and scalable, adapting to the evolving needs of web development.

Let's implement an injectable state service that allows us to post and receive success and failure messages.

Getting ready

Before you dive into an injectable state service, do the following:

- Create a Chapter05/Recipe03 directory – this will be your working directory
- Copy the Config class with customized PrerenderDisabled render mode from the *Implementing an in-memory state container* recipe or the Chapter05/Recipe03 directory in the GitHub repository

How to do it...

Follow this guide to implement an injectable state service in your application:

1. Add a `StateArgs` base record and define the `SuccessArgs` and `FailureArgs` state arguments deriving from that base:

```
public abstract record StateArgs;
public record SuccessArgs : StateArgs;
public record FailureArgs : StateArgs;
```

2. Introduce a `StoreState` class with an `event` delegate that can be subscribed to and a `Notify()` method that accepts `StateArgs` and triggers the `OnChanged` event:

```
public sealed class StoreState
{
    public event Func<StateArgs, Task> OnChanged;
    public Task Notify(StateArgs args)
        => OnChanged?.Invoke(args);
}
```

3. Navigate to the `Program` class and register `StoreState` in the dependency injection container:

```
builder.Services.AddScoped<StoreState>();
```

4. Create a routable `Store` component that leverages `PrerenderDisabled` render mode and implements the `IDisposable` interface:

```
@page "/ch05r03"
@rendermode Config.PrerenderDisabled
@implements IDisposable
```

5. In the `Store` component @code block, inject `StoreState` and initialize a `Message` variable:

```
[Inject] private StoreState State { get; init; }
protected string Message = string.Empty;
```

6. Still in the @code block, implement a `ReactAsync()` method to convert `StateArgs` into user-friendly messages and apply UI changes:

```
private Task ReactAsync(StateArgs args)
{
    Message = args is SuccessArgs
        ? "Success"
        : "Failure";
    return InvokeAsync(StateHasChanged);
}
```

7. In the @code block, override the OnInitialized() life cycle method to subscribe the ReactAsync() method to the StoreState event:

```
protected override void OnInitialized()
    => State.OnChanged += ReactAsync;
```

8. Lastly, within the @code block, implement the Dispose() method as required by IDisposable and unsubscribe ReactAsync() from the StoreState event:

```
public void Dispose()
    => State.OnChanged -= ReactAsync;
```

9. In the Store component's markup, add two buttons that, upon being clicked, call the Notify() method with either SuccessArgs or FailureArgs. Include a paragraph to display the current value of the Message variable as well:

```
<button @onclick="@(() =>
        State.Notify(new SuccessArgs()))">
    Buy!
</button>
<button @onclick="@(() =>
        State.Notify(new FailureArgs()))">
    Buy!
</button>
<p>@Message</p>
```

How it works...

In *step 1*, we define three object types – StateArgs, SuccessArgs, and FailureArgs – to represent states within our application. Leveraging inheritance and having SuccessArgs and FailureArgs inherit from StateArgs allows us to maintain simplicity in our state-handling logic. In *step 2*, we implement the StoreState class, which acts as an application state service. We expose an event – encapsulating an invocation of an asynchronous method with a StateArgs parameter and a Notify() method – allowing any component to communicate state changes. We've effectively encapsulated the complexities of state transitions behind a simple, intuitive interface. With StoreState ready to go, in *step 3*, we integrate it into our application's dependency injection container within the Program class.

In *step 4*, we create a routable Store component to demonstrate the practical use of our application state service. We opt for custom PrerenderDisabled render mode to avoid potential rendering pitfalls; you learned about that in the *Implementing an in-memory state container* recipe. We also declare Store to implement the IDisposable interface, indicating that there will be a custom cleanup logic to execute. In *step 5*, we inject StoreState as State and initialize the Message variable, where we will capture user-friendly snapshots of the application's state for display. In *step 6*, we implement a `ReactAsync()` method that acts as a dynamic resolver of `StateArgs`. We update the `Message` variable based on the `args` type, pivoting between success and failure states. Afterward, we invoke `StateHasChanged()` to notify that the UI state has changed, but we wrap it inside the `InvokeAsync()` method to ensure that our UI remains responsive and thread-safe.

In *step 7*, we enable the `Store` component to listen to state changes broadcasted by `StoreState`. We override the `OnInitialized()` method and subscribe our `ReactAsync()` to `State.OnChanged`. In *step 8*, we implement the `Dispose()` method, enforced by the `IDisposable` interface. Here, we unsubscribe `ReactAsync()` from `State.OnChanged` to prevent memory leaks and guarantee graceful component disposal.

In *step 9*, we put the `Store` markup in place. We add two buttons – one signals success while the other signals failure. Both utilize the `State.Notify()` method to orchestrate state changes. Below these buttons, we add paragraph tags and render `Message` to visualize the impact of our button's interactions. To keep the example simple, we're triggering state changes with buttons within the same component that listens to those state changes. However, you could place these buttons in any component across the application, and our `Store` will still accurately receive and react to the state notifications. That's the true strength and agility of having an injectable application state service.

See also

In this recipe, we've touched on the topic of events in .NET. We won't dive deep into the .NET fundamentals in that book, but if you're curious to learn more, check out the official Microsoft Learn resources: `https://learn.microsoft.com/en-us/dotnet/csharp/programming-guide/events/`.

Invoking state changes from anywhere

In this recipe, we're exploring injecting state service globally in your Blazor application. State service can cover anything from a user's app personalization to user session details or processing indicators. In our example, we're implementing an overlay covering our interface during a long-running task. **Overlay** serves as a visual cue to users, signaling that their request is being executed and preventing any user interactions that could disrupt the ongoing process.

Getting ready

Before we explore the strategy to globally inject state service and trigger an overlay, do the following:

- Create a `Chapter05/Recipe04` directory – this will be your working directory
- Copy `Api` and `Event` files from the `Chapter05/Data` directory in the GitHub repository

- Copy the `Overlay.css` file from the `Chapter05/Data` directory in the GitHub repository and rename it `Overlay.razor.css`; after renaming, your IDE might display a compilation error – we will explain that behavior and fix the error by the end of this recipe

- Register the `Api` service as scoped in the application's dependency injection container (check out the *Having a bookmarkable state* recipe to see how)

How to do it...

Follow these instructions to add a globally injected overlay state handler:

1. Create an `OverlayState` class with an `OnChanged` event for subscribers to listen to and an `ExecuteAsync()` method that triggers `OnChanged`, both before and after executing any job passed to it:

```
public class OverlayState
{
    public event Func<bool, Task> OnChanged;

    public async Task ExecuteAsync(Func<Task> job)
    {
        await OnChanged.Invoke(true);
        await job.Invoke();
        await OnChanged.Invoke(false);
    }
}
```

2. Navigate to the `Program` class and register `OverlayState` in the dependency injection container.

```
builder.Services.AddScoped<OverlayState>();
```

3. Navigate to the main `_Imports.razor` file at the project level and inject the `OverlayState`, making it available across all components. You might need to reference the missing assembly as well:

```
@inject
    BlazorCookbook.App.Client.Chapters.Chapter05
    .Recipe04.OverlayState OverlayState
```

4. Create an `Overlay` component that implements the `IDisposable` interface:

```
@implements IDisposable
```

5. In the @code block of Overlay, initialize an IsVisible variable and define a ReactAsync()
    method to update IsVisible, based on state changes:

    ```
    protected bool IsVisible;
    public Task ReactAsync(bool isVisible)
    {
        IsVisible = isVisible;
        return InvokeAsync(StateHasChanged);
    }
    ```

6. Override the OnInitialized() life cycle method in the @code block of the Overlay,
    and subscribe the ReactAsync() method to the OverlayState.OnChanged event
    for state change notifications:

    ```
    protected override void OnInitialized()
        => OverlayState.OnChanged += ReactAsync;
    ```

7. Still within the @code block, implement a Dispose() **method to unsubscribe** ReactAsync()
    from the OverlayState.OnChanged event:

    ```
    public void Dispose()
        => OverlayState.OnChanged -= ReactAsync;
    ```

8. In the Overlay markup, include an <overlay> section that visually represents the overlay,
    and use the IsVisible variable to toggle the visibility of this section with:

    ```
    <overlay class="@(IsVisible ? "visible" : "")">
        Loading...
    </overlay>
    ```

9. Create a routable Store component that renders in InteractiveWebAssembly mode:

    ```
    @page "/ch05r04"
    @rendermode InteractiveWebAssembly
    ```

10. In the Store component's @code block, inject the Api service, and implement a SyncAsync()
    method to engage the OverlayState for managing overlay visibility while executing the
    Api service request:

    ```
    [Inject] private Api Api { get; init; }

    private Task SyncAsync()
        => OverlayState.ExecuteAsync(()
            => Api.SynchronizeAsync(default));
    ```

11. In the `Store` markup, embed the `Overlay` component, and include a button to trigger the `SyncAsync()` method:

```
<Overlay />
<button @onclick="@SyncAsync">
    Synchronize data
</button>
```

How it works...

In *step 1*, we create an `OverlayState` service. As we expect our overlay to have a binary nature – visible or hidden – we build a `bool`-based logic. We add a subscribable event of type `Func<bool, Task>` and implement an `ExecuteAsync()` method, which accepts an asynchronous `job` as a parameter. Within `ExecuteAsync()`, we toggle the overlay's visibility by invoking the `OnChanged` event before and after the `job` execution, effectively showing the overlay during processing and hiding it upon completion. In *step 2*, we integrate `OverlayState` into the dependency injection container, and in *step 3*, we achieve `OverlayState` global accessibility by injecting it into the `_Imports.razor` file. `_Imports.razor` files in a Blazor application act as encapsulators of adding namespaces and directives, enabling them to be accessible across sibling or nested Razor components without declaring them explicitly in each.

In *step 4*, we create an `Overlay` component, interacting with `OverlayState`. As we will implement event-driven logic in `Overlay`, we declare it to implement the `IDisposable` interface. In *step 5*, we initiate an `IsVisible` variable to track the overlay's visibility state and a `ReactAsync()` method to respond to those state changes. Now, we can leverage the `ReactAsync()` method to listen to the `OverlayState` event. In *step 6*, we override the `OnInitialized()` life cycle method to subscribe to the `OverlayState.OnChanged` event with `ReactAsync()`. Now, Blazor will communicate any changes in the overlay state to the `Overlay` UI. In *step 7*, we address potential memory leaks and unsubscribe from the `OnChanged` event within the `Dispose()` method. In *step 8*, we implement the `Overlay` markup. We introduce a custom `<overlay>` tag to avoid conflicts with other, standard DOM elements. We use the `IsVisible` flag to toggle the `visible` class, deciding whether an overlay is currently visible. Blazor will automatically associate the `Overlay.razor.css` collocated styles (which you've copied from the sample directory) and scope that styling to the `Overlay` component we just implemented.

In *step 9*, we shift to showcasing the practical application of `OverlayState` and `Overlay`. We create a `Store` component and set it to render in `InteractiveWebAssembly` mode. In *step 10*, we inject the `Api` service and implement a `SyncAsync()` method. In the `SyncAsync()` method, we leverage `OverlayState.ExecuteAsync()` to encapsulate the execution of potentially time-consuming operations and display a visual cue in the form of an overlay, ensuring that the user is aware that their request is processing. In *step 11*, we introduce the `Store` markup by adding the `Overlay` component and a trigger button for the `SyncAsync()` method.

There's more...

As we've injected the `OverlayState` globally across all components, we can decouple the `Overlay` presence from any component state. We can achieve that by incorporating the `Overlay` tag within the application's layout file. With that, the overlay functionality is omnipresent – you can leverage the overlay from any application area with minimal fuss.

Here's what the layout could look like:

```
@inherits LayoutComponentBase
<Overlay />
<main>
    @Body
</main>
```

Persisting state

In modern web development, the ability to persist application and session states is no longer a luxury but a necessity. Whether it's to enhance user experience, safeguard user progress, or maintain preferences across sessions, state persistence plays a pivotal role in creating seamless and engaging digital experiences. Consider the convenience of saving local application configurations on the client side, such as a user's preference for dark mode or their choice to receive push notifications. Similarly, persisting parts of the session state can be crucial for ensuring that users don't lose valuable progress due to unexpected disruptions – imagine the frustration it would cause. These small touches can significantly boost the usability and personalization of any application. Let's see how to persist state in your Blazor app.

Let's implement an option to switch between light and dark modes and persist a proper setting flag in a user's browser.

Getting ready

Before implementing state persistence, do the following:

- Create a `Chapter05/Recipe05` directory – this will be your working directory

How to do it...

Follow these steps to implement state persistence:

1. Add an {ASSEMBLY_NAME}.lib.module.js file within the wwwroot directory of your client application, and define a browserStorage object with a set function that is capable of storing a key-value pair in either session storage or local storage, based on a type parameter:

```
window.browserStorage = {
    set: function (type, key, value) {
        if (type === 'sessionStorage') {
            sessionStorage.setItem(key, value);
        }
        if (type == 'localStorage') {
            localStorage.setItem(key, value);
        }
    }
};
```

2. Create a generic, abstract StorageValue class with the Key and Value properties, aligning with the parameters expected by the browserStorage.set function:

```
public abstract record StorageValue<T>
{
    public string Key { get; init; }
    public T Value { get; init; }
}
```

3. Create LocalStorageValue and SessionStorageValue records – specific implementations of StorageValue for different browser storage types:

```
public record LocalStorageValue<T> : StorageValue<T>;
public record SessionStorageValue<T> :
    StorageValue<T>;
```

4. Create a BrowserStorage class within your application, and inject the IJSRuntime service available in Blazor by default:

```
public class BrowserStorage
{
    private readonly IJSRuntime _js;
    public BrowserStorage(IJSRuntime js)
    {
        _js = js;
    }
}
```

5. Inside the `BrowserStorage`, define `const` values to ensure the consistency of the logic:

    • `_setFunc` to store the JavaScript function name

    • `_local` and `_session` to reference the storage types:

    ```
    private const string
        _setFunc = "browserStorage.set",
        _local = "localStorage",
        _session = "sessionStorage";
    ```

6. Still inside `BrowserStorage`, implement a `PersistAsync()` method, accepting a `StorageValue<T>` parameter. Utilize `JsonSerializer` to convert the value to JSON and determine the appropriate storage location, before invoking the `browserStorage.set` function:

    ```
    public ValueTask PersistAsync<T>(
        StorageValue<T> @object)
    {
        var json = JsonSerializer
            .Serialize(@object.Value);

        var storage = @object is LocalStorageValue<T>
            ? _local : _session;

        return _js.InvokeVoidAsync(_setFunc,
            storage, @object.Key, json);
    }
    ```

7. Navigate to the application's `Program` class and register the `BrowserStorage` service in the dependency injection container:

    ```
    builder.Services.AddTransient<BrowserStorage>();
    ```

8. Create a routable `Settings` component that renders in `InteractiveWebAssembly` mode:

    ```
    @page "/ch05r05"
    @rendermode InteractiveWebAssembly
    ```

9. Within the `@code` block of `Settings`, inject `BrowserStorage` and declare constant keys dedicated to managing view mode persistence:

    ```
    [Inject] private BrowserStorage Storage { get; init; }
    private const string _key = "viewMode",
                         _light = "lightMode",
                         _dark = "darkMode";
    ```

10. Still in the @code block, implement a SetViewModeAsync() method that takes a mode parameter, encapsulates it within a LocalStorageValue<string> object, and persists it using the BrowserStorage.PersistAsync() method:

```
public async Task SetViewModeAsync(string mode)
{
    var value = new LocalStorageValue<string>
    {
        Key = _key,
        Value = mode
    };
    await Storage.PersistAsync(value);
}
```

11. In the Settings component's markup, introduce two buttons that utilize the SetViewModeAsync() method to adjust the application's view mode – one to set light mode and the other for dark mode:

```
<button @onclick="@(() => SetViewModeAsync(_light))">
    Turn the light on!
</button>
<button @onclick="@(() => SetViewModeAsync(_dark))">
    Turn the light off!
</button>
```

How it works...

In this recipe, we will require a piece of custom **JavaScript** to lay the foundation of our process. We utilize the {ASSEMBLY_NAME}.lib.module.js file, which resides in the wwwroot folder of our client-side project; if you don't have it yet, create one. Blazor will automatically embed it, so explicit registration is not required. In *step 1*, we navigate to that .js file and define a browserStorage API. For now, we implement just a set function that accepts the type, key, and value parameters, and depending on the specified type, it invokes the setItem function of either the sessionStorage or localStorage instance.

In *step 2*, we create a StorageValue generic record with the Key and Value properties. By marking this record as abstract, we signal our intention to use it as a foundation for more specific storage values. And we implement just that in *step 3*, where we add LocalStorageValue and SessionStorageValue, both inheriting from StorageValue.

In *step 4*, we initiate the BrowserStorage service. As we need to call a JavaScript function from our C# code, we inject Blazor's baked-in IJSRuntime into our service. In *step 5*, we introduce a few const values to anchor our persistence logic. With _setFunc, we encapsulate the naming of the JavaScript function we want to call, while _local and _session identify the two available browser storage types. In *step 6*, we finalize the `BrowserStorage` implementation with the `PersistAsync()` generic method. However, browser storage allows us to store `string` types only. We address that constraint by leveraging the `JsonSerializer` to transform our `value` object into a **JSON** format. Then, using the `is` operator and our constant values, we resolve the appropriate browser storage type. Having all the required payload, we end the `PersistAsync()` logic by delegating work to the `browserStorage.set` function, with the help of the `IJSRuntime` reference and its `InvokeVoidAsync()` method. Now, we need to make our `BrowserStorage` available for components. In *step 7*, we navigate to the `Program` class and register `BrowserStorage` within the dependency injection container. Given the stateless nature of `BrowserStorage`, we opt for a `Transient` lifetime to avoid unnecessary memory use.

In *step 8*, we create a `Settings` component and set it to render in `InteractiveWebAssembly` mode, ensuring the component's interactivity. Then, in *step 9*, we inject `BrowserStorage` into the `Settings` and declare a few constant variables – `_key`, which holds the storage value key, and `_light` and `_dark`, which outline the available view modes. In *step 10*, we implement the `SetViewModeAsync()` method, where we initialize the `LocalStorageValue` variable with our `_key` and the `mode` parameter and invoke the `PersistAsync()` method of the injected `BrowserStore` service. To wrap it up, in *step 11*, we add two buttons to the `Settings` component markup. With these buttons, users can invoke the `SetViewModeAsync()` method and set the selected view mode in the browser's local storage.

Steps may vary a little between browsers, but here's how you can peak the `viewMode` key value with Chrome DevTools:

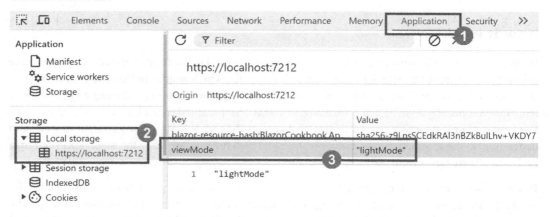

Figure 5.1: Peaking the value persisted in a browser's local storage with Chrome DevTools

There's more...

We've developed a custom JavaScript function to enable access to a browser's storage, as this implementation remains functional across both server and client-side scenarios, offering broad compatibility and flexibility. When integrating JavaScript into Blazor applications, you must remember that services depending on `IJSRuntime` cannot be registered as singletons. `IJSRuntime` requires access to each user's browser session, which makes it architecturally incompatible with the singleton initialization pattern and lifetime model.

However, for projects strictly confined to server-side Blazor, you should consider leveraging the built-in `ProtectedBrowserStorage` API. `ProtectedBrowserStorage` is a Blazor-native mechanism that enables browser storage access with a data encryption layer that doesn't require custom JavaScript at all.

Resolving persisted state

In the previous recipe, you explored persisting application state within a browser's storage. Building upon this foundation, in this recipe, we'll focus on an equally crucial aspect – restoring that persisted state. That functionality is invaluable when dealing with user-specific local application personalization, such as the preference between dark or light mode or the consent to receive push notifications. With state persistence and resolution, you offer users the convenience of rejoining their sessions exactly where they left them. This continuity is fundamental in crafting a user-centric application and offering a personalized experience.

With the light or dark mode persisted in the last recipe, let's implement an option to resolve a persisted view mode value when a component renders.

Getting ready

Before you start resolving persisted state, do the following:

- Create a `Chapter05/Recipe06` directory – this will be your working directory
- Copy the `BrowserStorage`, `Settings`, and all `StorageValue` records from the *Persisting state* recipe or the `Chapter05/Recipe05` directory of the GitHub repository
- If you're not following along the entire chapter but starting with this recipe, copy the `BlazorCookbook.App.Client.lib.module.js` file from the `wwwroot` directory of the `BlazorCookbook.App.Client` in the GitHub repository to the `wwwroot` of your project, and rename it to match your project assembly
- Register the `BrowserStorage` as transient in your application's `Program` class (check out the *Persisting state* recipe to see how)

How to do it...

Follow these instructions to implement the resolution of persisted state:

1. Open the {ASSEMBLY_NAME}.lib.module.js script file, and enhance browserStorage by adding a get function that retrieves the persisted value from storage, specified by the type parameter:

    ```
    get: function (type, key) {
        if (type === 'sessionStorage') {
            return sessionStorage.getItem(key);
        }
        if (type === 'localStorage') {
            return localStorage.getItem(key);
        }
        return '';
    },
    ```

2. In the BrowserStorage class, introduce a new _getFunc variable to hold the name of the newly created browserStorage.get JavaScript function:

    ```
    private const string _getFunc = "browserStorage.get";
    ```

3. Within the BrowserStorage, implement a ResolveAsync() generic method, accepting a StorageValue parameter that fetches the persisted value from the appropriate browser storage. Utilize JsonSerializer to transform the retrieved string into the expected object type:

    ```
    public async ValueTask<T> ResolveAsync<T>(
        StorageValue<T> @object)
    {
        var storage = @object is LocalStorageValue<T>
            ? _local : _session;

        var value = await _js.InvokeAsync<string>(
            _getFunc, storage, @object.Key);

        return JsonSerializer.Deserialize<T>(value);
    }
    ```

4. Move to the Settings component. Extend the @code section with a new ViewMode variable, and override the OnAfterRenderAsync() life cycle method with logic to resolve the persisted viewMode value in ViewMode:

```
protected string ViewMode = string.Empty;

protected override async Task
    OnAfterRenderAsync(bool firstRender)
{
    if (!firstRender) return;

    var value = new LocalStorageValue<string>
    {
        Key = _key
    };

    ViewMode = await Storage.ResolveAsync(value);
    StateHasChanged();
}
```

5. Enhance the Settings component's markup by adding a paragraph below the buttons to display the current ViewMode value:

```
<p>@ViewMode</p>
```

How it works...

We start by enhancing our browserStorage API. In *step 1*, we navigate to the {ASSEMBLY_NAME}.lib.module.js script file and expand the browserStorage functionality with a get function. We mirror the set function's implementation, utilizing the type parameter to select the appropriate storage type and fetching the value associated with the specified key.

In *step 2*, we refine our BrowserStorage service implementation by introducing a _getFunc variable to store the name of our newly created browserStorage.get function, safeguarding against potential typo errors in future references. Following this, in *step 3*, we implement a ResolveAsync() generic method that mirrors the logic of the existing PersistAsync() method. ResolveAsync() takes a StorageValue parameter, identifies the correct storage using the is operator, and calls the InvokeAsync() generic method provided by IJSRuntime to pull the value from browser storage. Since this value returns as a JSON string, we utilize the JsonSerializer API to convert this string back into the desired data type.

In *step 4*, we shift to the Settings component, where we initialize a ViewMode variable to hold the resolved value of the user's persisted view mode choice. We then override the OnAfterRenderAsync() life cycle method, where we use the injected Storage service and the newly introduced ResolveAsync() method to resolve the ViewMode value when the Settings component initially renders. Leveraging the **fast-return pattern**, we ensure that the method exits immediately during subsequent component state changes. Since Blazor executes our resolving logic post-render, we must invoke the StateHasChanged() method to refresh the UI with the updated values. Finally, in *step 5*, for the sake of simplicity, we add a paragraph below the action buttons within the Settings markup to display the current ViewMode value. Alternatively, you can apply CSS classes for light and dark modes to the DOM elements, should you have the supporting CSS in place.

There's more...

We used the OnAfterRenderAsync() method to resolve the ViewMode value for an architectural reason. Blazor blocks all IJSRuntime interactions in the initial phases of component initialization. Before the DOM is created, the component is essentially in a setup phase, initializing and fetching required data. Once rendering completes and the DOM structure is in place, Blazor allows us to invoke the IJSRuntime API and interact with loaded JavaScript functions.

Sharing state across interactive render mode boundaries

Navigating state management in Blazor apps becomes complicated when you switch from running solely in one render mode to mixing render modes, or using InteractiveAuto mode. The challenge arises from the recreation of a scoped state with every render mode change, due to the lack of automatic state sharing between server and client environments. You can tackle this fragmentation by designating a single, consistent source for state persistence. In this recipe, we will dive into a strategy where the client is the source of truth, and we will restore state from the browser storage.

Let's implement a generic component base that allows us to share state across interactive render mode boundaries.

Getting ready

Before you dive into state sharing, do the following:

- Create a Chapter05/Recipe07 directory – this will be your working directory
- Copy the BrowserStorage and StorageValue objects from the *Resolving persisted state* recipe or from the Chapters05/Recipe06 directory of the GitHub repository

- If you're not following along the entire chapter but starting with this recipe, copy the `BlazorCookbook.App.Client.lib.module.js` file from the `wwwroot` directory of the `BlazorCookbook.App.Client` in the GitHub repository to the `wwwroot` of your project, and rename it to match your project assembly

- Register the `BrowserStorage` as transient in your application's `Program` class (check out the *Persisting state* recipe to see how)

How to do it...

Follow these steps to implement sharing state across interactive render mode boundaries:

1. Create a `CartState` class, with an `UpdateTime` property and an `Add()` method that mimics adding to the cart and refreshes `UpdateTime`:

```
public sealed class CartState
{
    public DateTime UpdateTime { get; set; }
    public void Add() => UpdateTime = DateTime.UtcNow;
}
```

2. Navigate to the `Program` class and register a global `CascadingValue` for `CartState`:

```
builder.Services
    .AddCascadingValue(it => new CartState());
```

3. Create a generic `CrossingInteractiveBoundary` component that implements the `IAsyncDisposable` interface:

```
@implements IAsyncDisposable
@typeparam T
```

4. Within the component's @code section of `CrossingInteractiveBoundary`, define a unique state identifier, `_key`, inject `BrowserStorage`, and use `CascadingParameter` to intercept the generic `State`:

```
private const string _key = "state";
[Inject] private BrowserStorage Storage { get; init; }
[CascadingParameter] public T State { get; set; }
```

5. Still within the @code block, override the `OnAfterRenderAsync()` life cycle method to hydrate `State` by fetching the persisted value with `SessionStorageValue`, via the `ResolveAsync()` method of `Storage`:

```
protected override async Task
    OnAfterRenderAsync(bool firstRender)
{
    if (!firstRender) return;

    var value = new SessionStorageValue<T>
    {
        Key = $"{_key}_{State.GetType()}"
    };
    try
    {
        State = await Storage.ResolveAsync(value);
        StateHasChanged();
    }
    catch { }
}
```

6. Lastly, in the @code block, to preserve state upon disposal, implement a `DisposeAsync()` method, as mandated by the `IAsyncDisposable` contract, and send the updated `State` back to the browser storage through the `PersistAsync()` method:

```
public ValueTask DisposeAsync()
{
    var value = new SessionStorageValue<T>
    {
        Key = $"{_key}_{State.GetType()}",
        Value = State
    };
    return Storage.PersistAsync(value);
}
```

7. Create a routable `Cart` component that operates in `InteractiveAuto` render mode and inherits from the `CrossingInteractiveBoundary<CartState>` type:

```
@page "/ch05r07"
@rendermode InteractiveAuto
@inherits CrossingInteractiveBoundary<CartState>
```

8.   In the layout of the Cart component, add a button that triggers the Add() method of State and a paragraph to display the current value of the UpdateTime property:

```
<button @onclick="@(() => State.Add())">
    Add to cart
</button>
<p>Last cart change: @State.UpdateTime</p>
```

How it works...

In *step 1*, we create a CartState state class with an UpdateTime property and an Add() method that refreshes UpdateTime with the current UTC, demonstrating the dynamic state interactions. In *step 2*, we navigate to the Program class, and by leveraging Blazor's AddCascadingValue() extension method, we declare CartState as a globally accessible CascadingValue, ensuring that the state object is available throughout the application. We declare that the initial state of the cart is represented by a new instance of the CartState object.

In *step 3*, we introduce the cornerstone of our state-sharing mechanism – the CrossingInteractiveBoundary component. By implementing the IAsyncDisposable interface, we prepare CrossingInteractiveBoundary to have an asynchronous disposal logic. In *step 4*, we define a unique _key storage identifier and inject BrowserStorage to persist state beyond traditional life cycle boundaries. With the CascadingParameter attribute, we dynamically capture the State value, regardless of the currently expected type. In *step 5*, we override the OnAfterRenderAsync() life cycle method of the CrossingInteractiveBoundary to rehydrate State with previously persisted values from the browser's session storage. We utilize the try-catch structure to gracefully handle scenarios where the user initializes state for the first time, so there's no value to restore. In *step 6*, we complete the implementation with the DisposeAsync() method, but instead of releasing resources, we add logic to persist the State value with the PersistAsync() method of Storage. This way, we ensure that the state remains updated and recoverable, regardless of navigation actions or rendering mode transitions.

In *step 7*, we introduce the Cart component that renders in dynamic InteractiveAuto mode and inherits from CrossingInteractiveBoundary, with state represented by the CartState object. Blazor will seamlessly alternate between server-side and client-side rendering, which makes it a perfect environment to showcase the adaptive state-sharing logic of CrossingInteractiveBoundary. In *step 8*, we add the Cart markup – a button that invokes the Add() method of CartState and a paragraph displaying the current UpdateTime value.

There's more...

The strategy we've explored in this recipe is not limited to cascading parameters. You can also leverage `BrowserStorage` to hydrate and persist the state of the state injected as a service (you learned how to implement injectable state in the *Injecting application state as a service* recipe). Depending on your architectural requirements, you can leverage a **REST API** or **gRPC** service and persist state on the server as well. Moreover, as the complexity and size of the state object grows, you'll see that state hydration can cause a visible delay before the UI refreshes with the correct data. That's where the `Overlay` component, which we implemented in the *Invoking state changes from anywhere* recipe, comes in handy. By temporarily obscuring the UI until state resolution completes, we ensure that users experience a seamless and cohesive interface.

6

Building Interactive Forms

In this chapter, we will focus on the essential skills needed to construct interactive forms in Blazor. Forms are a critical component of many web applications, and Blazor provides tools that significantly simplify form creation and handling.

We will start by learning how to bind simple and nested models to a form for capturing and managing user input. Next, we will explore the built-in input components provided by Blazor. These components help standardize form behavior across different platforms, ensuring consistency and reducing the amount of custom code needed. We will also cover techniques for interpreting keystrokes and making the form intuitive. At the end of the chapter, we will address the security aspect of form handling and the role of the **anti-forgery** token. Implementing these security measures is crucial for protecting your applications from common web threats such as **Cross-Site Request Forgery** (**CSRF**) attacks.

By the end of this chapter, you will have the practical knowledge to create, manage, and secure forms in Blazor applications – all vital for developing reliable, interactive, and user-friendly web applications.

Here's the list of recipes we'll cover in this chapter:

- Binding a simple model to a form
- Submitting static forms without full page reload
- Binding nested models to a form
- Utilizing built-in input components
- Handling file uploads with a form

Technical requirements

We will keep the examples simple and focus on showcasing all the angles of setting up forms in Blazor. At the beginning of each recipe, you will find instructions on where to find required samples and which directories to create. With that said, you will need these basic tools for Blazor development:

- A modern IDE (that supports Blazor development)
- A modern web browser (that supports WebAssembly)
- Browser DevTools (that could be a part of the modern browser already)
- A Blazor project (where you'll write your code)

In the *Handling file uploads with a form* recipe, we'll utilize a NuGet package – `Microsoft.AspNetCore.Http.Features` – that's not pre-installed by default, so you might as well add it to your project now.

You can find all the code samples on GitHub at: `https://github.com/PacktPublishing/Blazor-Web-Development-Cookbook/tree/main/BlazorCookbook.App.Client/Chapters/Chapter06`

Binding a simple model to a form

In the development of modern web applications, forms are ubiquitous and essential. Whether registering user details, collecting feedback, or entering information, forms serve as the primary interface for user input. Blazor supports a traditional HTML `<form>` markup but elevates the experience with its native `EditForm` component. `EditForm` integrates seamlessly with Blazor's data binding capabilities and provides a streamlined, efficient approach to form management.

Let's add the first small form that binds to a simple data model and allows the user to create a new event by providing its name.

Getting ready

Before we start creating a form and bind it to a simple model, do the following:

- Create a `Chapter06/Recipe01` directory – this will be your working directory
- Copy the `Models.cs` file from the `Chapter06/Data` directory in the GitHub repository

How to do it...

To implement a form supporting a simple data model, follow these steps:

1. Create a routable `EventManager` component:

   ```
   @page "/ch06r01"
   ```

2. Within the @code block of EventManager, declare a Model object and decorate it with a SupplyParameterFromForm attribute:

```
[SupplyParameterFromForm]
protected Event Model { get; set; }
```

3. Still inside the @code block, override the OnInitialized() lifecycle method with conditional initialization of the Model parameter if it's unset. Additionally, implement a Save() method as a placeholder to simulate saving the form:

```
protected override void OnInitialized()
    => Model ??= new();
private void Save()
    => Console.WriteLine($"Saved {Model.Name}.");
```

4. In the markup of EventManager, embed an EditForm component and bind it to the Model parameter. Include an input field for entering Model.Name and a submit button that triggers the Save() method:

```
<EditForm FormName="event-form"
          Model="@Model"
          OnSubmit="@Save">
    <label>
        Name:
        <InputText @bind-Value="@Model.Name" />
    </label>
    <button type="submit">Save</button>
</EditForm>
```

How it works...

In *step 1*, we create a routable EventManager component, which will serve as the container for our form.

In *step 2*, within the @code block of EventManager, we declare a Model parameter for our form with a form-specific attribute – SupplyParameterFromForm – enabling Blazor to automatically populate the Model object with values from the associated form. In *step 3*, we finalize the @code block of EventManager. We override the OnInitialized() lifecycle method to seamlessly initialize the Model parameter to an empty object unless it already carries a value. Additionally, we introduce a Save() method, acting as a placeholder to mimic the saving of changes made to the form.

In *step 4*, we tackle the implementation of the EventManager markup, leveraging Blazor's built-in EditForm component. We assign our Model object to the Model parameter of the EditForm component and the Save() method to the OnSubmit callback, automating the invocation of Save() upon form submission. Crucially, we set a unique value for the FormName parameter of

EditForm, allowing Blazor to properly resolve the form data. Within the form, we incorporate a simple input box, binding it to the Model.Name property, and include a submit button to facilitate form submission.

We opted not to declare any render mode intentionally, resulting in static server-side rendering of our page. While this approach ensures quick rendering and minimal resource utilization on the server, submitting the form requires a full page reload – similar to **MVC** or **Razor pages** applications.

There's more

Each parameter of the EditForm component has a corresponding Blazor attribute, compatible with standard HTML, which means you can customize the behavior of your forms extensively without relying on the EditForm component. You can retain the standard HTML <form> markup and customize it to your needs.

To give you a practical example, here's how you can implement our form using the HTML <form> markup:

```
<form method="post"
      @onsubmit="@Save"
      @formname="event-form">
    <AntiforgeryToken />
    <label>
        Name:
        <InputText @bind-Value="@Model.Name" />
    </label>
    <button type="submit">Save</button>
</form>
```

We construct a simple form, leveraging the default HTML form element. We declare the form's unique name, the method to call on submit, and that Blazor should execute a post action when submitting the data. However, as we no longer leverage the EditForm component, Blazor will force us to provide an anti-forgery token for security reasons. For that, we leverage a built-in AntiforgeryToken component, but we will explore that component in detail in the *Securing a form with an anti-forgery token* recipe, at the end of the chapter.

Submitting static forms without full page reload

Blazor, leveraging the diffing algorithm (we talked about it in the *Hooking into event delegates* recipe in *Chapter 3*), offers an **enhanced navigation** feature, which optimizes user interactions by reducing unnecessary re-renderings and updating only the parts of the UI that have changed rather than reloading entire pages. Interactive render modes have the diffing algorithm enabled by default, but forms rendered in **static server-side render** (**SSR**) mode do not. In this recipe, we will explore how to enable the enhanced navigation on the EditForm component using the Enhanced parameter.

Let's enable enhanced navigation on the Event creation form and prevent the form from reloading the entire page upon submission while maintaining its operation in SSR mode.

Getting ready

Before we explore form enhancing, do the following:

- Create a Chapter06/Recipe02 directory – this will be your working directory
- Copy the EventManager component from the *Binding a simple model to a form* recipe or from the Chapter06/Recipe01 directory of the GitHub repository
- Copy the Models.cs file from the Chapter06/Data directory in the GitHub repository

How to do it...

1. To enable enhanced navigation on your form, navigate to the EventManager component and set the Enhance parameter value of the EditForm component:

```
<EditForm FormName="event-form"
          Model="@Model"
          OnSubmit="@Save"
          Enhance>
    @* form body *@
</EditForm>
```

How it works...

In this recipe, we navigate to the EventManager component and set the value of the Enhance parameter on the EditForm component. Since Enhance is of type bool, merely stating the parameter name is equivalent to declaring Enhance="true". This simple adjustment is all it takes to enable the enhanced navigation on your form. If you've been developing MVC applications, you can conceptualize the enhancement using Html.BeginForm when the form is not enhanced and Ajax.BeginForm with the Enhance attribute in place.

Although the EventManager component continues to render statically on the server, with enhanced navigation activated, Blazor now monitors UI changes more effectively. Full-page reload is no longer required when a user submits the form, which results in a smoother and more responsive user experience while still leveraging the benefits of the SSR.

There's more...

The Enhance parameter, similar to other parameters of the EditForm component, has an equivalent attribute compatible with plain HTML forms – data-enhance.

Here's how you can attach data-enhance to your <form> tag:

```
<form method="post"
      @onsubmit="@Save"
      @formname="event-form"
      data-enhance>
    @* form body *@
</form>
```

We leverage the default HTML form element and declare the form's unique name, the method to call on submit, and that Blazor should execute a post action when submitting the data. Next to those already familiar attributes, we attach the data-enhance attribute. The order of attributes has no impact on the form's functionality.

Binding nested models to a form

In this recipe, we'll explore the management of **nested models** within forms in Blazor. Nested models are complex data structures where a model contains other models as properties. They're common when we capture detailed or structured information, such as a user profile with multiple addresses or an order with multiple items. However, managing forms with complex and nested data models can get out of hand as the depth of the data structure grows. Keeping track of each input field and ensuring proper binding can be challenging, making the form less maintainable and more prone to errors. The Editor<T> component simplifies the handling of complex object scenarios as it encapsulates the binding of each field to its corresponding property, giving you a narrowed view of the current form context.

Let's enhance our event creation form with a nested object, allowing us to add information about the event's duration.

Getting ready

Before we start the implementation of a nested form, do the following:

- Create a Chapter06/Recipe03 directory – this will be your working directory
- Copy the EventManager component from the *Submitting static forms without full page reload* recipe or from the Chapter06/Recipe02 directory of the GitHub repository
- Copy the Models.cs file from the Chapter06/Data directory in the GitHub repository

How to do it...

Follow these steps to implement a maintainable nested form:

1. Create an `EventDurationForm` component inheriting from `Editor<EventPeriod>`:

    ```
    @inherits Editor<EventPeriod>
    ```

2. In the markup of the `EventDurationForm` component, utilize the `InputDate` component and add two fields for setting the `Start` and `End` properties of the base `EventPeriod` model:

    ```
    <label>
        From: <InputDate @bind-Value="@Value.Start" />
    </label>
    <label>
        To: <InputDate @bind-Value="@Value.End" />
    </label>
    ```

3. In the `EventManager` component, navigate to the `@code` block and extend the `Save()` method to log `Model.Period` details to the console:

    ```
    private void Save()
    {
        Console.WriteLine($"Saved {Model.Name}.");
        Console.WriteLine(
            $"{Model.Period.Start} - {Model.Period.End}"
        );
    }
    ```

4. In the `EventManager` markup, integrate an instance of the `EventDurationForm` component within `EditForm`, between the existing label and the `submit` button, and bind it to the `Model.Period` nested property:

    ```
    <label>
        Name: <InputText @bind-Value="@Model.Name" />
    </label>
    <EventDurationForm @bind-Value="@Model.Period" />
    <button type="submit">Save</button>
    ```

How it works...

In *step 1*, we create the `EventDurationForm` component, dedicated to handling the period settings of an event. To properly reference the necessary model, we include a `@using` directive for the assembly of the `EventPeriod` model and use the `@inherits` directive to derive from the generic `Editor<T>` component, setting T as our `EventPeriod` model. Next, in *step 2*, we add the markup of the `EventDurationForm` component. As the `Editor<T>` component implements the

@bind-Value pattern, we can directly interact with the underlying model through the local Value property. We embed two date input fields using the InputDate component, binding them to the Value.Start and Value.End properties. For now, we will skip the built-in form components in Blazor as we explore them in a subsequent recipe.

In *step 3*, we shift our focus to the EventManager component. In the @code block, we extend the Save() placeholder method to log Model.Period details to the console. It will allow us to validate the binding of our nested model. Finally, in *step 4*, we jump to the markup of the EventManager component and integrate the EventDurationForm component into the existing EditForm markup, right before the submit button. By utilizing the bind-Value pattern, we bind the Model.Period object directly to EventDurationForm.

We've effectively encapsulated the markup and logic of managing the event period without complexifying the main EditForm instance.

There's more...

Throughout all the recipes exploring the EditForm capabilities, we have consistently utilized static server rendering. It's a strategic choice, allowing you to highlight any potential edge cases and particularities of the SSR mode and providing a comprehensive understanding of how forms behave under different rendering conditions.

However, if you choose to employ any of the interactive rendering modes available in Blazor, forms will continue to function correctly. By adding the @renderMode directive to your components, you can easily switch between rendering modes depending on the needs of your application. Whether you need server-side rendering for its robustness and security or client-side rendering for its interactivity and speed — EditForm will operate smoothly and efficiently.

Utilizing built-in input components

In this recipe, we'll explore how quickly you can set up both simple and complex forms using Blazor's native form support and built-in input components. The benefit of using Blazor lies in its ability to handle much of the heavy lifting involved in form creation, such as data binding, event handling, maintaining state, or parsing user input to expected values. You're then free to focus on other aspects of the user interface.

Let's showcase Blazor's built-in input components by creating a comprehensive form where the system administrator provides a detailed definition of the events they are planning.

Getting ready

Before we build the event creator, do the following:

- Create a Chapter06/Recipe04 directory – this will be your working directory

- Copy the EventManager and EventDurationForm components from the *Binding nested models to a form* recipe or copy their implementation from the Chapter06/Recipe03 directory of the GitHub repository

- Copy the Models.cs file from the Chapter06/Data directory in the GitHub repository

How to do it...

Follow these steps to implement the event creator with built-in input components:

1. Open the EventManager component and, in the @code block, update the Save() method:

    ```
    private void Save()
        => Console.WriteLine($"Saved: {Model.Json}");
    ```

2. Navigate to the markup section of the EventManager component and locate the EditForm markup. All subsequent steps will take place within this form.

3. Wrap the existing InputText instance, EventDurationForm instance, and the save button in separate paragraph <p> tags:

    ```
    <p>
        Name:
        <InputText @bind-Value="@Model.Name" />
    </p>
    <p>
        <EventDurationForm @bind-Value="@Model.Period" />
    </p>
    <p>
        <button type="submit">Save</button>
    </p>
    ```

4. In a new paragraph, below the EventDurationForm paragraph, add an InputCheckbox component and bind it to the Model.IsActive property:

    ```
    <p>
        <InputCheckbox @bind-Value="@Model.IsActive" />
        Active
    </p>
    ```

5. Add another paragraph – this time with an InputNumber component – and bind it to the Model.Capacity property:

    ```
    <p>
        Capacity
        <InputNumber @bind-Value="@Model.Capacity" />
    </p>
    ```

6. Create another paragraph and embed the `InputSelect` component within it, binding it to the `Model.Type` property. Render the select options using values from the `EventType` enum:

```
<p>
    <InputSelect @bind-Value="@Model.Type">
        @foreach (var type in
            Enum.GetValues<EventType>())
        {
            <option value="@type">@type</option>
        }
    </InputSelect>
</p>
```

7. In another paragraph, incorporate an `InputRadioGroup` component and bind it to the `Model.Location` property. Use `EventVenues.All` values and an `InputRadio` component to render each radio option:

```
<p>
    <InputRadioGroup @bind-Value="@Model.Location">
        @foreach (var venue in EventVenues.All)
        {
            <InputRadio Value="@venue" />@venue
        }
    </InputRadioGroup>
</p>
```

8. In a separate paragraph, place an `InputTextArea` component and bind it to the `Model.Description` property:

```
<p>
    <InputTextArea @bind-Value="@Model.Description" />
</p>
```

How it works...

In this recipe, we enhance the `EventManager` component. In *step 1*, we navigate to the `@code` block and update the `Save()` method, where, leveraging the `Model.Json` auto-property, we convert the entire `Model` object to JSON and write out the result to the console, so we can peek at the state of the saved `Model` instance.

In *step 2*, we shift to the `EditForm` markup available in the markup of the `EventManager` component. In *step 3*, we wrap the existing fields into organized paragraphs with `<p>` tags. We use the `InputText` component to render a text input element bound to the `Model.Name` property, allowing a user to set the name of an event. Next, with the `EventDurationForm` component, we encapsulate the setting of the event period, utilizing `InputDate` components for date entries.

InputDate supports a variety of time formats and includes a built-in calendar picker – out of the box. We conclude the structurization of the form by wrapping the submit button in another set of <p> tags.

In *step 4*, we introduce an InputCheckbox component in a new paragraph, binding it to the Model.IsActive property. InputCheckbox renders a checkbox input type that's perfect for handling bool properties, so we allow the user to toggle the active status of the event.

In *step 5*, we add an InputNumber component in another paragraph, linking it to the Model.Capacity property. InputNumber accepts any primitive numeric type, which makes it ideal for setting the maximum number of event participants. In *step 6*, we embed an InputSelect component within another paragraph and bind it to the Model.Type property to facilitate selecting the event type. InputSelect is a generic component, so you can easily cover a variety of objects within. However, remember that the select option value must be of a primitive type. In our form, we populate the drop-down menu by iterating over the EventType enum from the sample Data directory.

In *step 7*, we allow the user to choose the event venue. We render an InputRadioGroup component and bind it to the Model.Location property. We also render multiple InputRadio components, each representing a venue from the EventVenues.All sample collection. Blazor automatically scopes all InputRadio components to the nearest parent element but wrapping them inside InputRadioGroup exposes additional functionalities of the checkbox group and gives us more control.

In *step 8*, we add an InputTextArea component within the final paragraph, providing a text area for the Model.Description property. InputTextArea generates an input of type textarea – ideal for longer descriptions, although it's not a rich text editor.

The form we've just built appears simple, but it renders fully functional, secured, and organized markup with little coding effort:

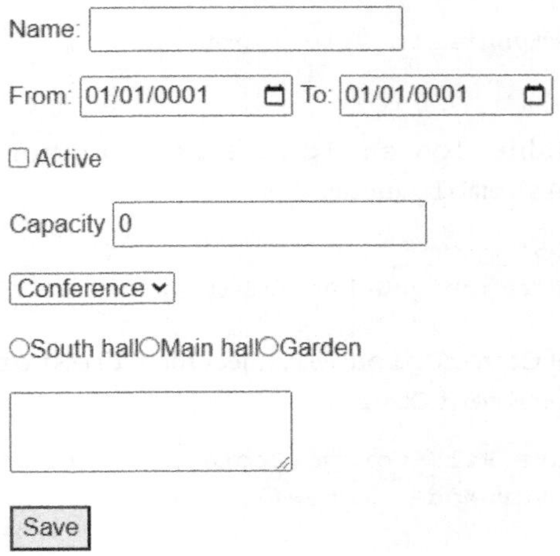

Figure 6.1: Functional, secure, and structured form using only built-in input components

Handling file uploads with a form

In this recipe, we dive into managing file uploads in Blazor applications. File uploading is crucial for any modern web application that requires users to upload documents or images. The `InputFile` component simplifies the integration of file uploads with its simple but comprehensive API. Moreover, with a little additional coding, you can enable **drag-and-drop** behavior for file uploads.

Let's add a simple form that allows users to upload a file representing an event cover.

Getting ready

Before we implement the form with file uploads, do the following:

- Create a `Chapter06/Recipe05` directory – this will be your working directory
- Copy `FileStorage` from the `Chapter06/Data` directory in the GitHub repository

How to do it...

Follow these steps to enable file uploads in an interactive form:

1. Open your application's `Program` file and add the `FileStorage` service to the dependency injection container:

   ```
   builder.Services.AddTransient<FileStorage>();
   ```

2. Create an `EventCover` class with a single `File` property of type `IBrowserFile`:

   ```
   public class EventCover
   {
       public IBrowserFile File { get; set; }
   }
   ```

3. Create a new routable `CoverUploader` component that renders in the `InteractiveWebAssembly` mode:

   ```
   @page "/ch06r05"
   @rendermode InteractiveWebAssembly
   ```

4. In the `@code` block of `CoverUploader`, inject the `FileStorage` service and initialize a `Model` variable of type `EventCover`:

   ```
   [Inject] private FileStorage Storage { get; init; }
   public EventCover Model = new();
   ```

5. Still within the @code block, implement a FileChanged() method that takes the InputFileChangeEventArgs parameter and assigns the file data to Model.File:

```
private void FileChanged(InputFileChangeEventArgs e)
    => Model.File = e.File;
```

6. Lastly, in the @code block, implement a SaveAsync() method that initializes a file upload from the Model instance, using the FileStorage service:

```
private Task SaveAsync()
{
    using var stream = Model.File.OpenReadStream();
    return Storage.UploadAsync(stream);
}
```

7. In the CoverUploader markup, add an EditForm component, bind it to the Model instance, and attach the SaveAsync() method to the OnSubmit form callback:

```
<EditForm FormName="cover-upload"
          Model="@Model"
          OnSubmit="@SaveAsync">
</EditForm>
```

8. Inside the EditForm markup, add an InputFile component that invokes the FileChanged() method with its OnChange event and a simple submit button. Wrap both elements in paragraphs:

```
<p><InputFile OnChange="FileChanged" /></p>
<p><button type="submit">Save</button></p>
```

How it works...

In *step 1*, we navigate to the application's Program file and register the FileStorage service into the dependency injection container. FileStorage is a fake service that pretends to upload a file to the storage of your choice. In *step 2*, we create an EventCover class with a single File property of type IBrowserFile. The IBrowserFile interface represents a file received from the user, encapsulating properties such as the file's name, content type, size, and methods to access the file's content.

In *step 3*, we create a routable CoverUploader component and set it to render in InteractiveWebAssembly mode to enable interactivity on our form. In *step 4*, within the @code block of the CoverUploader component, we inject the FileStorage service to utilize its API for managing incoming files. We then initialize a Model object of type EventCover, which forms the backbone of our form. In *step 5*, within the same @code block, we implement a FileChanged() method that handles InputFileChangeEventArgs. The InputFileChangeEventArgs object contains an `IBrowserFile` payload, which we assign to the `File` property of our `Model` instance, capturing the user-selected file. In *step 6*, we add a `SaveAsync()` method where we read the `File` value into a stream and use the `FileStorage.UploadAsync()` method to upload the file bytes to our selected storage. We leverage the `using` keyword to ensure efficient resource management and no memory leaks. The `using` keyword, inside a method, works together with an `IDisposable` object and creates a temporary, disposable scope that automatically disposes of the attached object when the method execution completes.

In *step 7*, we set up the markup for `CoverUploader` using the `EditForm` component. We give the form a unique name, bind it to our `Model` instance, and assign the `SaveAsync()` method as the submission fallback. Finally, in *step 8*, we build the body of the `EditForm` component. We incorporate the `InputFile` component and attach the `FileChanged()` method to its `OnChange` callback. The `OnChange` event seamlessly integrates with the `FileChanged()` logic in our `@code` block, handling the file selection initiated by the user. We also add a simple submit button that activates the form's `OnSubmit` callback.

At the end, your form should look similar to mine:

Figure 6.2: Form containing the InputFile component and a submit button

What about the drag-and-drop feature? Actually, the `InputFile` component inherently supports drag-and-drop functionality! Even though it looks like a button, `InputFile` renders an `input` area that has the drag-and-drop feature already enabled – you don't need to add any additional code or any additional attributes. You may want to add additional styling to make `InputFile` look like a drop zone, but the functionality is available out of the box.

Lastly, we didn't implement any file type or size validation for the uploading (we will explore validation in *Chapter 7*). For the enterprise-ready application, you must consider putting such boundaries in place to protect your infrastructure as well as server resources.

There's more...

What if you want to support file uploads and leverage the newest SSR render mode? In the SSR mode, Blazor pre-renders components on the server and serves only a static markup without any interactivity, so you can't intercept the file the user tries to upload. However, if we consider enabling enhanced navigation and leveraging the `enctype` attribute, uploading files will work even in the SSR mode. The `enctype` HTML attribute specifies how the browser should encode the form data when submitting it to the server.

Let's modify our existing interactive form to render in the SSR mode and still allow users to upload a file:

1. Update the `EventCover` class by changing the `File` property type from `IBrowserFile` to `IFormFile`. That's part of the `Microsoft.AspNetCore.Http.Features` package, so you may need to add it to your project beforehand:

```
public class EventCover
{
    public IFormFile File { get; set; }
}
```

2. Next, adjust the `CoverUploader` component to render in SSR mode by removing the `@renderMode` directive.

3. In the `@code` block of the `CoverUploader` component, transform `Model` into a property and decorate it with `SupplyParameterFromForm` to enable automatic binding of the form data:

```
[SupplyParameterFromForm]
public EventCover Model { get; set; }
```

4. Still within the `@code` block, override the `OnInitialized()` lifecycle method to adhere to the SSR form binding pattern and remove the `FileChanged()` method, as we won't need it anymore:

```
protected override void OnInitialized()
    => Model ??= new();
```

5. Within the `CoverUploader` markup, enhance the `EditForm` component by adding the `Enhance` attribute, which activates enhanced navigation, and include the `enctype` attribute with the value `multipart/form-data`:

```
<EditForm FormName="cover-upload"
          Model="@Model"
          OnSubmit="@SaveAsync"
          Enhance
          enctype="multipart/form-data">
    @* ... *@
</EditForm>
```

6. Lastly, replace the assignment of the `OnChange` callback on the `InputFile` component with the `name` HTML attribute and set its value to match the `Model.File` property so Blazor knows how to bind the selected file directly from the form:

```
<p><InputFile name="Model.File" /></p>
```

Securing a form with an anti-forgery token

In this recipe, we explore an essential aspect of web security — protecting your application from CSRF attacks. CSRF attacks exploit the trust between our app and a user's browser, making the browser perform unwanted actions using the user's identity. An **anti-forgery token**, also known as a CSRF token, is a crucial security measure you must use to ensure that the requests sent to a server are genuine and originated from a legitimate user, not an attacker. Embedding an anti-forgery token in your forms practically creates a unique key sent with each post request. The server checks this token upon receiving a request; if the token is not present or is incorrect, the request is rejected, thus preventing unauthorized actions.

Let's secure our event creation form with the anti-forgery token implementation offered in Blazor.

Getting ready

Before we explore securing a form with the anti-forgery token, do the following:

- Create a `Chapter06/Recipe06` directory – this will be your working directory
- Copy the `Models.cs` file from the `Chapter06/Data` directory in the GitHub repository

How to do it...

Follow these instructions to secure your form with the anti-forgery token:

1. On the server side of your solution, navigate to the `Program` file and, in the middleware configuration area, register the anti-forgery middleware:

    ```
    var app = builder.Build();
    //...
    app.UseStaticFiles();
    app.UseAntiforgery();
    //...
    app.Run();
    ```

2. Create a routable `EventManager` component:

    ```
    @page "/ch06r06"
    ```

3. Inside the `@code` block of the `EventManager` component, declare a `Model` object of type `Event` and decorate it with the `SupplyParameterFromForm` attribute:

    ```
    [SupplyParameterFromForm]
    protected Event Model { get; set; }
    ```

4. Still within the @code block of EventManager, override the OnInitialized() lifecycle method to conditionally initialize the Model instance if it is not already set and implement a Save() method to simulate the process of saving the form data:

```
protected override void OnInitialized()
    => Model ??= new();
private void Save()
    => Console.WriteLine($"Saved {Model.Name}.");
```

5. In the markup section of the EventManager component, construct a standard HTML form with a unique name that triggers the Save() method when submitted:

```
<form method="post"
      @onsubmit="@Save"
      @formname="event-form">
</form>
```

6. Within the <form> area, include a text input field linked to the Model.Name property and a submit button. Most crucially, embed an AntiforgeryToken component within the form:

```
<AntiforgeryToken />
<label>
    Name: <InputText @bind-Value="@Model.Name" />
</label>
<button type="submit">Save</button>
```

How it works...

In *step 1*, we navigate to the Program file of the server-side project to enable anti-forgery security. We leverage the app.UseAntiforgery() extension method within the middleware area. The order of middleware registration is crucial; you must position the anti-forgery middleware thoughtfully based on other middleware in use. If your application includes authentication and authorization, ensure app.UseAntiforgery() is placed after app.UseAuthentication() and app.UseAuthorization(). If you have routing configured, place anti-forgery middleware after app.UseRouting(), but before app.UseEndpoints() if you register endpoint middleware.

In *step 2*, we create a routable EventManager component and include the necessary assembly reference with the @using directive to access the Event type. In *step 3*, within the @code block of the EventManager component, we declare a Model property of type Event to support our form. We leverage the SupplyParameterFromForm attribute to enable an automatic data binding between the Model and form fields. In *step 4*, we override the OnInitialized() method to conditionally initialize the Model instance if it's still empty. We also implement a Save() method as a placeholder to simulate saving changes to the form. In *step 5*, we move to the markup of the EventManager component. We construct a standard HTML form, using <form> tags, that triggers the Save() method upon submission. In Blazor, each form must have a unique name, so we use the @formname attribute and name ours event-form. In *step 6*, we implement the form body.

First, we embed the `AntiforgeryToken` component. Next, we add a text input field for the user to provide the event name and bind it to the `Model.Name` property. Finally, we include a `Save` button to enable submitting the form.

With the `AntiforgeryToken` component in place, Blazor generates a hidden form field containing the anti-forgery token. We've embedded the `AntiforgeryToken` instance at the top of the form, but as it's a hidden field, you can place it anywhere, as long as it remains part of the form. The token itself is part of the DOM, so you can inspect its value using your browser's development tools:

```
▼<article class="content px-4" b-ly3ap3nnel>
  ▼<form method="post" action="/ch06r06">
      <input type="hidden" name="_handler" value="event-form">
      <input type="hidden" name="__RequestVerificationToken"
      value="CfDJ8BWDTOWN9XZHqQEDsEJj_Kpks05SdxfJjtT9x9gTiVsC8
      uQL-lGInX5zDIqpSvdqAezdvwvCzSEF5V7dse7beJ6Lb2nuQqNT6IabQ
      jUUw4rDm17pjvqH_8iMzZLiZQasbfIE_E7t34e-Jm_LO44w4Y0">
    ▼<label>
        " Name: "
```

Figure 6.3: Inspecting the anti-forgery token generated as part of the from markup

There's more...

I recommend using the `EditForm` component for all your forms due to its native Blazor integration and extensive API. So, why have we not covered adding the anti-forgery token to the `EditForm` markup? The reason is straightforward: `EditForm` comes with built-in anti-forgery support. Blazor automatically secures the `EditForm` instance, saving you the hassle of explicitly handling CSRF protection.

Furthermore, we entirely skipped the implementation of anti-forgery tokens for client-side applications. Blazor WebAssembly apps run entirely in the browser and do not have a server-side processing pipeline where you would typically configure a middleware such as `app.UseAntiforgery()`. If your Blazor WebAssembly app interacts with server-side APIs, you should manage anti-forgery at the API level. However, if you already use **token-based authentication** to secure communication, anti-forgery tokens are generally not necessary. Token-based authentication, by its nature, mitigates the risks associated with CSRF, making additional anti-forgery tokens redundant. We will explore authentication and authorization further in *Chapter 8*.

See also

If you'd like to learn more about token-based authentication, you can check this resource:

https://learn.microsoft.com/en-us/xandr/digital-platform-api/token-based-api-authentication

7

Validating User Input Forms

In this chapter, we explore the essential aspect of ensuring the accuracy and integrity of data submitted through forms in Blazor applications. With effective validation, you'll prevent erroneous data entry and enhance user interactions and application security. Throughout this chapter, we will explore a comprehensive range of techniques and strategies you can employ while validating user inputs.

We begin with the fundamental process of adding validation to a form, setting the stage for more complex validation scenarios. You will learn how Blazor handles basic validation scenarios and how you can extend them to meet specific domain needs. After that, we explore the use of data annotations for form validation. You'll uncover how to simplify form validation using built-in annotations and how to leverage them to enforce rules and constraints directly on data models, reducing boilerplate code. Right after, you will see how to implement custom validation attributes, which provide the flexibility to address unique business requirements. Then, we address the validation of complex data models, ensuring that data integrity is maintained even in intricate scenarios.

At the end of the chapter, we focus on improving the user experience of your forms. We cover the styling of validation messages and modernizing validation summaries. Good styling makes validation messages clear and more aligned with the application's design, while toasts offer a dynamic way to alert users about issues without disrupting their workflow. Lastly, we explore how to dynamically control form actions based on validation results, ensuring that users can only submit forms in a valid state, thereby avoiding unnecessary submissions and server load.

By the end of this chapter, you'll know how to implement effective validation strategies in your Blazor applications, ensuring correct user inputs and enhancing the usability and reliability of your application.

Here's the list of recipes we're going to cover in this chapter:

- Adding validation to a form
- Leveraging data annotations for form validation
- Implementing custom validation attributes
- Validating complex data models
- Styling validation messages
- Displaying a toast when validation fails
- Enabling the submit option based on the form state

Technical requirements

In this chapter, recipes build on each other, so you can follow the entire journey within the same directory. However, for clarity and easier initial setup, at the beginning of each recipe, you will find instructions on what working directory to create and which files are required to execute the task at hand. But before diving in, make sure you have all the basic tools for Blazor development:

- A modern IDE (that supports Blazor development)
- A modern web browser (that supports WebAssembly)
- Browser dev tools (which can be a part of the modern browser already)
- A Blazor project (where you'll write your code)

In the *Validating complex data models* recipe, we utilize the `Microsoft.AspNetCore.Components.DataAnnotations.Validation` NuGet package, which is not pre-installed by default, so you might as well add it to your project now. Keep in mind that the validation package is still in preview, so you'll have to include prerelease packages in the NuGet feed in your IDE.

You can find all the code written in this chapter and code samples on GitHub at:

```
https://github.com/PacktPublishing/Blazor-Web-Development-Cookbook/
tree/main/BlazorCookbook.App.Client/Chapters/Chapter07
```

Adding validation to a form

In this recipe, we'll explore the basics of user input validation in Blazor. Validation is critical for preventing errors and security vulnerabilities, maintaining data consistency, and enhancing the user experience. The Blazor community has created various NuGet packages for handling input validation, offering a range of features and configurations. However, Blazor provides extensive built-in support for validating forms and displaying validation results in a user-friendly manner. The native functionalities are lightweight and integrate directly with Blazor's data binding and UI features.

Let's implement a small event creation form, where a user must provide the event name. We will also display a validation message when the event name is empty.

Getting ready

Before we add the first, basic validation to a form, create a `Chapter07/Recipe01` directory – this will be your working directory.

How to do it...

Follow these steps to add a simple validation to a form:

1. Create an `Event` class with a `Name` property – we will use it as a form model:

    ```
    public class Event
    {
        public string Name { get; set; }
    }
    ```

2. Create a routable `EventManager` component that implements the `IDisposable` interface. You will see compilation errors now, but we will resolve them later:

    ```
    @page "/ch07r01"
    @implements IDisposable
    ```

3. In the `@code` block of `EventManager`, declare an `Event` model to serve as the backing model for the form:

    ```
    [SupplyParameterFromForm]
    public Event Model { get; set; }
    ```

4. Below the `Model` parameter declaration, introduce the `Context` and `Store` variables for the form's state management:

    ```
    protected EditContext Context;
    protected ValidationMessageStore Store;
    ```

5. Still within the `@code` block, implement a `Save()` placeholder method to simulate form submission:

    ```
    private void Save()
        => Console.WriteLine($"Saved {Model.Name}.");
    ```

6. Alongside `Save()`, implement a `ValidateForm()` method, with a signature matching the response of a `EventHandler` validation, which checks whether the `Model.Name` property has a valid value:

```
private void ValidateForm(object sender,
ValidationRequestedEventArgs args)
{
    Store.Clear();
    if (string.IsNullOrWhiteSpace(Model.Name))
        Store.Add(() => Model.Name,
            "You must provide a name.");
}
```

7. Continuing in the `@code` block, override the `OnInitialized()` life cycle method to initialize the `Model` instance if needed and set up both the form context and the validation message container:

```
protected override void OnInitialized()
{
    Model ??= new();
    Context = new(Model);
    Context.OnValidationRequested += ValidateForm;
    Store = new(Context);
}
```

8. Finalize the `@code` block by implementing the `Dispose()` method to adhere to the `IDisposable` requirement and unsubscribe from the validation event handler:

```
public void Dispose()
{
    if (Context is not null)
        Context.OnValidationRequested -= ValidateForm;
}
```

9. In the `EventManager` markup, include an `EditForm` component, attaching `Context` to the appropriate parameter and linking the `Save()` method to handle the form submission:

```
<EditForm EditContext="@Context"
        event-form="forEvent-form"
        OnValidSubmit="@Save">
</EditForm>
```

10. Inside `EditForm`, add an `InputText` component and bind it to the `Model.Name` property. Alongside `InputText`, add a `ValidationMessage` component to display validation errors for the attached property:

```
<p>Name: <InputText @bind-Value="@Model.Name" /></p>
<p><ValidationMessage For="() => Model.Name" /></p>
```

11. Lastly, complete `EditForm` by adding a submit button below the form fields:

```
<button type="submit">Save</button>
```

How it works...

In *step 1*, we create a simple `Event` class with a single `Name` property. We will use `Event` as a model for our form. Next, in *step 2*, we create a routable `EventManager` component, not specifying any render mode, which leads Blazor to default to static server-side mode. As form validation is event driven, `EventManager` must implement the `IDisposable` interface, which we apply using the `@implements` directive. You will see compilation errors now, but we will resolve them later.

Moving to *step 3*, within the `@code` block of `EventManager`, we utilize the `Event` class to declare the `Model` parameter, tagging it with the `SupplyParameterFromForm` attribute to enable an automatic binding with the form. In *step 4*, we introduce two form-backing variables: `EditContext` and `ValidationMessageStore`. The `EditContext` instance tracks changes to form inputs and manages the validation state, while `ValidationMessageStore` holds and displays validation messages, simplifying the validation process.

Proceeding to *step 5*, we implement a `Save()` placeholder method. Data persistence isn't the focus of this chapter, so we log a brief message to the console to simulate a save operation. In *step 6*, we implement the `ValidateForm()` method with a signature that matches the validation handler required by `EditForm`. Whenever Blazor invokes `ValidateForm()`, we first clear any messages in `Store` to handle multiple validation attempts smoothly. Then, we check whether the user provided the `Model.Name` property; if not, we add a **You must provide a name.** message to `Store` and identify the invalid property with a delegate, `() => Model.Name`. Under the hood, Blazor breaks down this delegate into the object (`Model`) and the property path string (`Name`) to efficiently track and manage validation and error association.

In *step 7*, we override the `OnInitialized()` life cycle method to set up the form's underlying logic. We resolve the `Model` value, supporting the pattern for the parameter with the `SupplyParameterFromForm` attribute. We then initialize `Context` with the `Model` object and subscribe `ValidateForm()` to the `OnValidationRequested` event handler that `Context` exposes. With that, Blazor will automatically invoke `ValidateForm()` every time the user submits the form. Finally, we initialize `Store` by passing `Context`, so the validation container can access the `Model` fields. In *step 8*, we wrap up the `@code` block by implementing the `Dispose()` method, adhering to the `IDisposable` pattern. Within `Dispose()`, we safely unsubscribe `ValidateForm()` from the validation trigger of `Context` to prevent potential memory leaks.

Having the backend logic in place, we proceed to the `EventManager` markup. In *step 9*, we add an `EditForm` component, but instead of attaching the backing `Model` instance directly, we attach `Context` to the `EditContext` parameter. Blazor will not allow attaching both `Model` and `EditContext` since `Context` already encompasses an instance of `Model`. We also use the `OnValidSubmit` callback rather than the standard `OnSubmit`. Blazor invokes `OnValidSumbit` only when all validations pass successfully, making it ideal for our needs. In *step 10*, within `EditForm`, we place an `InputText` component and bind it to the `Model.Name` property, enabling the user to provide the required event name. Alongside `InputText`, we position a `ValidationMessage` component that displays validation messages for the specific form field. As `ValidationMessage` requires a delegate to retrieve messages from the container, we leverage the same delegate we used in `ValidateForm()` for seeding a validation message into `Store`. Finally, in *step 11*, we complete the form implementation by adding a submit button.

When the user submits the form, Blazor triggers the `OnValidationRequested` event handler first. If validation results in errors, the `Save()` method is not activated, ensuring that only valid data is processed.

Here's what the validation error looks like in our form:

Name: [   ]

You must provide a name.

[Save]

Figure 7.1: Validation message when user submits the form without providing the name

There's more...

With the `ValidationMessage` component, we can control where Blazor renders validation messages for each field, providing granular feedback directly next to individual form elements. However, you might want to display a consolidated validation summary rather than scattered messages. That's where the `ValidationSummary` component comes in handy. The `ValidationSummary` component gathers and displays all validation messages within one container. You can see such summaries at the top or bottom of the forms or even as part of a validation popup.

To implement a summary in our form, we only need to replace `ValidationMessage` with `ValidationSummary` and add a `DataAnnotationsValidator` component within the form:

```
<EditForm EditContext="@Context"
          FormName="forEvent-form"
          OnValidSubmit="@Save">
    <DataAnnotationsValidator />
    <p>Name: <InputText @bind-Value="@Model.Name" /></p>
```

```
    <p><ValidationSummary /></p>
    <button type="submit">Save</button>
</EditForm>
```

We must embed `DataAnnotationsValidator` as it triggers the population and re-render of `ValidationSummary`. Without the validator, will get the red input styling, indicating that the value provided is invalid, but no message explaining why.

We explore `DataAnnotationsValidator` further in the next recipe.

Leveraging data annotations for form validation

In this recipe, we explore the role of **data annotations** in streamlining and enhancing the validation processes in a form in Blazor. Data annotations are attributes applied directly to model properties that enable a declarative way of specifying validation rules. By implementing data annotations, you can significantly simplify the validation logic and encapsulate it within the model rather than coupling it with any specific form. Such separation ensures that validation is consistently enforced across different parts of your application regardless of the context in which you use the model. Blazor has a built-in `DataAnnotationsValidator` component that seamlessly integrates data annotations into a form. `DataAnnotationsValidator` checks the data annotations applied to the model and produces validation results without additional coding.

Let's convert an explicit validation logic in a form into data annotations and leverage Blazor's native support to handle validation efficiently.

Getting ready

Before we encapsulate the validation logic into a separate component:

- Create a `Chapter07/Recipe02` directory – this will be your working directory
- Copy `EventManager` and `Event` from the *Adding validation to a form* recipe or from the `Chapter07/Recipe01` directory in the GitHub repository

How to do it...

Follow these steps to leverage data annotations for model validation:

1. Navigate to the `Event` class and decorate the `Name` property with the `Required` attribute with a user-friendly error message. You must reference a `System.ComponentModel.DataAnnotations` namespace, but your IDE might include it automatically:

    ```
    [Required(ErrorMessage = "You must provide a name.")]
    public string Name { get; set; }
    ```

2. Move to the EventManager component and remove the IDisposable declaration from the top of the file. You should have only a route declaration left.

3. In the EventManager markup, locate EditForm and embed the DataAnnotationsValidator component just below the submission button:

```
<EditForm EditContext="@Context"
          event-form="event-forEvent"
          OnValidSubmit="@Save">
    @* ... existing form body ... *@
    <button type="submit">Save</button>
    <DataAnnotationsValidator />
</EditForm>
```

4. Jump to the @code block of EventManager and do some cleanup:

- Remove the subscription to the OnValidationRequested event handler from the OnInitialized() method implementation

- Remove the Dispose() and ValidateForm() methods entirely

How it works...

In *step 1*, we enhance the Event class by implementing data annotations to enforce input validation. We decorate the Name property with the Required attribute to ensure a user always provides that value. Data annotations also accept the ErrorMessage parameter, where we can pass in a user-friendly validation message, so we extend the Required attribute with the **You must provide a name.** error message.

In *step 2*, we move to the EventManager component. With data annotations in place, we no longer need explicit event handling. Consequently, we remove the IDisposable declaration from the top of the EventManager file. In *step 3*, we enhance the EventManager markup and embed the DataAnnotationsValidator component at the end of EditForm, just below the submission button. DataAnnotationsValidator operates seamlessly within the form, carrying no distinct markup and relying on the cascading EditContext for validation operations. We placed DataAnnotationsValidator at the end of the form, but you can put it anywhere as long as it's within the EditForm tags. In *step 4*, we update the @code block of EventManager. With data annotations now managing validation, we can simplify the component code by removing most of the previously necessary validation logic. We remove the OnValidationRequested subscription within the OnInitialized() method, as DataAnnotationsValidator now automatically monitors the validation state. Following this, we also eliminate the ValidateForm() method, as the management of the validation message store and error messages has shifted to DataAnnotationsValidator as well. Lastly, we remove the Dispose() method because EventManager no longer implements the IDisposable interface or listens to any events.

With these few adjustments, we achieve the same validation scope as in the *Adding validation to a form* recipe but with significantly less code!

There's more...

With `DataAnnotationsValidator` in place, Blazor can perform two types of validation:

- The first type is **full-model validation** – Blazor executes when the user submits the form. This validation occurs when you click the **Save** button on the `EventManager` form. It involves checking every validation rule across all fields in the model, ensuring that all data meets the specified criteria before the form is processed. As we're working in the SSR render mode, which has inherently limited interactivity, only full-model validation is supported.

- However, should you opt to render `EventManager` in an interactive mode, `DataAnnotationsValidator` can execute another layer of validation – **field validation**. Blazor triggers field validation when the user moves the focus away from an individual form field, displaying immediate feedback on the input provided in that specific field.

Implementing custom validation attributes

In this recipe, we dive into the flexibility of customizing validation attributes. While built-in data annotations simplify validation logic, they cover only the most commonly used validation rules. You might find yourself missing the coverage for your specific needs. Fortunately, you can implement custom data validation attributes with unique rules beyond the standard validations provided by .NET. Additionally, Blazor's native `DataAnnotationsValidator` component seamlessly integrates with any custom attributes.

Let's implement an event name validation attribute that checks whether the user provided the event name and scans for any forbidden keywords.

Getting ready

Before we implement a custom validation attribute, do the following:

- Create a `Chapter07/Recipe03` directory – this will be your working directory
- Copy `EventManager` and `Event` from the *Leveraging data annotations for form validation* recipe or from the `Chapter07/Recipe02` directory in the GitHub repository

How to do it...

Follow these instructions to implement a custom validation attribute:

1. Create a new `EventNameValidationAttribute` class that inherits from a
   `ValidationAttribute` class. You must reference the `System.ComponentModel.`
   `DataAnnotations` assembly, but your IDE might include it automatically:

   ```
   using System.ComponentModel.DataAnnotations;
   public class EventNameValidationAttribute
       : ValidationAttribute
   {
   }
   ```

2. Inside the `EventNameValidationAttribute` class, declare a private variable, `_forbidden`,
   and initialize it with the `event` value:

   ```
   private const string _forbidden = "event";
   ```

3. Below the `_forbidden` variable, implement a `Failure()` method that accepts `message`
   and `member` parameters and returns an instance of `ValidationResult`:

   ```
   private static ValidationResult Failure(
       string message, string member)
       => new(message, [member]);
   ```

4. Complete the implementation of `EventNameValidationAttribute` by overriding
   the `IsValid()` method, which returns a `ValidationResult` object. Return the result
   of `Failure()` invocation if the incoming `value` was not provided or it contains the
   `_forbidden` keyword. Otherwise, return the default `ValidationResult.Success`:

   ```
   protected override ValidationResult IsValid(
       object value, ValidationContext validationContext)
   {
       var text = value?.ToString();

       if (string.IsNullOrWhiteSpace(text))
           return Failure("You must provide a name.",
               validationContext.MemberName);

       if (text.Contains(_forbidden,
           StringComparison.InvariantCultureIgnoreCase))
           return Failure(
               "You mustn't use the 'event' keyword.",
   ```

```
                    validationContext.MemberName);

        return ValidationResult.Success;
    }
```

5. Navigate to the `Event` class and update the decoration of the `Name` property by replacing the existing `Required` attribute with the newly implemented `EventNameValidation` attribute:

```
[EventNameValidation]
public string Name { get; set; }
```

How it works...

In *step 1*, we create an `EventNameValidationAttribute` class, inheriting from `ValidationAttribute`. The `ValidationAttribute` class is a base class for validation attributes, providing a framework for implementing custom validation rules in .NET applications. It allows for defining specific conditions that data must meet before being processed further. In *step 2*, we declare a `_forbidden` variable within our custom validation attribute class to store the forbidden keyword to check against the input value. In *step 3*, we implement a `Failure()` method that accepts the `message` and `member` parameters. `Failure()` creates and returns an instance of `ValidationResult`, representing a failure in validation. The `member` parameter allows associating the error message with specific fields, enhancing the clarity of feedback provided to the user.

In *step 4*, we implement the custom validation logic by overriding the `IsValid()` method from the `ValidationAttribute` class. Blazor triggers `IsValid()` when it validates the form model. We choose to override the overload that returns a `ValidationResult` object rather than a simple `bool`, as we want to provide detailed feedback on validation issues. We first convert the incoming `value` to a `text` variable. If `text` doesn't carry a meaningful value, we call the `Failure()` method to return a validation error with the message **You must provide a name.**. But `Failure()` also requires providing a `member` name. The `IsValid()` method accepts another parameter of type `ValidationContext`, which provides context about the validation operation, including `MemberName` identifying the validated field. With `MemberName`, we can conform to the `Failure()` method signature. We then check whether `text` contains the `_forbidden` keyword, ignoring case and culture differences. If the forbidden keyword is found, we invoke `Failure()` again with the message **You mustn't use the 'event' keyword.**. Lastly, if all checks pass successfully, we return `ValidationResult.Success` – a success indicator encapsulated inside the `ValidationResult` class.

In *step 5*, we navigate to the `Event` class and replace the existing `Required` attribute on the `Name` property with our newly created `EventNameValidation` attribute. Thanks to code generators and the C# and Blazor compilers, we can reference custom attributes using the class name without the `Attribute` suffix.

Now, we validate not only whether the user provides the event name but also whether they use the forbidden keyword:

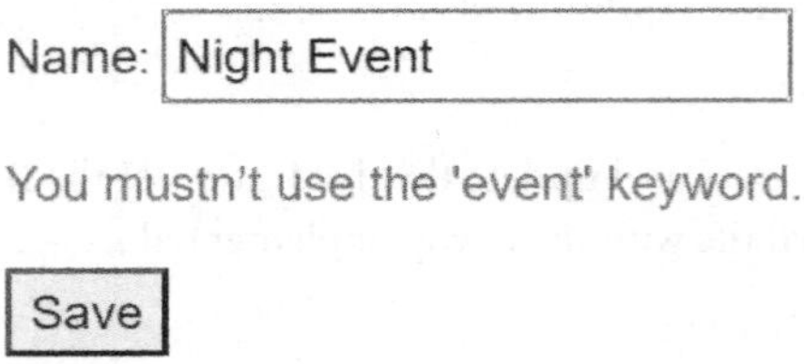

Name: | Night Event |

You mustn't use the 'event' keyword.

Save

Figure 7.2: Validation message when user submits a value containing a forbidden keyword

There's more...

When building multilingual applications, you might need to translate user-friendly error messages. Additionally, with continuous delivery trends, you may need to conditionally enable validation rules based on feature flags or application settings. You will require access to the dependency injection container to support such advanced scenarios. While in a class based on `ValidationAttribute`, you can reach dependency injection through the `ValidationContext` parameter, which encapsulates the behavior of `IServiceProvider` and exposes all the standard dependency injection methods available in .NET.

For example, assuming that you've registered an `Api` service in the service container, you can inject this dependency within your attribute in the following way:

```
protected override ValidationResult IsValid(object value,
    ValidationContext validationContext)
{
    var api = validationContext.GetRequiredService<Api>();
    //...
}
```

We override the `IsValid()` method, inherited from the `ValidationAttribute` class, and we get an instance of `ValidationContext`. As `ValidationContext` implements the `IServiceProvider` interface, we leverage the built-in generic `GetRequiredService()` extension method to retrieve an instance of our `Api` service.

It's important to note that custom validation attributes in .NET do not support asynchronous validation. This limitation is crucial to consider when designing your validation strategy to ensure performance and user experience are not adversely affected.

Validating complex data models

In this recipe, we tackle the validation of complex forms and data models. Having well-structured and modularized code makes the code base easier to maintain and reduces the likelihood of errors by clearly defining and isolating each component's responsibilities. In forms, complex models segment the data into manageable parts, each with its validation logic, making it easier to maintain the overall form's state and ensuring each segment adheres to specific business rules. The `Microsoft.AspNetCore.Components.DataAnnotations.Validation` package, although experimental, exposes Blazor-native validators and offers enhanced data annotations that integrate smoothly with complex models.

Let's extend the event creation form to include a nested object that encapsulates details about the event location.

Getting ready

Before we set up nested, complex model validation, do the following:

- Create a `Chapter07/Recipe04` directory – this will be your working directory
- Copy `EventManager`, `Event`, and `EventNameValidationAttribute` from the *Implementing custom validation attributes* recipe or from the `Chapter07/Recipe03` directory in the GitHub repository

How to do it...

Follow these steps to enable validation of the nested model:

1. Add a reference to the `Microsoft.AspNetCore.Components.DataAnnotations.Validation` package to your project file:

    ```
    <ItemGroup>
      <PackageReference
        Include="Microsoft.AspNetCore.Components
          .DataAnnotations.Validation"
        Version="3.2.0-rc1.20223.4" />
    </ItemGroup>
    ```

2. Create a new `EventLocation` class and define two properties within it – `Venue` and `Capacity`:

    ```
    public class EventLocation
    {
        public string Venue { get; set; }
        public int Capacity { get; set; }
    }
    ```

3. Apply the `Required` attribute to the `Venue` property and include a meaningful error message when a user leaves the field blank:

```
[Required(ErrorMessage = "You must provide a venue.")]
public string Venue { get; set; }
```

4. For the `Capacity` property, decorate it with both the `Required` and `Range` attributes and provide a meaningful error message to ensure the user inputs only valid capacity values:

```
[Required, Range(1, 1000,
    ErrorMessage =
        "Capacity must be between 1 and 1000.")]
public int Capacity { get; set; }
```

5. Navigate to the `Event` class and add a new `Location` property. Decorate `Location` with a `ValidateComplexType` attribute:

```
[ValidateComplexType]
public EventLocation Location { get; set; } = new();
```

6. In the `EventManager` component, locate `EditForm` within the markup.

7. Inside `EditForm`, directly below the input field for `Name`, add a new paragraph with an `InputText` component bound to the `Model.Location.Venue` property:

```
<p>
    Venue:
    <InputText @bind-Value="@Model.Location.Venue" />
</p>
```

8. Below the `Venue` input field, add another paragraph containing an `InputNumber` component bound to the `Model.Location.Capacity` property:

```
<p>
    Capacity:
    <InputNumber
        @bind-Value="@Model.Location.Capacity" />
</p>
```

9. Still within `EditForm`, replace the existing `ValidationMessage` for the `Model.Name` property with `ValidationSummary`:

```
<p><ValidationSummary /></p>
```

10. Lastly, swap out the `DataAnnotationsValidator` component for `ObjectGraphDataAnnotationsValidator`:

```
<ObjectGraphDataAnnotationsValidator />
```

How it works...

In *step 1*, we open the `csproj` file of our project and add a reference to the `Microsoft.AspNetCore.Components.DataAnnotations.Validation` package that contains all the extensions required for seamless validation of complex, nested data models.

Next, in *step 2*, we create a new `EventLocation` class with the `Venue` and `Capacity` properties, representing event location details. In *step 3*, we decorate the `Venue` property with a `Required` attribute to ensure that users cannot submit the form without filling in the venue description. Should they forget to enter a `Venue` value, they will see a **You must provide a venue.** validation message to guide them. In *step 4*, we add validation to the `Capacity` property by applying both the `Required` and `Range` attributes. We enforce that users fill the capacity value and that it falls within a specified range (1 to 1,000). Users will receive a **Capacity must be between 1 and 1000.** error message if they enter a value outside the declared range.

For *step 5*, we turn to the `Event` class and extend it with a new property – `Location`, of type `EventLocation`. To ensure Blazor understands that this property represents a complex type requiring nested validation, we decorate it with the `ValidateComplexType` attribute. `ValidateComplexType` comes with the `Microsoft.AspNetCore.Components.DataAnnotations.Validation` package.

In *step 6*, we proceed to the `EventManager` component and locate the existing `EditForm` within the markup. We will extend the form to include fields for entering the event location details. In *step 7*, we embed a new paragraph just below the `Name` field where we insert an `InputText` component bound to `Model.Location.Venue` to allow users to input the venue details. In *step 8*, we add another paragraph, this time incorporating an `InputNumber` component bound to `Model.Location.Capacity` to allow users to specify the spots available in a given venue. In *step 9*, aiming to streamline the display of validation messages, we replace the `ValidationMessage` component previously dedicated to the `Name` property with a `ValidationSummary` instance. The `ValidationSummary` component consolidates all form validation messages into one area. Finally, in *step 10*, we enhance our validation setup by replacing the standard `DataAnnotationsValidator` with `ObjectGraphDataAnnotationsValidator`. The `ObjectGraphDataAnnotationsValidator` component is an advanced component capable of validating nested object graphs, allowing Blazor to trigger validation on every part of our complex `Event` model.

There's more...

When working with Blazor's built-in input components, you get an additional layer of flexibility. Any default input component, inheriting from the `InputBase` class, such as the `InputNumber` component we've used in this recipe, automatically intercepts any unmatched parameters and attaches them directly to the underlying HTML `input` element as attributes. With that, you can easily enhance the `InputNumber` component used for `Model.Location.Capacity` by declaring min and max attributes and disallowing users from manually increasing or decreasing the value beyond the specified range:

```
Capacity:
    <InputNumber min="1" max="1000"
        @bind-Value="@Model.Location.Capacity" />
```

By adding min and max attributes to the `InputNumber` component in the form and declaring their values to 1 and 1000, respectively, we ensure users won't be able to reduce the value in the input below 1 nor increment it above 1000. They can still type an invalid value by hand, but they'll trigger validation on the model properties. Following that example, you can leverage any other HTML input attributes you're familiar with.

Styling validation messages

In this recipe, we explore the styling of form validation in Blazor. You've probably noticed in previous recipes that Blazor automatically applies validation classes to form fields during validation. Default validation CSS classes align with default Bootstrap styles, where invalid fields get a red accent and valid ones get a green accent. While the default settings increase the delivery velocity, in most cases, you will still have to customize the visual feedback to suit your application branding or functional requirements. Fortunately, Blazor allows customizing styling and classes appended to fields upon validation. This customization maintains the integrity of your application's modular and loosely coupled architecture, ensuring that enhancements do not compromise the maintainability of your code.

Let's implement a custom validation class provider, making Blazor mark missing labels in red while missing location capacity in yellow.

Getting ready

Before implementing a custom validation class provider, do the following:

- Create a `Chapter07/Recipe05` directory – this will be your working directory
- Copy `Event`, `EventLocation`, `EventManager`, and `EventNameValidationAttribute` from the *Validating complex data models* recipe or from the `Chapter07/Recipe04` directory in the GitHub repository

How to do it...

Execute the following steps to add a custom validation class provider:

1. Add a new `EventManager.razor.css` file to the working directory. Your IDE might automatically nest that CSS file under `EventManager.razor`.

2. Within `EventManager.razor.css`, define an `invalid-warning` style class that adds an orange outline to any element we apply it to:

    ```css
    ::deep .invalid-warning {
        outline: 1px solid orange;
    }
    ```

3. Create a new `TypeValidationClassProvider` class, inheriting from `FieldCssClassProvider` available under the `Microsoft.AspNetCore.Components.Forms` namespace:

    ```csharp
    public class TypeValidationClassProvider
        : FieldCssClassProvider { }
    ```

4. In `TypeValidationClassProvider`, declare a private `_capacity` field holding the name of the `Capacity` property from the `EventLocation` class:

    ```csharp
    private static readonly string
        _capacity = nameof(EventLocation.Capacity);
    ```

5. To finalize the implementation of `TypeValidationClassProvider`, override the `GetFieldCssClass()` method and implement logic to return the `invalid-warning` class when the current field's value is invalid and corresponds to the `_capacity` property; otherwise, fall back to the `base` implementation:

    ```csharp
    public override string GetFieldCssClass(
        EditContext editContext,
        in FieldIdentifier fieldIdentifier)
    {
        var isValid =
            editContext.IsValid(fieldIdentifier);
        var isCapacity =
            fieldIdentifier.FieldName == _capacity;

        if (!isValid && isCapacity)
            return "invalid-warning";

        return base.GetFieldCssClass(
            editContext, fieldIdentifier);
    }
    ```

6. Navigate to the `EventManager` component and find the `OnInitialized()` method. After the existing setup, use the `SetFieldCssClassProvider()` extension method of `EditContext` and attach `TypeValidationClassProvider` to `Context`:

```
protected override void OnInitialized()
{
    // ... existing form context building ...
    Context.SetFieldCssClassProvider(
        new TypeValidationClassProvider());
}
```

How it works...

In *step 1*, we add a new CSS file to our working directory, specifically naming it `EventManager.razor.css` to adhere to the CSS isolation requirements and match the name of the component it will style. In Blazor, **CSS isolation** allows styles defined in a component-specific CSS file to affect only that component, preventing styles from leaking. If you enable the file nesting in your IDE, you will see isolated CSS files wrapped under the parent component file. In *step 2*, within `EventManager.razor.css`, we introduce a `.invalid-warning` class, which applies an orange outline to fields we attach it to. We use the `::deep` combinator to ensure that styling penetrates DOM-like encapsulations and affects nested components.

In *step 3*, we initiate our custom validation class provider by creating a new `TypeValidationClassProvider` class, which inherits from `FieldCssClassProvider`. The `FieldCssClassProvider` class provides the necessary API to customize CSS classes that Blazor applies based on field validation states. In *step 4*, we persist the name of the `Capacity` field in a `_capacity` variable within `TypeValidationClassProvider`. By declaring it as `private` and `static`, we ensure that this value remains unchanged and consumes minimal memory throughout the application's life cycle, effectively becoming a singleton instance. In *step 5*, we complete our custom provider by overriding the `GetFieldCssClass()` method, which Blazor calls whenever it needs to determine the appropriate CSS class based on the validation state of a field. In our implementation, we first check whether the field's current state is valid and its name matches the `_capacity` value. If the field is invalid and refers to the capacity, we return `invalid-warning`, instructing Blazor to apply the orange outline to highlight the error. Otherwise, we default to the base implementation by returning the result of the `base.GetFieldCssClass()` call, preserving standard behavior for other fields.

Finally, in *step 6*, we jump to the `EventManager` component and locate the overridden `OnInitialized()` life cycle method, where we initialize the `Context` variable. After the initial configurations, we utilize the `SetFieldCssClassProvider()` extension method of `EditContext` to configure `Context` to employ our `TypeValidationClassProvider` for resolving CSS classes based on field validation. Our custom styling logic is now in place.

There's more...

We've implemented a custom CSS validation class and leveraged the CSS isolation feature that Blazor offers. However, if you have already integrated a CSS framework into your application, you can simply use the validation classes the framework provides instead of creating custom ones.

Bootstrap, being the most common CSS framework to date, offers `border` and `border-warning` CSS classes, which you can use to highlight invalid input fields. Navigate to `TypeValidationClassProvider` and update the `GetFieldCssClass()` implementation as follows:

```
public override string GetFieldCssClass(
    EditContext editContext,
    in FieldIdentifier fieldIdentifier)
{
    var isValid = editContext.IsValid(fieldIdentifier);
    var isCapacity =
        fieldIdentifier.FieldName == _capacity;

    if (!isValid && isCapacity)
        return "border border-warning";

    return base.GetFieldCssClass(
        editContext, fieldIdentifier);
}
```

The custom validation logic remains intact – we still check whether the validation context is valid and whether the validated field refers to the capacity. However, when the custom validation fails, instead of returning the custom warning class, we leverage the `border border-warning` classes combination and effectively delegate the styling to Bootstrap.

Displaying a toast when validation fails

In this recipe, we explore how to enhance form validation feedback with a custom display of validation errors. Blazor's `ValidationSummary` component provides a straightforward way to collect and display all validation messages from a form in a single container, typically rendered as a simple `div`. While functional, this default presentation might not always align with a desired user experience or the aesthetic standards of your application. You can replace the standard `ValidationSummary` component with a custom implementation to make validation messages more engaging and fit seamlessly with the broader notification strategy of your application.

Let's implement a custom component that displays validation errors inside a default Bootstrap toast, making a more modern version of `ValidationSummary`.

Getting ready

Before diving into the implementation of a custom validation summary, do the following:

- Create a Chapter07/Recipe06 directory – this will be your working directory
- Copy Event, EventLocation, EventManager, EventNameValidationAttribute, and TypeValidationClassProvider from the *Styling validation messages* recipe or from the Chapter07/Recipe05 directory in the GitHub repository

How to do it...

Follow these steps to introduce a custom validation summary:

1. Create a ValidationToast component that implements the IDisposable interface:

```
@implements IDisposable
```

2. Inside the @code block of the ValidationToast component, declare a CascadingParameter parameter of type EditContext and an IsDisplayed property:

```
[CascadingParameter]
public EditContext Context { get; set; }
protected bool IsDisplayed { get; set; }
```

3. Still within the @code block, implement a Rerender() method, matching the signature of a subscriber of an EventHandler<ValidationStateChangedEventArgs> handler:

```
private void Rerender(object sender,
ValidationStateChangedEventArgs args) { }
```

4. Inside Rerender(), set the IsDisplayed property based on whether there are any validation messages in Context and invoke the StateHasChanged() to trigger a UI refresh:

```
IsDisplayed = Context.GetValidationMessages().Any();
StateHasChanged();
```

5. Below Rerender(), override the OnInitialized() life cycle method and subscribe to the OnValidationStateChanged event of EditContext:

```
protected override void OnInitialized()
    => Context.OnValidationStateChanged += Rerender;
```

6. Complete the @code block by implementing the Dispose() method and unsubscribe from the OnValidationStateChanged event:

```
public void Dispose()
    => Context.OnValidationStateChanged -= Rerender;
```

7. In the `ValidationToast` markup, below the `@implements` directive, include a fast-return clause to prevent any markup rendering based on the `IsDisplayed` value:

```
@if (!IsDisplayed) return;
```

8. Below the fast-return clause, construct a frame of a default Bootstrap toast notification:

```
<div class="position-fixed bottom-0 end-0 p-3"
    style="z-index: 1">
    <div class="toast text-white bg-danger show">
        @* toast area *@
    </div>
</div>
```

9. Within the toast area, add an empty header for aesthetics, and in the toast body, implement logic to dynamically render the list of validation messages retrieved from `EditContext`:

```
<div class="toast-header" />
<div class="toast-body">
    @foreach (var message in
        Context.GetValidationMessages())
    {
        <div>@message</div>
    }
</div>
```

10. Navigate to the `EventManager` component, above the form submit button, and remove the existing `ValidationSummary` paragraph. Replace it with an instance of the new `ValidationToast` component:

```
<ValidationToast />
```

How it works...

In *step 1*, we create a new `ValidationToast` component that implements the `IDisposable` interface to ensure a proper resource clean-up as we will work with an event handler.

From *step 2*, we work on the `@code` block of the `ValidationToast` component. We declare a `CascadingParameter` parameter of type `EditContext` to gain access to the parent form's context. We also declare an `IsDisplayed` property, which will help us control the visibility of the toast based on validation results. In *step 3*, we initialize a `Rerender` method, accepting the `sender` parameter and `args` of type `ValidationStateChangedEventArgs`, so we can subscribe it later to a matching `EventHandler`. In *step 4*, we implement the `Rerender` logic, where we determine whether there are any validation messages in the `Context` instance and set the `IsDisplayed` property, indicating that there are errors to display. We then invoke `StateHasChanged()` to prompt

Blazor to refresh the UI and reflect the updated state. In *step 5*, we override the `OnInitialized()` life cycle method to subscribe the `Rerender()` method to the `OnValidationStateChanged` event of `EditContext`. Blazor will execute `Rerender()` every time the form's validation state changes, allowing our toast notification to update reactively. In *step 6*, we implement the `Dispose()` method, where we unsubscribe from the `OnValidationStateChanged` event, ensuring that `ValidationToast` does not continue to react to events after it has been removed from the UI, thus preventing memory leaks.

In *step 7*, we focus on the markup of `ValidationToast`. We start below the `@implements` directive with a fast-return clause, based on the `IsDisplayed` value, which instructs Blazor to immediately exit the rendering process when there are no validation messages. In *step 8*, we construct a visual frame using default Bootstrap classes to create a toast notification. As it's standard Bootstrap code, we won't analyze it deeply. Shortly, we position the frame fixed at the bottom end of the viewport, ensuring that it is visible but non-intrusive. We also make the toast red to clearly indicate that there's a problem. In *step 9*, we implement the toast area. We add an empty header for visual balance and a body where we iterate over the result of the `Context.GetValidationMessages()` call and dynamically render each validation message.

Lastly, in *step 10*, we jump to the `EventManager` component. Here, we remove the existing `ValidationSummary` paragraph and replace it with the new `ValidationToast` component, which now handles the display of validation messages in a more interactive and visually engaging manner.

We arrive at a still simple but more modern validation summary that our users will appreciate:

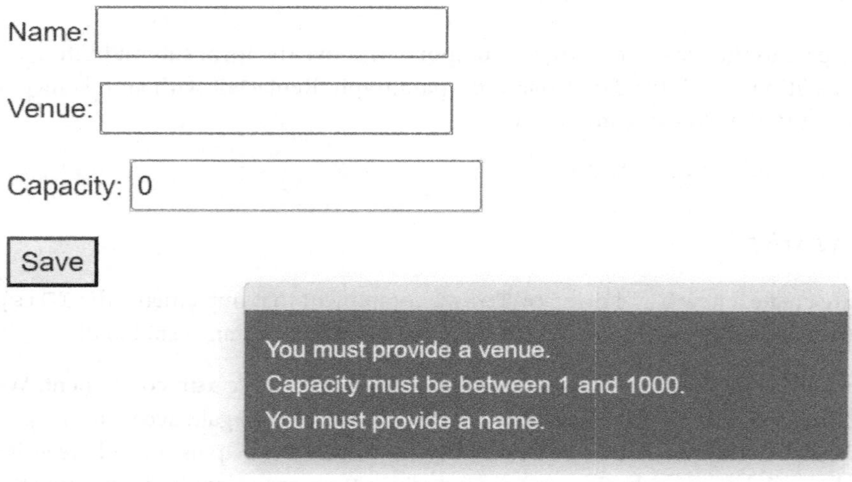

Name:

Venue:

Capacity: 0

Save

You must provide a venue.
Capacity must be between 1 and 1000.
You must provide a name.

Figure 7.3: Toast notification replacing a standard validation summary container

Enabling a submit option based on the form state

In this recipe, we dive into a strategy to enhance the user experience by dynamically controlling the state of the form's submit button. We use forms not only when creating a new object but also when modifying an existing one as well. It makes sense that we would prevent the form submission when a user didn't make any changes or if some input is invalid. Having that feature in place, we improve the user experience, conserve memory usage, and reduce unnecessary server requests.

Let's enhance a form with a mechanism that enables form saving only when there have been changes to the form data and all inputs are valid.

Getting ready

Before making the form submit button react to the form state, do the following:

- Create a `Chapter07/Recipe07` directory – this will be your working directory
- Copy `Event`, `EventLocation`, `EventManager`, `EventNameValidationAttribute`, `TypeValidationClassProvider`, and `ValidationToast` from the *Displaying toast when validation fails* recipe or from the `Chapter07/Recipe06` directory in the GitHub repository

How to do it...

Follow these steps to make the form submit button reactive to the form state:

1. Navigate to the `EventManager` component and update it to implement the `IDisposable` interface and to render mode in `InteractiveWebAssembly`:

    ```
    @rendermode InteractiveWebAssembly
    @implements IDisposable
    ```

2. Within the `@code` block of `EventManager`, introduce an `IsSubmittable` variable of type `bool`:

    ```
    protected bool IsSubmittable;
    ```

3. Still in the `@code` block, add a `FieldChanged()` method that conforms to the `EventHandler<FieldChangedEventArgs>` response pattern and resolve the form's current state into the `IsSubmittable` variable:

    ```
    private void FieldChanged(
        object sender, FieldChangedEventArgs args)
    {
        IsSubmittable =
            Context.Validate() && Context.IsModified();
        StateHasChanged();
    }
    ```

4. In the `OnInitialized()` method, initiate a default value for the `Model` instance to simulate a data-editing scenario:

```
Model ??= new()
{
    Name = "Packt Party",
    Location = new()
    {
        Venue = "Packt Room",
        Capacity = 150
    }
};
```

5. At the end of the `OnInitialized()` method, subscribe the `FieldChanged()` method to the `OnFieldChanged` event, exposed by the `EditContext` API:

```
Context.OnFieldChanged += FieldChanged;
```

6. Complete the `IDisposable` implementation by adding a `Dispose()` method at the end of the `@code` block and unsubscribe `FieldChanged()` from the `OnFieldChanged` handler:

```
public void Dispose()
    => Context.OnFieldChanged -= FieldChanged;
```

7. Switch to the `EventManager` markup and locate the submit button. Set the button's `disabled` attribute to the negated value of the `IsSubmittable` variable:

```
<button type="submit" disabled="@(!IsSubmittable)">
    Save
</button>
```

How it works...

In *step 1*, we start by enhancing the interactivity of our form located in `EventManager`. We configure `EventManager` to render in an `InteractiveWebAssembly` mode, enabling component interactivity, and we declare that it will implement the `IDisposable` interface allowing a custom cleanup implementation.

In *step 2*, we move to the `@code` block of `EventManager` and declare an `IsSubmittable` variable that we will leverage in managing the state of the form's submit button. In *step 3*, we implement a `FieldChanged()` method that takes the `sender` and `args` parameters of type `FieldChangedEventArgs`. Inside `FieldChanged()`, we utilize the `EditContext` API through the `Context` instance to dynamically evaluate the form's state. We set the `IsSubmittable` variable by checking whether all form fields are valid, using `Context.Validate()`, and the form was modified, using `Context.IsModified()`. Given that this operation can affect the state of the form's submit button, we call `StateHasChanged()` to notify Blazor that the UI might need updating.

In *step 4*, we adjust how `EventManager` initializes. Instead of resetting the `Model` object to a new instance, we simulate editing an existing model by setting initial properties, reflecting a typical data-editing scenario. In *step 5*, as part of the initialization process, we also subscribe `FieldChanged()` to the `Context.OnFieldChanged` event handler. Blazor triggers `OnFieldChanged` whenever the form field's value changes, ensuring our form responds to every edit. In *step 6*, we finalize the `IDisposable` implementation. We implement the `Dispose()` method, where we unsubscribe `FieldChanged()` from the `OnFieldChanged` event handler to prevent memory leaks and ensure that the `EventManager` component is disposed of gracefully when it is no longer needed.

In *step 7*, we jump to the `EventManager` markup to reflect our backend logic in the UI. We locate the form's submit button and attach a `disabled` attribute, setting its value to the `IsSubmittable` negation. Whenever the user changes focus between fields in the form, we will recalculate the value of `IsSubmittable` – and since `IsSubmittable` indicates whether the user made changes and the form is in a valid state, negating this value determines when the submit button should be disabled, preventing unnecessary submission until all conditions for a valid and modified form are met.

There's more...

`EditContext` in Blazor plays a crucial role in managing form states and validations but has some limitations. One significant caveat is that it does not track the initial state of model properties. `EditContext` monitors changes to input fields, marking them as modified when their values change. However, if the user reverts a field's value to its original state, `EditContext` still considers it modified. This behavior can lead to scenarios where forms may incorrectly allow submission or display validation states because they do not recognize that the field value has returned to its initial state.

To address this limitation and refine the behavior of form modifications, you must implement an equality comparer, inheriting from `IEqualityComparer<T>` to customize how equality for reference types is determined. Having an explicit comparison logic, we can persist the initial value of the model in an `_initialModel` variable and replace the standard `Context.IsModified()` check with an `_initialModel != Model` evaluation. Blazor will disable the submit button when the user's input returns to the initial values, ensuring that the form is only submittable with actual changes.

8

Keeping the Application Secure

In this chapter, we focus on essential security practices for Blazor applications, as protecting user data and maintaining trust is crucial for any commercial success.

We will start by scaffolding identity – setting up the necessary infrastructure for user authentication and management by leveraging the template provided by the .NET team. We will look at strategies to prevent unauthorized access and protect your component from unwanted actors. Additionally, we will cover a more granular approach and secure markup areas to customize the component behavior and ensure that sensitive information is only accessible to authorized users. We will explore how to define and enforce **roles** and **policies** to centralize and encapsulate access levels that align with your security requirements. Next, we will learn how to determine users' **authentication state** and their current access context, allowing us to secure and enhance backend logic. We will also discuss how to update user identity safely and securely.

By the end of this chapter, you will understand various security mechanisms in Blazor and have the best security practices in your skillset.

Here's a list of the recipes we will cover:

- Scaffolding identity
- Securing pages
- Securing markup areas
- Creating roles
- Modifying a user's identity
- Supporting roles' and policies' authorization
- Resolving authentication state in procedural logic

Technical requirements

In this chapter, recipes build on one another, resulting in a guide through the most often required identity features. For clarity, at the beginning of each recipe, you will find instructions on how to set up a working directory and where to get the sample objects from. On top of that, this chapter requires that you have a working **Structured Query Language** (**SQL**) database, a connection string to the database instance, and a SQL IDE as you will need to run a few custom migrations. Most of the tables will be scaffolded for you, so don't stress if you don't have much experience with SQL itself.

All the code samples are available on GitHub at: `https://github.com/PacktPublishing/Blazor-Web-Development-Cookbook/tree/main/Chapter08/BlazorCookbook.Auth`

Scaffolding identity

The .NET team provides a template that enables adding authentication to your Blazor application rapidly. This template is not only quick to set up but also highly customizable. You can streamline the implementation of user authentication, registration, and profile management, ensuring that your application is secure from the get-go. You get essential features such as login and logout functionality, password recovery, and user data management – all crucial for any authentication system.

Let's scaffold a new Blazor project with authentication enabled and explore the features it offers out of the box. By the end of this recipe, you will have a solid foundation and understanding of the identity system. Whether you're building a simple app or a complex enterprise solution, this approach will save you time and effort while ensuring your application meets modern security standards.

Getting ready

We will showcase initializing the project with identity, leveraging the GUI provided as part of Visual Studio, so the only pre-requirement in this recipe is that you start your IDE. Let's dive in.

If you're using the .NET CLI in your environment, you can refer to the *There's more...* section at the end of the recipe, where I'll provide equivalent commands.

How to do it...

Follow these steps to scaffold a new Blazor project with identity:

1. Select **Create a new project** from the welcome window:

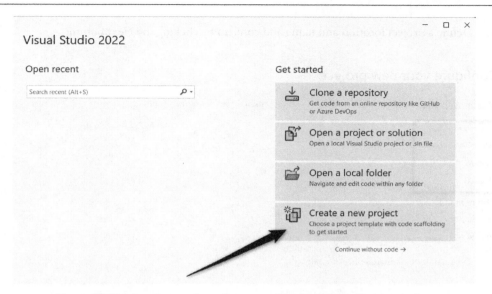

Figure 8.1: Starting the creation of a new project from the welcome window

2. Use the search bar at the top of the panel to find the **Blazor Web App** position and confirm by clicking the **Next** button:

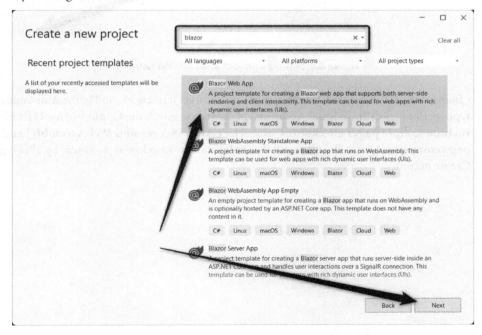

Figure 8.2: Selecting Blazor Web App from available project templates

3.   Define a project location and name and confirm by clicking the **Next** button:

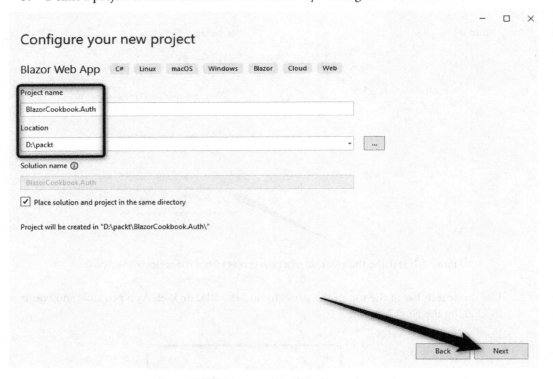

Figure 8.3: Setting a project location and name

4.   Choose **.NET 9.0 (Standard Term Support)** as the target framework, and in the **Authentication type** section, select **Individual Accounts**. Make sure to check the **Configure for HTTPS** and **Include sample pages** checkboxes, and select **Auto (Server and WebAssembly)** and **Per page/component** from the interactivity configuration dropdowns. Confirm by clicking the **Create** button:

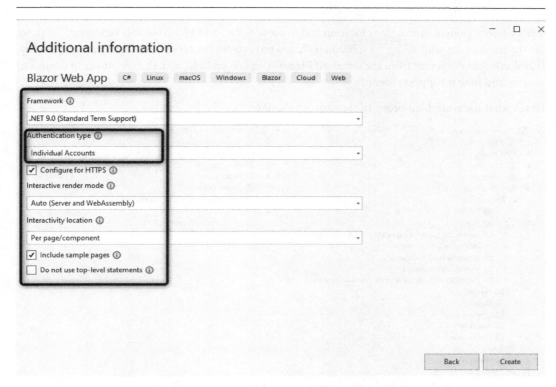

Figure 8.4: Configuring the project's framework, interactivity, and authentication

You will arrive at a similar project setup, which may vary depending on the name of your project:

Figure 8.5: Initial solution structure

How it works...

The entire process is almost the same as we explored in the *Initializing a project* recipe in *Chapter 1*. Navigate there for the first three steps. Here, we focus on *step 4*.

In *step 4*, we land on the project configuration panel. First, we select **.NET 9 (Standard Term Support)** as our target framework. Then, we have an **Authentication type** section. Here, we opt for the **Individual Accounts** option, instructing Visual Studio to scaffold the code supporting identity in our application. We also enable HTTPS and generate sample pages by checking the respective checkboxes. Lastly, to complete the configuration setup, we define the interactivity of our application – we will use a per-page/component interactivity location and a mix of Server and WebAssembly rendering. Next, we see the result of the scaffolding – a solution with two projects for the server and client side, respectively. It looks nothing different from the standard Blazor template scaffold, so let's dive into each project to understand how it supports identity.

Here's what the scaffolded projects' structures look like:

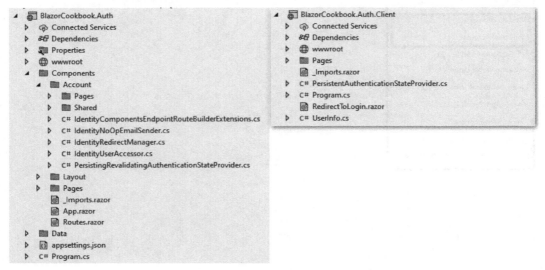

Figure 8.6: Scaffolded server- and client-side projects, with enabled authentication

Let's first unpack the client-side project (on the right side in *Figure 8.6*), as it's significantly smaller. On the components' side, we're getting just one relevant to manage identity – `RedirectToLogin`. As the name implies, `RedirectToLogin` safely redirects a user to the login page, persisting the initial URL so that Blazor can return there. We're also getting a `UserInfo` class – a model containing the user identity details we want to share between server- and client-side communication, and one we can easily extend. The backbone of sharing the authentication state across render mode boundaries is the `PersistentAuthenticationStateProvider` service, which we will explore in the *Supporting roles' and policies' authorization* recipe. Lastly, we're getting a minimal setup in the `Program.cs` file. The `PersistentAuthenticationStateProvider` service is registered as a singleton in the **dependency injection container** (**DI**), and with the `AddAuthorizationCore()` extension method, all services required to enable authorization in our app are registered for us. We also get an invocation of the `AddCascadingAuthenticationState()` extension method to add an authentication state as a root-level cascading value and make it interceptable in the entire WebAssembly application.

The server-side project (on the left side in *Figure 8.6*) contains the `Data` directory, with an `ApplicationDbContext` class, an `ApplicationUser` class, and a `Migrations` subdirectory, indicating that the server-side project is responsible for persisting and managing users and their identities. That means you must provide a valid connection string to the database where you want to store identity data. You'll find a placeholder `DefaultConnection` node generated in the `appSettings.json` file, which you must replace with the connection details of your database resource. Next to the `Data` directory, we get a chunk of generated components, including an `Account` area, with pages and UI, handling all actions required to manage identity in our application. There are components for logging in, logging out, managing accounts, and even enabling **two-factor authentication** (**2FA**), and they're all Razor-native components. You'll notice that regardless of the interactivity declared when configuring, all the identity components are rendered in **server-side rendering** (**SSR**) mode by default. As is currently an industry standard for applications with a server-side to leverage cookies for identity management, we're also getting a custom `IdentityRedirectManager` wrapper, which leverages the default Blazor `NavigationManager` class, extending it with identity status cookies and a few redirection resolvers. The `IdentityRedirectManager` class is also designed to throw an `InvalidOperationException` exception when used outside of the static SSR. In SSR, contrary to other rendering modes, we can access an `HttpContext` instance of each request. The `IdentityUserAccessor` class is another wrapper class, allowing us to resolve the current user identity from the `HttpContext` instance. In the `IdentityComponentsEndpointRouteBuilderExtensions` class, we get a mapping for three additional identity endpoints for logging in with an external **identity provider** (**IdP**), downloading personal user data, and logging out. These are missing in the default identity API implementation, as they're native for applications with a UI. The `IdentityNoOpEmailSender` class is a placeholder service for sending identity-related emails: confirming user email or resetting passwords. You have to implement your own `IEmailSender` client before going live. We also get a `PersistingRevalidatingAuthenticationStateProvider` class that Blazor uses to share the authentication state across render boundaries between server and client code – we will explore that in the *Supporting roles' and policies' authorization* recipe too. The `Program.cs` file gets a bit more complex. We will find here the default setup of interactive server and WebAssembly components and a default middleware pipeline. However, on top of that, we're setting up the server-side identity features. We register the custom identity services (discussed earlier in this section) and invoke the `AddCascadingAuthenticationState()` extension method to enable the cascading of the authentication state at a root level. We configure the authentication leveraging the `AddAuthentication()` extension method. Here's also where we inform Blazor to use cookies for identity persistence with the help of the `AddIdentityCookies()` extension method. In `Program.cs`, we also configure the database access for our `ApplicationDbContext` class. Lastly, and most importantly, we leverage the `AddIdentityCore()` method and the `IdentityBuilder` API to configure the required identity services.

Now that you understand the structure of each of the projects, let's visualize how the authentication workflow works:

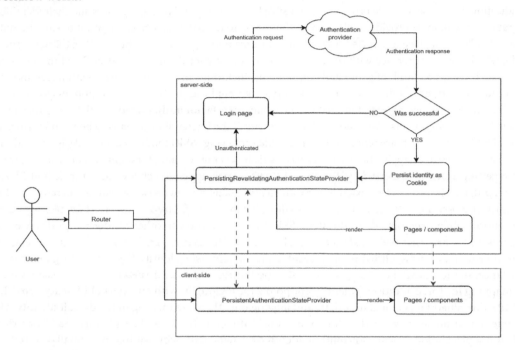

Figure 8.7: Authentication workflow between server and client sides of the Blazor web app

When a user tries to access the application, their identity is checked. The authentication state provider service validates the available authentication cookie or lack thereof. If validation is successful, the user gets redirected to the page they intended to visit; otherwise, the user lands on the login page. After submitting the login form and receiving a successful authentication response from the IdP, Blazor persists the user's identity in the authentication cookie. That cookie gets attached to every request between the server and client side, allowing `PersistingRevalidatingAuthenticationStateProvider` and `PersistentAuthenticationStateProvider` to effectively monitor and recognize the current user and their permissions.

When you run the application for the first time and try to create an account, your application will fail. But in a developer-friendly way, you will see an exception page, informing you that you didn't run the initial migration yet, so your backing database can't support identity features:

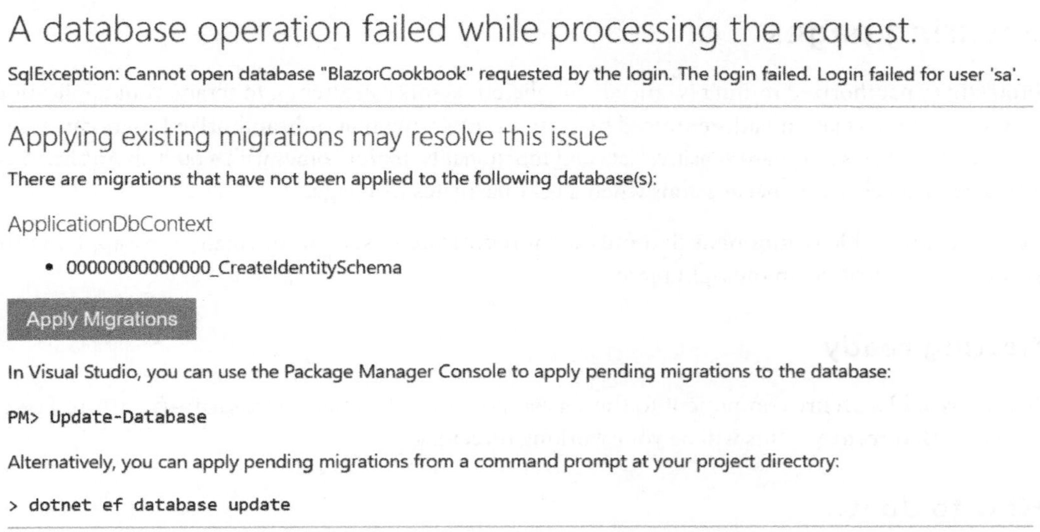

A database operation failed while processing the request.

SqlException: Cannot open database "BlazorCookbook" requested by the login. The login failed. Login failed for user 'sa'.

Applying existing migrations may resolve this issue

There are migrations that have not been applied to the following database(s):

ApplicationDbContext

- 00000000000000_CreateIdentitySchema

Apply Migrations

In Visual Studio, you can use the Package Manager Console to apply pending migrations to the database:

PM> Update-Database

Alternatively, you can apply pending migrations from a command prompt at your project directory:

> dotnet ef database update

Figure 8.8: Exception page when you try to create an account without the initial migration

You will also get a simple **Apply Migrations** button allowing you to apply the migrations immediately!

All that code and functionality are ready to use, and you haven't written a single line of your own code yet. Leveraging solution templates and scaffolding increases the velocity of the delivery of your application.

There's more...

In case you're not using a GUI or Visual Studio, you can leverage the cross-platform .NET CLI and scaffold the same template with a single command line. Navigate to your working directory and run the following command:

```
dotnet new blazor -o BlazorCookbook.Auth -int Auto --framework net9.0
-au Individual
```

You will get the same format of a project that we did through the Visual Studio walk-through, with one difference. The project scaffolded with the .NET CLI utilizes the SQLite database rather than SQL Server. You can quickly adjust that by navigating to the Program.cs file of the server-side project and updating the ApplicationDbContext registration options to use SQL Server:

```
builder.Services.AddDbContext<ApplicationDbContext>(
    options => options.UseSqlServer(connectionString));
```

Securing pages

Protecting unauthorized routing is crucial as malicious actors can attempt to scrape your application, bypassing the navigation paths enforced by your UI. Ensuring that only authorized users can access specific routes helps safeguard sensitive data and functionality. Blazor comes with a built-in `Authorize` attribute to check access permissions when a user navigates to a page.

Let's add a routable component that only an authenticated user can navigate to by applying the `Authorize` attribute in the right place.

Getting ready

Before we add a secure component to the server-side project, create a `Components/Recipes/Recipe02` directory – this will be your working directory.

How to do it...

Follow these instructions to protect a component:

1. Create a routable `Settings` component with a `/ch08r02` path:

   ```
   @page "/ch08r02"
   ```

2. Reference the `Microsoft.AspNetCore.Authorization` assembly and attach an `Authorize` attribute to the `Settings` component:

   ```
   @using Microsoft.AspNetCore.Authorization
   @attribute [Authorize]
   ```

3. Add placeholder markup to the `Settings` component, informing the user that they are authorized to see this content:

   ```
   <h3>Settings</h3>
   <p>You're authorized to see settings.</p>
   ```

How it works...

In *step 1*, we execute a routine step and create a new routable `Settings` component, leveraging `@page`. Next, in *step 2*, we reference the `Microsoft.AspNetCore.Authorization` assembly with the help of the `@using` directive right below the `@page` declaration. Then, we use `@attribute` to attach the `Authorize` attribute. Now, only authenticated users can access the `Settings` page. However, it's important to note that Blazor performs a verification of the `Authorize` attribute only as part of the routing process and does not apply it to child components' rendering flow. Lastly, in *step 3*, we add some placeholder content to inform users that they are authorized to view this page. In the `Settings` markup, we render the page header and a **You're authorized to see settings.** message.

There's more...

If you're building a markup-less component or simply working in a code-behind fashion, you can still leverage the `Authorize` attribute. Here's how we would implement a markup-less version of the `Settings` component:

```
[Route("/ch08r02")]
[Authorize]
public class Settings : ComponentBase
{
    // ...
}
```

As we're no longer in a Razor file, we're using the syntax of C# attributes. By decorating the `Settings` class with a `[Route]` attribute, we enable navigation to the `/ch08r02` path. Additionally, by adding the `[Authorize]` attribute, we ensure that Blazor only allows routing to this component for authenticated users. We effectively achieve the same logical behavior as in the initial implementation. As a side note, when you're working in Razor files, the Razor compiler translates all the dedicated `@directive` declarations to attributes – similar to what we did with the markup-less component.

Securing markup areas

Sometimes, restricting access to an entire page can be too limiting. You might want to expose your landing page to everyone while fine-tuning the elements users see in the navigation menu. For example, authenticated users might have access to a back office feature that standard users cannot see despite viewing the same page. Blazor supports protecting specific markup areas with an `AuthorizeView` component. The `AuthorizeView` component allows you to control the visibility of content based on the user's authentication state. It supports various states and works seamlessly with `RenderFragment` objects, making it highly flexible and versatile.

Let's leverage the `AuthorizeView` component and add a status message visible only to authenticated users.

Getting ready

Before we add a protected status message to a component, do the following:

- In the server-side project, create a `Components/Recipes/Recipe03` directory – this will be your working directory
- Copy the `Settings` component from the *Securing pages* recipe or from the `Components/Recipes/Recipe02` directory in the GitHub repository

How to do it...

Follow these steps to add a protected markup area in a component:

1. Navigate to the `Settings` component and remove the `Authorize` attribute and the existing `@using` directive.

2. Locate the authorization status message in the `Settings` markup and wrap it in `AuthorizeView` component tags:

```
<h3>Settings</h3>
<AuthorizeView>
    <p>You're authorized to see settings.</p>
</AuthorizeView>
```

How it works...

In *step 1*, we remove the existing `Authorize` attribute and the `@using` directive, required to reference the attribute, from the `Settings` component, allowing all users to access the page.

In *step 2*, we locate the **You're authorized to see settings.** authorization status message in the `Settings` markup. We then wrap this message inside `AuthorizeView` component tags. The `AuthorizeView` component manages content visibility based on the user authentication state and accepts `ChildContent`, meaning Blazor will render the status message only for authenticated users. This approach ensures that only users with the proper credentials see certain content, enhancing the security and user experience of your application. You can find more details on the `ChildContent` pattern in the *Creating components with customizable content* recipe of *Chapter 1*.

Blazor will effectively obscure everything inside the `AuthorizeView` component from unauthorized users. That means markup, as well as any event handlers or method calls. Consequently, you can secure your UI and entire features and functionalities, preventing unauthorized users from even knowing they exist.

There's more...

Apart from `ChildContent`, `AuthorizeView` supports providing the `Authorized`, `Authorizing`, and `NotAuthorized` fragments explicitly. With that, you can define distinct content for authenticated and unauthenticated users within the same component. You would leverage the `Authorizing` fragment to display a temporary message indicating that resolving of user's identity is in progress, as you might need to execute some asynchronous and long-running logic. In our case, we could opt for the following markup in the `Settings` component:

```
<h3>Settings</h3>
<AuthorizeView>
    <Authorized>
```

```
        <p>You're authorized to see settings.</p>
    </Authorized>
    <Authorizing>
        <p>Give us a few moments...</p>
    </Authorizing>
    <NotAuthorized>
        <p>You can't be here, sorry.</p>
    </NotAuthorized>
</AuthorizeView>
```

The `AuthorizeView` component will evaluate the user's authentication state normally, but this time give the user a feeling of each stage of the process. When authenticating the user, Blazor will render the content in `Authorizing` tags – a **Give us a few moments…** message. When authentication is complete, for the authenticated user, Blazor will render the markup in the `Authorized` section and display the expected **You're authorized to see settings.** message. However, contrary to the `Authorized` attribute, an anonymous user will also see some content – one within `NotAuthorized` tags, saying **You can't be here, sorry.**, offering meaningful feedback to unauthenticated users.

Creating roles

Roles in web applications are predefined categories assigned to users that determine their access permissions and functionalities within the application. By categorizing users into roles, you can manage and control what each user can view and do, enhancing security and user experience. Roles provide a clear and structured way to enforce access control. Instead of managing permissions for each user, you can assign roles and define access rules based on these roles. This approach simplifies the administration of user permissions and ensures consistent security policies across the application.

Let's add a small form where authenticated users can create new roles in the application.

Getting ready

Before we implement the role creation form, do the following:

- In the server-side project, create a `Components/Recipes/Recipe04` directory – this will be your working directory
- Copy the `Settings` component from the *Securing markup areas* recipe or from the `Components/Recipes/Recipe03` directory in the GitHub repository
- If you haven't scaffolded your project, copy the `StatusMessage` component from the `Components/Account/Shared` directory of the GitHub repository to the same path in your server-side project

How to do it...

Follow these instructions to set up roles' support and management:

1. Navigate to the server-side project's `Program.cs` file. Find the section where we register identity services, starting with the `AddIdentityCore()` method.

2. After the `AddIdentityCore()` method, invoke the `AddRoles()` method and leverage the default `IdentityRole` model to declare the application role model. Below the `AddEntityFrameworkStores()` method, register a role manager with the help of an `AddRoleManager()` builder method with the default `RoleManager` service for the `IdentityRole` model:

```
builder.Services.AddIdentityCore<ApplicationUser>()
    .AddRoles<IdentityRole>()
    .AddEntityFrameworkStores<ApplicationDbContext>()
    .AddRoleManager<RoleManager<IdentityRole>>()
    .AddSignInManager()
    .AddDefaultTokenProviders();
```

3. Open the `Settings` component, and below the `@page` directive, add a set of `@using` directives referencing the necessary assemblies:

```
@using BlazorCookbook.Auth.Components.Account
@using BlazorCookbook.Auth.Components.Account.Shared
@using Microsoft.AspNetCore.Identity
```

4. Below the section with `@using`, inject `RoleManager` and `Navigation` services:

```
@inject RoleManager<IdentityRole> RoleManager
@inject IdentityRedirectManager Navigation
```

5. In the `Settings` component, initialize the `@code` block and construct an `InputModel` class with a single `RoleName` property:

```
@code {
    private sealed class InputModel
    {
        public string RoleName { get; set; }
    }
}
```

6. Below the service injections, intercept a cascading value of `HttpContext`:

```
[CascadingParameter]
private HttpContext HttpContext { get; set; }
```

7. Below `HttpContext`, declare an `Input` parameter supplied from a form and override the `OnInitialized()` lifecycle method to complete the form initialization pattern:

```
[SupplyParameterFromForm]
private InputModel Input { get; set; } = new();
protected override void OnInitialized()
    => Input ??= new();
```

8. Complete the `@code` block with the implementation of a `SaveAsync()` method, where you initialize a new `IdentityRole` object and leverage the `RoleManager` service to save the new role. Use the `Navigation` service to perform a self-redirect and display the operation status:

```
private async Task SaveAsync()
{
    var role = new IdentityRole(Input.RoleName);
    await RoleManager.CreateAsync(role);

    Navigation.RedirectToCurrentPageWithStatus(
        $"'{role.Name}' role has been created",
        HttpContext);
}
```

9. In the `Settings` component markup, locate the `AuthorizeView` tags and declare a custom name for the `Context` parameter. Also, replace the authentication status message with a `StatusMessage` component:

```
<AuthorizeView Context="auth">
    <StatusMessage />
</AuthorizeView>
```

10. Below `StatusMessage`, initialize an `EditForm` component, attaching the `Input` model and the `SaveAsync()` method to the `Model` and `OnValidSubmit` parameters. Remember to declare a unique `EditForm` name as well:

```
<EditForm FormName="creator"
          OnValidSubmit="@SaveAsync"
          Model="@Input">
</EditForm>
```

11. Within the `EditForm` component, add a paragraph with an editable input box binding to the `Input.RoleName` property:

```
<p>Role name
  <InputText @bind-Value="@Input.RoleName" />
</p>
```

12. Complete the EditForm component by adding a form submit button below the role name input:

```
<p><button type="submit">Save</button></p>
```

How it works...

In *step 1*, we navigate to the Program.cs file of the server-side project and locate the section where we register identity services. It's a section starting with an AddIdentityCore() method and producing an IdentityBuilder object. In *step 2*, we invoke the AddRoles() method to add role management capabilities to the identity system. The AddRoles() method is a generic method requiring an identity role model class. We leverage the default IdentityRole model, provided with an identity package. The IdentityRole model is enough for our needs. Next, below the AddEntityFrameworkStores() method, we register the role manager using the AddRoleManager() builder method with the default RoleManager service for the IdentityRole model. We've effectively enabled roles' support and roles' management in the app.

In *step 3*, we move to the Settings component. First, we add a set of @using directives below @page to reference the necessary assemblies, allowing access to the scaffolded Account area and built-in identity services. In *step 4*, we inject the RoleManager and Navigation services, handling role management and navigation, respectively. In *step 5*, we initialize the @code block in the Settings component. Within the @code block, we construct an InputModel class with a single RoleName property. The InputModel class will hold the details of the new role when a user fills out the form. In *step 6*, we intercept a cascading value of HttpContext to access the current HTTP context – necessary for communicating role creation status later. The HttpContext object didn't appear magically – when Blazor renders in SSR mode, it exposes the HttpContext instance cascadingly by default. In *step 7*, below HttpContext, we declare an Input parameter supplied from a form and override the OnInitialized() lifecycle method to complete the form initialization pattern. You can learn more about building forms in *Chapter 6*. In *step 8*, we complete the @code block by implementing a SaveAsync() method. In SaveAsync(), we initialize a new IdentityRole object and leverage RoleManager to save the new role to a database. We use the Navigation service and HttpContext to perform a self-redirect and send an operation status back to the user.

In *step 9*, we switch to the Settings markup. First, we locate the AuthorizeView tags. The AuthorizeView component is a generic component, so it exposes a Context property. Likewise, EditForm, which we will use for our form, is also a generic component having a Context property. We will have a conflict, and the app will not compile! To resolve that issue, we give a custom name to the Context property of AuthorizeView. We also replace the existing authentication status message with a StatusMessage component. The StatusMessage component intercepts HttpContext and resolves the status message from a designated cookie. That's why we needed HttpContext in the @code block – to attach that status cookie correctly. In *step 10*, we initialize an EditForm component below StatusMessage, attaching the Input model and the SaveAsync() method to the Model and OnValidSubmit parameters, respectively. We also declare a unique FormName class for EditForm. Within EditForm, in *step 11*, we add a paragraph with an editable input box binding to the `Input.RoleName` property, allowing the user to enter the new role name. Finally, in *step 12*, we complete the `EditForm` component by adding a form submit button below the role name input.

Modifying a user's identity

Modifying a user's identity can be crucial for tailoring your application's functionality and improving user experience. Having additional identity properties, you can enable more personalized interactions and better manage user-specific information. In many applications, a username is equivalent to a user's email, and that's not enough details for displaying personalized greetings, sending customized notifications, or generating reports. But worry not. In Blazor, identity is highly flexible.

Let's allow a user to fill in their first and last name.

Getting ready

Before extending the user's identity, do the following:

- In the server-side project, create a `Components/Recipes/Recipe05` directory – this will be your working directory
- Copy the `Settings` component from the *Creating roles* recipe or from the `Components/Recipes/Recipe03` directory in the GitHub repository
- Find the `seed-work.sql` script in the `Samples` directory of the server-side project in the GitHub repository and run it on your database
- If you haven't scaffolded your project, copy the `StatusMessage` component from the `Components/Account/Shared` directory of the GitHub repository to the same path in your server-side project

How to do it...

Follow these steps to extend the default user identity model:

1. Navigate to the `ApplicationUser` class in the `Data` directory of the server-side project and extend it with `FirstName` and `LastName` properties:

```
public class ApplicationUser : IdentityUser
{
    public string FirstName { get; set; }
    public string LastName { get; set; }
}
```

2. Using the **Package Manager Console**, call an Entity Framework command to generate a new `AddedUserFullName` database migration:

```
add-migration AddedUserFullName
```

Alternatively, if you're using the .NET CLI, generate the same migration using the following command:

```
dotnet ef migrations add AddedUserFullName
```

You will get a few new files in the `Data/Migrations` directory:

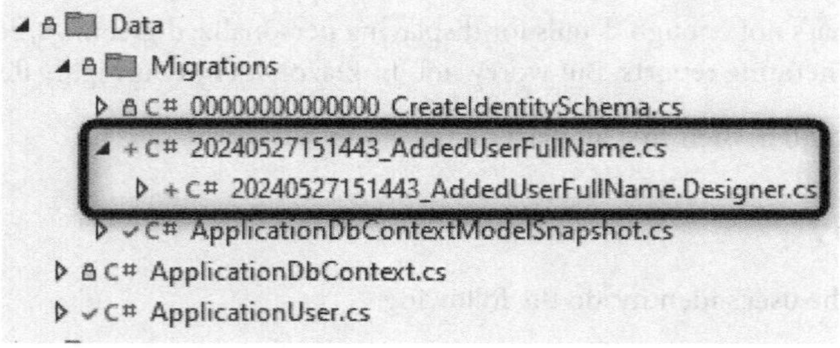

Figure 8.9: Migration files adding FirstName and LastName properties to ApplicationUser in database

3. Apply the `AddedUserFullName` migration to the database by calling another command in the **Package Manager Console**:

```
update-database
```

Alternatively, if you're using the .NET CLI, update the database using the following command:

```
dotnet ef database update
```

4. Open the `Settings` component and add one more `@using` directive, next to the existing ones:

```
@using BlazorCookbook.Auth.Data
```

5. Below, in the section with injections, replace the `RoleManager` service with `IdentityUserAccessor`, `UserManager`, and `SignInManager` services. Keep the already available `Navigation` service:

```
@inject IdentityUserAccessor UserAccessor
@inject UserManager<ApplicationUser> UserManager
@inject SignInManager<ApplicationUser> SignInManager
@inject IdentityRedirectManager Navigation
```

6. In the @code block, update the InputModel class by replacing the existing properties with FirstName and LastName:

```
private sealed class InputModel
{
    public string FirstName { get; set; }
    public string LastName { get; set; }
}
```

7. Above the existing SaveAsync() method, declare a private ApplicationUser field:

```
private ApplicationUser _user;
```

8. Below the _user declaration, override the OnInitializedAsync() lifecycle method. Leverage the UserAccessor instance to get the user details from the database and hydrate the Input model:

```
protected override async Task OnInitializedAsync()
{
    _user = await UserAccessor
        .GetRequiredUserAsync(HttpContext);
    Input.FirstName ??= _user.FirstName;
    Input.LastName ??= _user.LastName;
}
```

9. To complete the @code block, update the SaveAsync() method so that it updates _user details from the filled Input model, persist changes with the help of UserManager, and refresh the user context using SignInManager. Lastly, update the status message returned to the user:

```
private async Task SaveAsync()
{
    _user.FirstName = Input.FirstName;
    _user.LastName = Input.LastName;
    await UserManager.UpdateAsync(_user);
    await SignInManager.RefreshSignInAsync(_user);

    Navigation.RedirectToCurrentPageWithStatus(
        "Your profile has been updated",
        HttpContext);
}
```

10. Jump to the Settings markup area and locate the content area of the existing EditForm component.

11. Update the existing input label to First Name and fix the binding to the Input.FirstName property:

```
<p>First Name
  <InputText @bind-Value="@Input.FirstName" />
</p>
```

12. Below the first name, add a paragraph displaying another editable input binding to the Input.LastName property:

```
<p>Last Name
  <InputText @bind-Value="@Input.LastName" />
</p>
```

How it works...

In *step 1*, we navigate to the ApplicationUser class in the Data directory of the server-side project. The ApplicationUser class represents the user of our application and currently inherits from the default IdentityUser class to be compatible with the identity schema. Now, we extend our user identity details with FirstName and LastName properties. In *step 2*, we extend the identity database using a database migration. Database migrations are a way to manage and apply incremental changes to the database schema over time. They allow developers to define changes to the database structure, such as adding or modifying tables and columns, in code, ensuring that the database is in sync with the application. We open the **Package Manager Console**, available in Visual Studio, and generate a new AddedUserFullName database migration. The Entity Framework tool will generate two new files in the Data/Migrations directory. In *step 3*, we apply the AddedUserFullName migration to the database using the **Package Manager Console** again. We will not explore generated migrations or migration commands as they're not in the scope of this book, but you can find additional resources in the *See also* section at the end of the recipe.

Next, in *step 4*, we open the Settings component and extend the set of already existing @using directives with a reference to a BlazorCookbook.Auth.Data assembly, where we have the ApplicationUser class. In *step 5*, we remove the RoleManager service injection, as we won't work with roles. Instead, we're adding a few other identity services. We need IdentityUserAccessor to resolve the user context from the application HttpContext instance. With the help of UserManager and SignInManager, we can safely manipulate and refresh user details. In *step 6*, we update the InputModel class to support our new requirements and replace all existing properties with FirstName and LastName properties, matching the details we want to see on the new form later. At this point, you will see some IDE errors, as the existing form is no longer compatible with the updated InputModel class. We will fix that shortly. In *step 7*, we declare a backing field – a private ApplicationUser variable to store a reference to the database object representing the currently logged-in user. We will use it to persist the first and last name the user provides. In *step 8*, we override the OnInitializedAsync() lifecycle method. We leverage the injected UserAccessor service to resolve the ApplicationUser object from HttpContext into the _user instance and hydrate the `Input` model with the found details. That way, we ensure the form is pre-populated with the current user's details before the UI renders. To complete the `@code` block, in *step 9*, we update the `SaveAsync()` method so that it supports the updated `Input` model and saves user identity details. We update the persisted `_user` object with data coming from the form, filled by the user, and save those changes to the database with the help of `UserManager`. After updating, we refresh the user context using `SignInManager` and perform a self-redirect to display a **Your profile has been updated** message on the UI.

Next, in *step 10*, we jump to the `Settings` markup area and locate the existing `EditForm` component. We will adjust the form to support filling in the user's first and last names. In *step 11*, we fix the no longer compatible input box by binding it to the `Input.FirstName` property. We also update the label to `First name`, to make it clear which field the user is updating. Similarly, in *step 12*, we add a paragraph with another editable input box with a `Last name` label and binding to the `Input.LastName` property.

With the form in place, you can run the app and update the first and last name of the account you'll be using. When you fill the inputs and save the changes, you'll receive a friendly confirmation message:

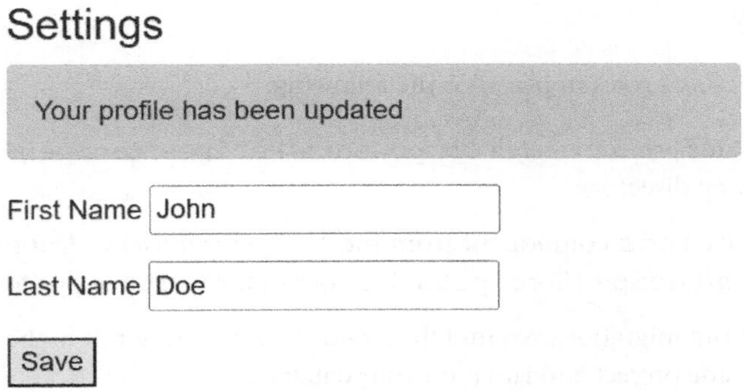

Settings

Your profile has been updated

First Name | John

Last Name | Doe

Save

Figure 8.10: Status message confirming that changes were successfully applied

You can also check changes in the database by displaying the records in the `AspNetUsers` table:

	Id	Email	FirstName	LastName
1	48E4DCD8-091B-4683-9F0D-163FCC8AF8BB	user@packt.com	NULL	NULL
2	7178EE03-B961-42FF-833A-3680590C83CA	user@annonymous.com	NULL	NULL
3	7A092C54-4046-4311-A300-D6501296CA15	admin@packt.com	John	Doe
4	A3F922DA-2903-42CC-9885-D69E986606A8	support@packt.com	NULL	NULL

Figure 8.11: Reviewing first and last name updates in the database

See also

In this recipe, we've touched on the concept of database migrations. It's a topic deserving a book of its own, but if you'd like to learn more, go to the learning resources prepared by the Microsoft team: `https://learn.microsoft.com/en-us/ef/core/managing-schemas/migrations`.

Supporting roles' and policies' authorization

Securing your application might not be just about having an authenticated user; it often requires more granular control. You may need to grant access to specific features or pages based on the user's role. Blazor's native authorization APIs – the `Authorize` attribute and the `AuthorizeView` component – support both roles and policies that you will find familiar from MVC applications or REST APIs.

Let's implement roles and policies, fine-tuning a settings page to display different content for administrators and standard users.

Getting ready

Before we put policies and roles in place, do the following:

- In the server-side project, create a `Components/Recipes/Recipe06` directory – this will be your working directory.

- Copy the `Settings` component from the *Modifying a user's identity* recipe or from the `Components/Recipes/Recipe05` directory in the GitHub repository.

- If you haven't run migrations yet, find the `seed-work.sql` script in the `Samples` directory of the server-side project and run it on your database.

- If you're not following along, make sure you have roles' support enabled in your server-side project; you must leverage the `AddRoles()` builder API method, which we discussed in the *Creating roles* recipe.

How to do it...

To add roles' and policies' support, both on the server and client side, follow these steps:

1. Navigate to the `Program.cs` file in the `BlazorCookbook.Auth.Client` project – the client-side application.

2. In the `Program.cs` file, find the `AddAuthorizationCore()` method call and overload it with `options` to configure the `InternalEmployee` policy that checks if a user's email belongs to the `@packt.com` domain:

```
builder.Services.AddAuthorizationCore(options =>
{
    options.AddPolicy("InternalEmployee", policy =>
        policy.RequireAssertion(context =>
            context.User?.Identity?.Name?
                .EndsWith("@packt.com") ?? false));
});
```

3. Still on the client side, open the `UserInfo` class and extend it with a `Role` property:

```
public class UserInfo
{
    //... existing properties ...
    public required string Role { get; set; }
}
```

4. Next, navigate to the `PersistentAuthenticationStateProvider` class, and in the constructor, extend the `claims` array to include the newly added `Role` value:

```
Claim[] claims = [
    // ... existing properties ...
    new Claim(ClaimTypes.Email, userInfo.Email),
    new Claim(ClaimTypes.Role, userInfo.Role),
];
```

5. Switch to the server-side application and open the `Program.cs` file of the `BlazorCookbook.Auth` project.

6. Locate where the app is built, and just before that, use the authorization builder to add the same `InternalEmployee` policy as on the client side:

```
builder.Services
    .AddAuthorizationBuilder()
    .AddPolicy("InternalEmployee",
        policy => policy.RequireAssertion(context =>
            context.User?.Identity?.Name?
                .EndsWith("@packt.com") ?? false));
var app = builder.Build();
```

7. Navigate to an OnPersistingAsync method of a PersistingRevalidatingAuthenticationStateProvider class and extend the logic executed for the authenticated user to append the role to the UserInfo class that Blazor will send over to the client side:

```
var userId = principal.FindFirst(
    options.ClaimsIdentity.UserIdClaimType)?.Value;
var email = principal.FindFirst(
    options.ClaimsIdentity.EmailClaimType)?.Value;
var role = principal.FindFirst(
    options.ClaimsIdentity.RoleClaimType)?.Value;

state.PersistAsJson(nameof(UserInfo), new UserInfo
{
    UserId = userId,
    Email = email,
    Role = role
});
```

8. Open the Settings component, and below the @page directive, add the Authorize attribute overloaded with the InternalEmployee policy:

```
@using Microsoft.AspNetCore.Authorization
@attribute [Authorize(Policy = "InternalEmployee")]
```

9. In the Settings markup, find the existing AuthorizeView opening tag and set the Roles parameter to allow Support and Admin roles:

```
<AuthorizeView Context="user" Roles="Support,Admin">
    @* here's still the existing EditForm *@
</AuthorizeView>
```

10. Below the EditForm protected area, construct another AuthorizeView section, protecting a **Shut down the app** button and rendering the content only for users in the Admin role:

```
<AuthorizeView Roles="Admin">
    <p><button>Shut down the app</button></p>
</AuthorizeView>
```

How it works...

We're starting with the client-side application, so in *step 1*, we navigate to the Program.cs file in the BlazorCookbook.Auth.Client project. In *step 2*, we extend the authorization registration by finding the AddAuthorizationCore() method call and overloading it with options to configure the InternalEmployee policy. We leverage the AuthorizationPolicyBuilder class, which we call `policy`, to check if a currently logged-in user's email belongs to the `@packt.com` domain. The `AuthorizationPolicyBuilder` class supports custom assertions (which we used) as well as checking claims, usernames, or .NET native `IAuthorizationRequirement` objects. In *step 3*, we open the `UserInfo` class and extend it with a `Role` property. The `UserInfo` class is a model that Blazor uses to share user identity details across render mode boundaries. As we need the WebAssembly side to resolve user roles correctly, we must pass them there explicitly. In *step 4*, we complete the client-side configuration by extending the constructor of the `PersistentAuthenticationStateProvider` class. Blazor uses `PersistentAuthenticationStateProvider` to determine the user's authentication state that arrives from the server side. In the constructor, we deserialize the state into a `UserInfo` object and extend the `claims` array to include the value of the newly added `Role` property. Now, whenever our application runs locally in the browser, the user's role will still be available to verify against.

In *step 5*, we switch to the server-side application and open the `Program.cs` file of the `BlazorCookbook.Auth` project. In *step 6*, we locate where we invoke the `builder.Build()` method to build the app. Right before that, we add the same `InternalEmployee` policy as on the client side with the help of the authorization builder. As the policy assertion is indeed the same, the server API for configuring authorization is slightly different. We invoke the `AddAuthorizationBuilder()` method to access the `AuthorizationBuilder` instance as it exposes the `AddPolicy()` builder method. In *step 7*, we complete the server-side implementation by navigating to the `OnPersistingAsync` method of the `PersistingRevalidatingAuthenticationStateProvider` class. That's the service Blazor uses when passing the user's identity to the browser. We locate the logic for the authenticated user. It already contains the sharing of the user's ID and email. We follow the same implementation pattern by grabbing the value of `RoleClaimType` from the current `principal` value and passing it on to the `UserRole` object that Blazor will persist as JSON inside the outgoing response.

Now, we put all that authorization implementation to the test. In *step 8*, we open the `Settings` component and add the `Authorize` attribute. It requires a reference to the `Microsoft.AspNetCore.Authorization` assembly, so we grant that with the `@using` directive. Then, we leverage the overloading of the `Authorize` attribute. We can set the `Policy` property so that the user must meet it to access the `Settings` page. That's where we finally use the `InternalEmployee` policy. In *step 9*, we continue to the `Settings` markup. We find the existing `AuthorizeView` opening tag, wrapping the form where users can fill in their first and last names. We set the `Roles` parameter to `Support` and `Admin` values, ensuring that the form renders only when the current user is in any of the expected roles. The `Roles` parameter accepts a `string` object, so you can provide one or multiple comma-separated roles. You can also have as many protected markup areas as you need within the same component. In *step 10*, we construct another `AuthorizeView` area below the one already existing. Inside, we construct an idle **Shut down the app** button, but we ensure it renders only for users in the `Admin` role.

We arrive at a fully functional, secure view that adjusts dynamically to whoever is viewing it.

Figure 8.12 shows the store settings to the user with the Admin role:

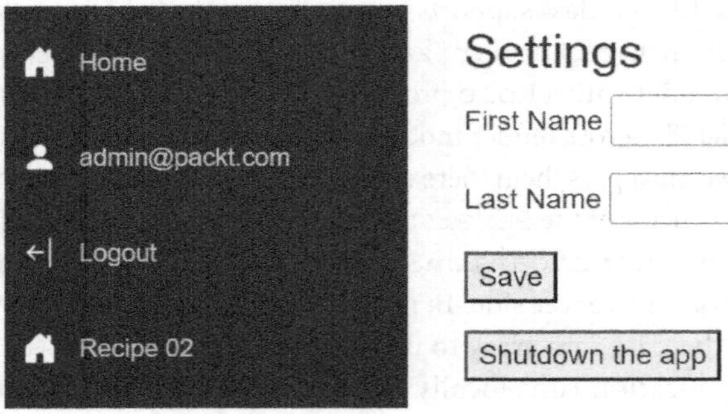

Figure 8.12: Store settings that an admin@packt.com user sees

Figure 8.13 shows the store settings to the user with the Support role:

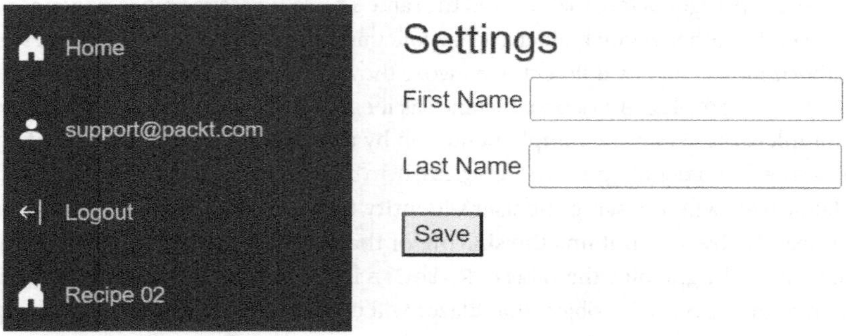

Figure 8.13: Store settings that a support@packt.com user sees

As you can see, when I log in as admin@packt.com, which has the Admin role, I can see both the edit form and the most restricted **Shut down the app** button. But the moment I change to support@packt.com, the **Shut down the app** button is gone! I encourage you to check how the UI changes when you log in as user@packt.com.

There's more...

The Authorize attribute supports the same authorization APIs that AuthorizeView does. Both can use Roles and Policy to verify the user's identity against specific criteria. You can even use both Roles and Policy at the same time!

```
@attribute [Authorize(Roles = "User,Support,Admin")]
<h3>Settings</h3>
<AuthorizeView Context="user" Policy="InternalEmployee">
    @* here's still the existing EditForm *@
```

```
</AuthorizeView>
<AuthorizeView Policy="InternalEmployee" Roles="Admin">
    <p><button>Shutdown the app</button></p>
</AuthorizeView>
```

With the `Authorize` attribute, we now verify whether the logged-in user has any of the three allowed roles: `User`, `Support`, or `Admin`. Additionally, we've updated the rendering of the user details edit form. Now, `AuthorizeView` displays the form to anyone meeting the `InternalEmployee` policy and having any of the available roles. We've also updated the restrictions on the **Shut down the app** button – the user has to have the `Admin` role and belong to the `@packt.com` domain, enforced by the `InternalEmployee` policy.

The parameters of `Authorize` and `AuthorizeView` work similarly but are applied at different levels. The question remains when to use the attribute and when the component suits best. Use `Authorize` when protecting navigation to a given resource or page, ensuring that only authorized users can access it. On the other hand, use `AuthorizeView` when you need to restrict access to certain areas of the markup without affecting the overall routing. This approach provides a comprehensive way to secure your Blazor application, ensuring that only authorized users can access specific features and content.

Resolving authentication state in procedural logic

Incorporating authentication and authorization into the procedural logic of your application is often necessary. Simply manipulating markup visibility may not suffice in these scenarios; you need to resolve the current authentication state to make informed decisions within your code. That's where a cascading `AuthenticationState` class comes in. The `AuthenticationState` class is a built-in Blazor feature that provides information about the user's authentication status and claims.

Let's add a button that redirects internal employees to different areas of a ticketing system based on their roles.

Getting ready

Before we leverage authentication state in procedural logic, do the following:

- In the server-side project, create a `Components/Recipes/Recipe07` directory – this will be your working directory
- Copy the `FakePages` directory from the `Components/Recipes/Recipe07` directory in the GitHub repository
- If you haven't run migrations yet, find the `seed-work.sql` script in the `Samples` directory of the server-side project and run it on your database
- As we will need to enable interactivity, we can't use any of the existing `Settings` components anymore, so we will create a totally new one

How to do it...

Follow these instructions to leverage authentication state in procedural logic:

1. Create a new routable `Settings` component with server-side interactivity and an injected `Navigation` service:

```
@page "/ch08r07"
@rendermode InteractiveServer
@inject NavigationManager Navigation
```

2. Add a `@code` block to intercept the cascading authentication state:

```
@code {
    [CascadingParameter]
    private Task<AuthenticationState> AuthState
    {
        get; set;
    }
}
```

3. Below the `AuthState` parameter, initialize a `GoToTicketsAsync()` method and resolve the `user` context:

```
private async Task GoToTicketsAsync()
{
    var user = (await AuthState).User;
    //we will continue building logic here
}
```

4. Below the `user` context, check if the user's `Identity` property has a value and redirect to the login page if it's missing:

```
if (user.Identity is null)
{
    Navigation.NavigateTo("/Account/Login");
    return;
}
```

5. Below the `Identity` verification, check if the user is correctly authenticated and redirect to the login page if not:

```
if (!user.Identity.IsAuthenticated)
{
    Navigation.NavigateTo("/Account/Login");
    return;
}
```

6. After authentication verification, check if the value of the user's Name property belongs to the @packt.com domain and, if not, redirect them to the landing page of the ticketing system:

```
if (!user.Identity.Name.EndsWith("@packt.com"))
{
    Navigation.NavigateTo("/tickets");
    return;
}
```

7. After the user's domain check, check if the user is in the Support or Admin role and redirect them to the admin panel of the ticketing system:

```
if (user.IsInRole("Support") ||
    user.IsInRole("Admin"))
{

    Navigation.NavigateTo("/tickets/admin");
    return;
}
```

8. Lastly, if the user's identity doesn't fit any of the handled cases, redirect them to the access denied page:

```
Navigation.NavigateTo("/tickets/denied");
```

9. Jump to the markup of the Settings component and add a button to navigate to the ticketing system:

```
<p>
    <button @onclick=@GoToTicketsAsync>
        Support tickets
    </button>
</p>
```

How it works...

In *step 1*, we create a new routable Settings component, rendering in an InteractiveServer mode as we want our users to navigate to the ticketing system with a button click.

If you follow along the entire chapter or have scaffolded your project, you will already have a cascading authentication state registered. But to give you a comprehensive overview, in both server- and client-side projects, in their Program.cs files, you will find (or add, if it's missing) the builder. Services.AddCascadingAuthenticationState() command that explicitly enables cascading authentication state in your application.

In *step 2*, we initialize the @code block in the Settings component. Firstly, we intercept the authentication state. Blazor shares AuthenticationState as a Task parameter – in line with modern web development, where all operations are inherently asynchronous and as the AuthenticationStateProvider implementation might contain asynchronous logic constructing the authentication state. We also inject a NavigationManager service to help us redirect the user to the intended destination. For the next couple of steps, still inside the @code block, we implement a GoToTicketsAsync() method to resolve the redirection destination based on the user's identity context. In *step 3*, we resolve the user object by awaiting AuthState and grabbing the User property from the result. In *step 4*, we check if the current user has an Identity value set, which can be null if the user hasn't logged in yet. If the Identity value is missing, we immediately redirect the user to the login page. In *step 5*, we perform an additional check on the Identity value using the IsAuthenticated property to verify if the user is logged in and correctly authenticated. If that check fails, we redirect the user to the login page to revalidate their authentication state. Now that we are sure the current user has a valid identity, in *step 6*, we check if the user is actually an internal employee. We leverage the Name property of the user object, representing the user's login in the application. As, in our case, the Name property is equivalent to the user's email, we verify if the user account of the current user we check belongs to the @packt.com domain. If that check fails, we redirect the user to the /tickets page, where they can create new support tickets as standard application users. In *step 7*, knowing that an internal employee is using the application, we check if they have an Admin or Support role. If they do, we redirect them to the /tickets/admin page, where they can access the admin panel of the ticketing system. In *step 8*, we close the implementation of the GoToTicketsAsync() method. When all the previous authentication and authorization checks fail, we assume the user's account is incomplete and redirect them to the /tickets/denied page, indicating they can't access the ticketing system.

In *step 9*, we extend the Settings component markup. Below the existing h3 header, we add a paragraph with a button property that invokes the GoToTicketsAsync() method upon click, allowing the user to navigate to the ticketing system. Effective redirection depends on the result of the procedural logic we added and the user's identity.

9

Exploring Navigation and Routing

Routing and navigation are essential features in any modern web application. In a Blazor Web App, routing is the process that maps URLs to Razor components, allowing users to navigate between different views. Navigation refers to the actions and processes involved in moving from one route to another, whether through user interactions, programmatic commands, or other means. Blazor provides a flexible routing system that supports both static and interactive routing, depending on how you configure the application.

Static routing occurs during static server-side rendering when prerendering is enabled. In this mode, the Blazor router, defined by the `Router` component in `Routes.razor`, performs routing based on the HTTP request path, mapping URLs directly to components. Conversely, when the Blazor router is set to an interactive render mode, it automatically transitions from static to **interactive routing** after the initial rendering on the server is completed. Interactive routing uses the document's URL (the URL in the browser's address bar) to determine which component to render dynamically, allowing an application to respond to user interactions and navigate without performing full HTTP requests. This approach enables dynamic content updates and seamless navigation within the application.

When comparing routing in Blazor to routing in ASP.NET Core, there are both similarities and key differences to consider. ASP.NET Core primarily uses controllers and actions for routing, where routes are typically defined in a centralized manner, often using attribute-based or conventional routing. In contrast, Blazor's routing is component-based, directly mapping URLs to Razor components instead of controller actions. This component-based approach in Blazor allows a more modular and encapsulated routing experience, where each component can manage its own navigation logic. Additionally, Blazor supports navigation within a client-side browser, without requiring full-page reloads, which is a significant difference from traditional server-side routing in ASP.NET Core.

In this chapter, we will cover aspects of routing and navigation in Blazor web apps using .NET 9. We will begin with enabling routes from multiple assemblies, essential for building modular applications and scenarios where you'll leverage external NuGet packages. Then, we will explore parameterized routes, where you will learn to create dynamic and flexible URLs with route parameters. Then, we will discuss implementing unified **deep linking** for centralizing route definitions for easier management. We will also cover handling incorrect navigation requests and controlling navigation history to enhance the user experience. Near the end, we will explain how to execute asynchronous operations during navigation and cancel long-running tasks when users navigate away. Lastly, we will explore how to prevent unintentional data loss by prompting users about unsaved changes before navigating away from forms.

By the end of this chapter, you will understand how routing works in Blazor and how to implement various routing and navigation scenarios.

Routing and navigation are critical components that often impact entire application behavior. However, the recipes in this chapter are fully independent and don't build on one another. This approach also means you can review and implement each recipe in isolation. Recipes begin with instructions on what working directory you should create and which sample files you need to execute the following task.

In this chapter, we're going to cover the following recipes:

- Enabling routes from multiple assemblies
- Working with parameterized routes
- Working with query parameters
- Implementing unified deep linking
- Handling incorrect navigation requests
- Executing an asynchronous operation with navigation
- Canceling a long-running task when users navigate away
- Controlling navigation history

Technical requirements

Before diving in, make sure that you have the following:

- .NET 9 SDK installed
- A modern IDE (that supports Blazor development)
- A modern web browser (that supports WebAssembly)
- A Blazor project

We will build all recipes in a `BlazorCookbook.App` project, so all references will reflect that assembly. Make sure you adjust assembly references to match your project.

You can find all the code written in this chapter and code samples on GitHub at: `https://github.com/PacktPublishing/Blazor-Web-Development-Cookbook/tree/main/BlazorCookbook.App.Client/Chapters/Chapter09`.

Enabling routes from multiple assemblies

You might want to modularize your Blazor application by spreading routes across multiple assemblies. **Modularization** is the practice of breaking down an application into smaller, manageable, and independent modules, each responsible for a specific functionality. It's an ideal development approach when working in big or distributed teams, as each team can deliver features independently. Modularization is also beneficial in larger applications, as you can encapsulate different features in separate assemblies. Blazor allows you to discover routable components from additional assemblies through the `Router` component's API, for interactive routing, and the endpoint convention builder, for static route setups.

Let's learn how to allow users to navigate to a component from an assembly different than our base project.

Getting ready

Before we extend assemblies, where Blazor scans for routable components, copy the `BlazorCookbook.Library` project from the GitHub repository to your solution.

How to do it...

Follow these steps to allow Blazor to discover routes from different assemblies:

1. Navigate to the `BlazorCookbook.App` server-side project of your solution.

2. Open `BlazorCookbook.App.csproj` and add a reference to the `BlazorCookbook.Library` project:

```
<ItemGroup>
  <ProjectReference
    Include="..\BlazorCookbook.App.Client\
    BlazorCookbook.App.Client.csproj" />
  <ProjectReference
    Include="..\BlazorCookbook.Library\
    BlazorCookbook.Library.csproj" />
</ItemGroup>
```

3. Open the `Program.cs` and locate a component mapping section. Use the `AddAdditionalAssemblies()` method to map routes from the `ExternalEventManager` assembly:

```
using BlazorCookbook.Library.Chapter09.Recipe01;

//other registrations and pipelines

app.MapRazorComponents<App>()
    .AddInteractiveServerRenderMode()
    .AddInteractiveWebAssemblyRenderMode()
    .AddAdditionalAssemblies(
        typeof(_Imports).Assembly,
        typeof(ExternalEventManager).Assembly
    );
```

4. Open the `Routes` component and extend the array attached to the `AdditionalAssemblies` parameter with the `ExternalEventManager` assembly:

```
@using BlazorCookbook.Library.Chapter09.Recipe01
<Router AppAssembly="@typeof(Program).Assembly"
        AdditionalAssemblies="new[]
        {
            typeof(Client._Imports).Assembly,
            typeof(ExternalEventManager).Assembly
        }">
    @* router configuration *@
</Router>
```

How it works...

In this recipe, we add all the configurations for routable component discoverability in the server-side project of the solution. In *step 2*, we find the BlazorCookbook.App project configuration file and reference the BlazorCookbook.Library project that you've copied from the GitHub repository. BlazorCookbook.Library contains an ExternalEventManager component, and we want our users to be able to navigate to it.

In *step 3*, we set up the discoverability of the static routing that might come from the BlazorCookbook.Library. We navigate to the Program.cs file of the BlazorCookbook.App project and locate where we build the endpoint convention of the application. The endpoint route builder starts from the MapRazorComponents() method call. At the end of the builder, we call the AddAdditionalAssemblies() method to map all the static routes from the BlazorCookbook.App.Client project. Now, we extend the additional assemblies' array with the ExternalEventManager assembly. To make the registration type-safe, rather than a simple string, we use the `typeof()` method. The `typeof()` method in .NET allows us to obtain the `Type` object for a given type name, enabling reflection and metadata access at runtime. Additionally, it allows retrieval of the assembly containing the type, which solves our requirement perfectly.

In *step 4*, we navigate to the `Routes` component, still in the server-side project, to extend the discoverability of interactive routes. Here, we find our application `Router` configuration. By specifying assemblies with the `AppAssembly` and `AdditionalAssemblies` parameters, `Router` dynamically discovers and maps routes to components defined in those assemblies. In our case, again, we find that the client-side project assembly is already attached to the `AdditionalAssemblies` parameter of the `Router`. We extend the `AdditionalAssemblies` with reference to the `ExternalEventManager` assembly.

Working with parameterized routes

In Blazor, parameterized routes allow you to pass parameters through the URL, making your application more dynamic and flexible. By leveraging route parameters, you can create components that respond to specific URL segments and render content based on those parameters. You can also use route parameters to persist the component state and allow users to bookmark it (which we explored at the beginning of *Chapter 5*).

Let's extend component routing with parametrized routes, enforcing parameter constraints.

Getting ready

Before exploring parametrized routing, do the following:

- Create a `Chapter09/Recipe02` directory – this will be your working directory
- Copy `ExternalEventManager` from the `Chapter09/Recipe01` directory in the `BlazorCookbook.Library` project or the matching directory in the GitHub repository

How to do it...

Follow these steps to implement routes with parameters and intercept their values:

1. Navigate to the `ExternalEventManager` component and extend its routes with parametrized options:

```
@page "/ch09r02"
@page "/ch09r02/{eventId:guid}"
@page "/ch09r02/{eventId:guid}/venues/{venue?}"
```

2. In `ExternalEventManager`, initialize the `@code` block with two parameters – `EventId` and `Venue`:

```
@code {
    [Parameter] public Guid EventId { get; set; }
    [Parameter] public string Venue { get; set; }
}
```

3. Extend the `ExternalEventManager` markup by constructing a conditional display of the `Venue` and `EventId` values:

```
@if (EventId == default) return;
<p>Event ID: @EventId</p>
<p>In @(Venue ?? "all venues")</p>
```

How it works...

In *step 1*, we navigate to `ExternalEventManager` and extend the routing there. We add a new route that expects an `eventId` parameter by placing the parameter name in curly braces. We also declare that it must be of type `guid`. Blazor also supports route parameter constraints, which enhance your application's security by automatically rejecting parameter values that don't meet the specified constraints. Users providing incompatible values will receive a `404` error status code. While the route parameter name is case-insensitive, the constraint must follow the configured casing. As constraint support is limited, in the *See also* section for this recipe, there's a link to all currently supported data types. In the last route we add, we declare the `venue?` optional route parameter by adding a `?` symbol at the end. Having an optional parameter means users can navigate to the page whether they provide the value of the `venue` or not, and we can adjust the display logic accordingly.

In *step 2*, we initialize a `@code` block in `ExternalEventManager` and declare two parameters, `EventId` and `Venue`, matching the names of the parameters added in the routes but following the Pascal case convention. That's all it takes to enable Blazor to bind route parameters to the component's properties.

In *step 3*, we construct a simple markup in `ExternalEventManager`. Below the existing `h1` element, we check whether `EventId` was set in the route and render its value in a paragraph. Lastly, we add another paragraph, below `EventId`, to display the current value of `Venue` or a message indicating that the user is viewing all venues (if `Venue` was not provided in the route). With this setup, you can test how different routes impact the component's behavior.

There's more...

Alternatively, you can implement a *catch'em all* pattern to intercept route parameters. You can intercept an entire route segment into a string parameter:

```
@page "/ch09r02/{*path}"
@code {
    [Parameter] public string Path {get; set; }
}
```

We still declare the route parameter in curly braces and a matching `string` parameter in the `@code` block, similar to other routing cases. However, to indicate that we want to intercept an entire route segment, we prefix the parameter name with a `*` symbol. For example, when a user navigates to `/ch09r02/im/definitely/lost`, Blazor assigns `im/definitely/lost` to the `Path` value. You can still mix standard route parameters and constraints as long as the catch-all route segment parameter is the last in the route path.

See also

For the full list of data types that Blazor supports as route parameter constraints, check out the following Microsoft documentation link: `https://learn.microsoft.com/en-us/aspnet/core/blazor/fundamentals/routing?view=aspnetcore-9.0#route-constraints`.

Working with query parameters

Query strings and parameters are parts of a URL that allow you to pass optional data to a web application. They appear after the `?` symbol in a URL and consist of key-value pairs, separated by `=` and joined by `&`. The use of query parameters is useful for filtering data, pagination, and passing user-specific information without altering the URL structure significantly.

Let's enhance the routing by allowing the conditional passing of an event date that will be loaded dynamically.

Getting ready

Before exploring query parameters, do the following:

- Create a `Chapter09/Recipe03` directory – this will be your working directory
- Copy `ExternalEventManager` from the *Working with parameterized routes* recipe or the `Chapter09/Recipe02` directory in the GitHub repository

How to do it...

Follow these instructions to intercept values from query parameters:

1. Navigate to the `@code` block of the `ExternalEventManager` and introduce a `Date` parameter, but use a `SupplyParameterFromQuery` attribute to indicate that Blazor should intercept it from the query string:

```
[SupplyParameterFromQuery]
public DateTime Date { get; set; }
```

2. At the end of the `ExternalEventManager` markup, check whether `Date` is available and render another paragraph with the `Date` value:

```
@if (Date == DateTime.MinValue) return;
<p>On @Date</p>
```

How it works...

In *step 1*, we navigate to `ExternalEventManager` and declare a `Date` parameter. Instead of using the standard `Parameter` attribute, we leverage the `SupplyParameterFromQuery` variant, instructing Blazor to intercept parameters from the query string. There's no need to manipulate routes; simply annotating the parameter with `SupplyParameterFromQuery` enables this functionality.

In *step 2*, we extend the `ExternalEventManager` markup. We check whether the `Date` value matches the default value of `DateTime`, which indicates that the parameter was not in the query string. If Blazor intercepts the `Date` parameter, we render a paragraph displaying its value. However, it's important to note that the format of the date provided in the query string needs to match the culture settings of the application. By default, Blazor and .NET expect dates in the `MM-DD-YYYY` format, which is a default format in the `en-US` culture, reflecting the United States standard. If the date is provided in a different format, such as `DD-MM-YYYY`, it may not be parsed correctly unless the application's culture is set appropriately. This can be adjusted either globally or within specific components by configuring the appropriate culture settings, ensuring that Blazor interprets the date in the desired format.

There's more...

When your C# parameter name differs from the one provided in a query string, or when a parameter key is present multiple times in a query string and you need to intercept all values into an array, you must explicitly declare the `Name` property of the `SupplyParameterFromQuery` attribute:

```
[SupplyParameterFromQuery(Name = "seat")]
public string[] Seats { get; set; }
```

With this code, Blazor will intercept all the query parameters attached to the `seat` key and store them in the `Seats` array. You can then use that array to highlight or reserve seats with specific numbers.

See also

If you'd like to learn more about globalization and culture settings in Blazor, check out the Microsoft Learn resource here: `https://learn.microsoft.com/en-us/aspnet/core/blazor/globalization-localization#globalization`.

Implementing unified deep linking

Deep linking in a web application is the ability to link directly to specific content or functionality. Implementing a unified deep linking service in your application centralizes route management, making the application more maintainable and scalable. It's much easier to manage routing changes and avoid inconsistencies with all routes in one place.

Let's move some routes to a static deep links container and update component routing to leverage these unified deep links.

Getting ready

Before we encapsulate routes into a dedicated container, do the following:

- Create a `Chapter03/Recipe04` directory – this will be your working directory
- Copy `ExternalEventManager` from the *Working with query parameters* recipe or the `Chapter09/Recipe03` directory in the GitHub repository

How to do it...

Follow these steps to introduce a container for routes in your application:

1. This time, create a `DeepLinks` static class, not a component:

```
public static class DeepLinks
{
    // you will define routes here
}
```

2. Inside the `DeepLinks` class, define three `const` routes that match the ones you have in `ExternalEventManager`:

```
public const string
    LandingPage = "/ch09r04",
    EventPage = "/ch09r04/{eventId:guid}",
    EventAtVenuePage =
        "/ch09r04/{eventId:guid}/venues/{venue?}";
```

3. Navigate to `ExternalEventManager`, and replace the `@page` directives with the `@attribute` and `[Route]` attributes. Instead of providing the routes explicitly, leverage the `DeepLinks` constants:

```
@attribute [Route(DeepLinks.LandingPage)]
@attribute [Route(DeepLinks.EventPage)]
@attribute [Route(DeepLinks.EventAtVenuePage)]
```

How it works...

In *step 1*, we create a new `DeepLinks` class. `DeepLinks` is not a component but, rather, a `static` class, as it represents a fixed library that should be easily accessible in the entire application and won't change through the application's lifetime. In *step 2*, we declare three `const` routes for the `LandingPage`, `EventPage`, and `EventAtVenuePage` pages inside `DeepLinks`. These routes match the ones we already have explicitly declared in `ExternalEventManager`, so we copy those values here.

In *step 3*, we navigate to `ExternalEventManager` and replace all `@page` directives with `@attribute`. With `@attribute`, we can leverage the `[Route]` attribute, which accepts a route as a parameter. We use the `DeepLinks` route repository to explicitly construct the same routing we had with `@page` directives. Even though we've encapsulated routes in `string` variables, Blazor still respects the constraints and optionality of the route parameters.

You can leverage the `DeepLinks` class to safely set up navigation links in the application menu or anywhere else. By having routes as named objects, you avoid mistyping and reduce the risk of errors in your routing configuration.

There's more...

You can extend the `DeepLinks` class with methods that allow you to generate stateful links and enable a more flexible and dynamic way to create URLs with route parameters. For instance, you can implement a method that accepts `EventId` and places it correctly in the `EventPage` route template:

```
public const string
    EventPage = "/ch09r04/{eventId:guid}";

public static string GetPage(Guid eventId)
    => EventPage.Replace("{eventId:guid}", $"{eventId}");
```

When rendering a grid with events, you can leverage the `GetPage()` method and safely generate links to the event page with details. `GetPage()` accepts the `eventId` parameter and uses the `Replace()` extension method to insert parameters into the `EventPage` route template.

Handling incorrect navigation requests

Graceful handling of incorrect navigation requests is mandatory in modern web development to ensure a smooth and user-friendly experience. By preventing users from encountering confusing error messages or broken links, you make your application feel professional and reliable. While we have already covered unauthorized navigation in *Chapter 8*, other error states might unexpectedly occur. How you handle broken links or mistyped URLs defines the quality of the user experience.

Let's implement a global, safe redirection to a friendly error page when users face unexpected navigation exceptions.

Getting ready

Before implementing the safe redirection, you must have something to redirect to. If you have been following along with the entire book or just scaffolded your project, you already have a routable `Error` component. Otherwise, you can get it from the `Modules` directory in the GitHub repository.

How to do it...

Follow these steps to add a global safe redirection when user navigation fails:

1. Navigate to the `Program` file of the server-side project.
2. After all the existing middleware registrations, use the `UseStatusCodePagesWithRedirects()` extension method of `WebApplication` to register an error redirection middleware and redirect users to the `/error` route:

```
//...
//other middleware registrations
app.UseAntiforgery();
app.UseStatusCodePagesWithRedirects("/error");
//...
```

How it works...

In Blazor apps, before the introduction of Blazor web apps, you would use the `NotFound` parameter of `Router` to handle users navigating to an unavailable route. Blazor web apps still support the `NotFound` parameter for backward compatibility, but leveraging the server-side middleware pipeline to resolve status codes provides much more flexibility.

In *step 1*, we navigate to the `Program` file of the server-side project, where we configure the server-side middleware pipeline. In *step 2*, we locate where the existing middleware registrations end and use the `UseStatusCodePagesWithRedirects()` method to extend the middleware pipeline. With `UseStatusCodePagesWithRedirects()`, we define that whenever a server request results in an unhandled error status code, users get redirected to an `/error` page. With the `Error` component, we can customize the message, details, and next steps that our users see.

The added benefit of `UseStatusCodePagesWithRedirects()` is that it covers all unsuccessful status codes, not just the *route not found* case.

See also

We've covered `UseStatusCodePagesWithRedirects()`, as it's the method most commonly used in UI-based applications. However, it's just one of the options from the `UseStatusCodePages()` family of methods. Handling ranges from simple text status representation to fully customized exception-handling logic and retries.

You can find all available options, with examples of when and how to use each, in the Microsoft docs: `https://learn.microsoft.com/en-us/aspnet/core/fundamentals/error-handling?view=aspnetcore-9.0#usestatuscodepages`.

Executing an asynchronous operation with navigation

In modern web applications, executing common logic during navigation can be crucial for maintaining a seamless user experience and gathering valuable insights. You can implement navigation event logging and achieve a better understanding of user behavior, identify the most frequently used features, and improve them accordingly. You can also implement periodic security checks and refresh a user's access token seamlessly.

Let's log all navigation requests inside the application to understand better which features users use the most so that you can prioritize them.

Getting ready

We will work inside the `Routes` component, which you must already have, as it's an integral part of the Blazor application. No preparation is required in this recipe.

How to do it...

Follow these instructions to trigger an operation on all navigation inside the app:

1. Navigate to the `Routes` component and inject a `Logger` instance:

   ```
   @inject ILogger<Routes> Logger
   ```

2. Initialize an `@code` block in the `Routes` component, and implement a `LogNavigation()` method that accepts `NavigationContext` and logs the path that the user entered:

   ```
   @code {
       private void LogNavigation(
           NavigationContext context)
           => Logger.LogInformation(
   ```

```
                        "User entered: {Path}",
                        context.Path);
    }
```

3. In the `Routes` markup, locate `Router` and attach the `LogNavigation()` method to its `OnNavigateAsync` callback:

```
<Router AppAssembly="@typeof(Program).Assembly"
        AdditionalAssemblies="new[]
        {
            typeof(Client._Imports).Assembly,
            typeof(ExternalEventManager).Assembly
        }"
        OnNavigateAsync="@LogNavigation">
    @* here's further router configuration *@
</Router>
```

How it works...

In *step 1*, we navigate to the `Routes` component. You learned about `Routes` in the *Enabling routes from multiple assemblies* recipe. First, we inject an instance of `ILogger`. The `ILogger` interface simplifies logging information in applications and allows you to log messages with different severity levels (such as information, warning, or error) without depending on a specific logging implementation. `ILogger` allows you to provide a logger category, which is then reflected in logs, implying the log source. In our case, we declare the `Routes` as the logger category. You can find more logging resources in the *See also* section at the end of the recipe.

In *step 2*, we initialize an `@code` block and implement a `LogNavigation()` method. `LogNavigation()` accepts `NavigationContext`, which provides information about the navigation event. By accessing the `Path` property of the `NavigationContext`, we can pass the navigation destination path to `Logger` and log the path the user navigated to.

In *step 3*, we move to the `Routes` markup. Here, we find the `Router` construction. The `Router` component exposes an `OnNavigateAsync` callback, so we attach the `LogNavigation()` method there. Now, with each navigation request, `Router` will invoke the `OnNavigateAsync` callback and trigger the `LogNavigation()` method, effectively logging every path our users enter inside the application.

By default, you will have a `Console` logger registered, but you can freely extend the logging behavior to cover your business use case. You can either implement your own logger or find multiple NuGet packages that support logging from different hosting models.

See also

You can learn more about logging by checking out the Microsoft learning resources: `https://learn.microsoft.com/en-us/dotnet/core/extensions/logging`.

Canceling a long-running task when users navigate away

Depending on the traffic in your application, long-running tasks can negatively impact performance and user experience if you don't properly manage them. With components rendered in SSR mode, the server handles cancellations for you, similar to what happens in web API projects. But in interactive modes, when state is persisted either on the server or the client side when users navigate away from a page where a long-running task is in progress, it's essential that you gracefully cancel the task to free up resources and prevent unnecessary processing.

Let's implement a graceful cancellation of long-running tasks with the help of Blazor's `NavigationManager` and `CancellationToken`.

Getting ready

Before we explore graceful cancellation of a long-running task when a user navigates away, do the following:

- Create a `Chapter09/Recipe07` directory – this will be your working directory
- Copy the `ExternalEventManager` and `DeepLinks` files from the *Implementing unified deep linking* recipe or the `Chapter09/Recipe04` directory in the GitHub repository
- As `DeepLinks` contains recipe-specific routes and routes in the application must be unique, update the paths with `ch09r07` to reflect the current recipe
- Copy the `Source` file from the `Chapter09/Data` directory in the GitHub repository

How to do it...

Follow these steps to trigger graceful cancellation when a user navigates away:

1. Navigate to the `ExternalEventManager` component, and then enhance it to render it in `InteractiveWebAssembly` mode and implement `IDisposable`. We will address the resulting compilation error shortly:

   ```
   @rendermode InteractiveWebAssembly
   @implements IDisposable
   ```

2. At the top of the `@code` block of `ExternalEventManager`, inject `NavigationManager`:

   ```
   [Inject] private NavigationManager Nav { get; init; }
   ```

3. Below the Nav injection, declare a _cts variable of type CancellationTokenSource:

```
private CancellationTokenSource _cts;
```

4. At the end of the @code block of ExternalEventManager, implement a CancelTask() method, matching the signature for an EventHandler object returning LocationChangedEventArgs, which acts as a proxy to call the Cancel() method of the _cts object:

```
private void CancelTask(object sender,
    LocationChangedEventArgs args) => _cts?.Cancel();
```

5. Below the CancelTask() method, override the OnInitialized() life cycle method and subscribe the CancelTask() method to the LocationChanged event exposed by the injected Nav:

```
protected override void OnInitialized()
    => Nav.LocationChanged += CancelTask;
```

6. Next to OnInitialized(), implement a Dispose() method required by the IDisposable interface, where you safely unsubscribe from the LocationChanged event and gracefully dispose of the _cts instance:

```
public void Dispose()
{
    Nav.LocationChanged -= CancelTask;
    _cts?.Dispose();
}
```

7. To complete the @code block, implement a GetAsync() method, where you get eventId from Source, and redirect the user to the event details page:

```
private async Task GetAsync()
{
    _cts = new();
    var eventId = await Source.LoadAsync(_cts.Token);
    if (_cts.IsCancellationRequested) return;
    Nav.NavigateTo($"/ch09r07/{eventId}");
}
```

8. Move to the ExternalEventManager markup area, and below the header, replace the fast-return clause when EventId is not set with a rendering of a button, allowing users to load an event if it has not yet loaded:

```
@if (EventId == default)
{
    <button class="btn btn-primary"
```

```
            @onclick="@GetAsync">
        Get event
    </button>
    return;
}
```

How it works...

In *step 1*, we navigate to the `ExternalEventManager` component and declare it to render in `InteractiveWebAssembly` mode, as we want to monitor the execution of a long-running task to cancel it if needed. We also need `ExternalEventManager` to implement `IDisposable`. Declaring the component as `IDisposable` results in a compilation error, but we will resolve it before the end of the recipe.

In *step 2*, we inject a `NavigationManager` instance at the top of the `@code` block of `ExternalEventManager`. The `NavigationManager` instance allows us to react to navigation and location changes. In *step 3*, we set up the backbone of graceful task cancellation by declaring a `CancellationTokenSource` variable. With `CancellationTokenSource`, we can signal and manage cancellation requests for asynchronous operations.

In *step 4*, we implement a `CancelTask()` method with a signature matching an `EventHandler` object returning `LocationChangedEventArgs`. The `CancelTask()` method's responsibility is to invoke `Cancel()` of the `_cts` instance and cancel all running operations, depending on that instance. We leverage the ? operator, called a **null-conditional operator**, as it allows us to invoke a method or access to a member only if the preceding object (`_cts` in this case) is not `null`. In *step 5*, we override the `OnInitialized()` life cycle method of `ExternalEventManager` and subscribe `CancelTask()` to the `LocationChanged` event exposed by `Nav`. Blazor triggers the `LocationChanged` event whenever a user navigates to a new location within the application. In *step 6*, we complete the implementation of `IDisposable` by constructing a `Dispose()` method. In the `Dispose()` method, we safely unsubscribe from the `LocationChanged` event to prevent memory leaks. We also dispose of the `_cts` instance using the `Dispose()` method it exposes. In *step 7*, we complete the `@code` block by implementing a `GetAsync()` method to test the graceful cancellation of a long-running task. As part of `GetAsync()`, we initialize a new `_cts` instance and call the `LoadAsync()` method of the `Source` class, passing in a `CancellationToken` sourced from the `_cts` instance. `CancellationToken` allows `LoadAsync()` to be aware of any cancellation requests as it executes. As we expect loading cancellations, we add a `_cts` state-check. With the `IsCancellationRequested` property, we can verify whether cancellation was requested and short-circuit the code execution. Lastly, if `LoadAsync()` completes, we redirect the user to the appropriate event details page.

In *step 8*, we move to the ExternalEventManager markup and add a simple button, allowing users to trigger GetAsync() and put the implementation to the test. You can run the application and click the **Get event** button. The LoadAsync() method from the Source has a hardcoded delay of five seconds and logs status messages to your browser console. If you navigate away from the ExternalEventManager page before the timer elapses, you will see that the saving request you've queued was gracefully canceled.

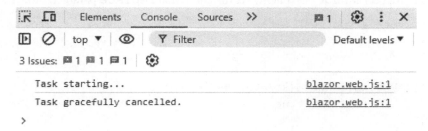

Figure 9.1: Messages in the browser console, indicating graceful task cancellation

Controlling navigation history

The NavigationManager in Blazor uses the browser's **History API** to maintain navigation history. Manipulating navigation history is particularly useful when authenticating users with external identity providers, where users are redirected back to an application after authentication. It's also beneficial when displaying intermediate pages that allow users to configure their application, but you want to restrict them from going backward in that process.

Let's simulate intermediate page removal from the browser history and force users to navigate to the last stable page when they try to return to the intermediate stage.

Getting ready

Before we explore browser navigation history manipulations, do the following:

- Create a Chapter09/Recipe08 directory – this will be your working directory
- Copy the ExternalEventManager and DeepLinks files from the *Canceling a long running task when users navigate away* recipe or the Chapter09/Recipe07 directory in the GitHub repository
- As DeepLinks contains recipe-specific routes and routes in the application must be unique, update the paths with ch09r08 to reflect the current recipe
- Copy the Source file from the Chapter09/Data directory in the GitHub repository

How to do it...

Follow these steps to replace an entry in the browser's navigation history:

1. Navigate to the @code block of ExternalEventManager and find the GetAsync() method.

2. Inside GetAsync(), when invoking the NavigateTo() method of the injected NavigationManager, explicitly set the additional replace parameter to true:

```
private async Task GetAsync()
{
    //... event getting logic

    Nav.NavigateTo($"/ch09r08/{eventId}",
        replace: true);
}
```

How it works...

In *step 1*, we navigate to the ExternalEventManager. Here, in the @code block, we have a GetAsync() method that users trigger when retrieving event details from an external source. In *step 2*, we extend the GetAsync() navigation logic by passing true as the replace argument. With the replace argument in NavigationManager.NavigateTo(), we ensure that the current entry in the browser's history is replaced with the new URL rather than adding a new entry.

If a user hasn't loaded any event yet, we will display a page with a button allowing them to load an event. After clicking the button, they get redirected to the event details page automatically. From there, when users try to navigate back, they will land on whatever page they were on before getting the event. The browser will not be aware of the intermediate step of loading the event in the first place.

10

Integrating with OpenAI

In this chapter, we will explore how to integrate advanced AI capabilities into your applications using OpenAI's powerful language models. You will learn to set up the Azure OpenAI service and deploy models, laying the foundation for integrating AI into your applications. By implementing AI-enhanced features in web applications, such as smart-pasting and smart text areas, you will enhance the user experience with intelligent data processing and content generation. Additionally, you'll build and integrate a ChatGPT-like chatbot for interactive AI-driven conversations. Finally, you will enable seamless data analysis by connecting your Azure OpenAI service to an existing Azure Search service data index.

Before we dive into recipes, it's crucial to highlight the ethical implications of using AI models, particularly concerning user data. In some cases, by using and deploying AI models, you consent to training those models on your application content. You must be vigilant about the privacy and security of your users' data and implement clear warnings and acceptance forms within your applications, allowing users to consent to or opt out of data sharing. By prioritizing transparency and user autonomy, you safeguard user trust and adhere to responsible AI practices.

Here are the recipes we will cover in this chapter:

- Setting up an Azure OpenAI service
- Implementing smart pasting
- Implementing a smart text area
- Adding a ChatBot
- Connecting an Azure OpenAI service to an existing data index

Technical requirements

In this chapter, we will rely heavily on the Azure services and a few NuGet packages that may still be in preview when you install them. You will find all the details and warnings described in detail in each of the impacted recipes, so you have nothing to worry about. Before you dive in, make sure you have the following:

- An active Azure account with access to the Azure Portal (if you don't have one yet, you can start with a time-limited, free account at `https://azure.microsoft.com/en-us/free`)
- A pre-created resource group in Azure
- A pre-installed Npm package manager, with globally available `npm` command
- A Blazor Web App project with per component/page render modes

You can find all the code examples (and data samples) from the following recipes in a dedicated GitHub repository at `https://github.com/PacktPublishing/Blazor-Web-Development-Cookbook/tree/main`. Just be aware that we will implement some recipes only on the server side – you'll understand why as you read through the chapter.

Setting up an Azure OpenAI service

Azure OpenAI Service is a cloud-based offering from Microsoft Azure that provides access to OpenAI's powerful language models. A **large language model** (**LLM**) is an optimized cost-function, trained on human texts, that can generate human-like text, allowing you to take chatbots, content generation, or language translation to the next level. By leveraging the Azure OpenAI service, you can integrate advanced AI capabilities into your Blazor application without managing the underlying infrastructure. You're also getting access to existing GPT models.

Let's set up an Azure OpenAI service in the Azure cloud using the Azure portal, deploy a dedicated GPT-4 model, and locate access details required for integration on the application side.

Getting ready

In this recipe, we won't write any code just yet; instead, we will focus on setting up the Azure OpenAI service. To get started, here are some prerequisites:

- You will need an Azure account and access to the Azure Portal
- You should create a resource group beforehand; we will use one named `blazor-cookbook` dedicated to this chapter

At the time of writing, the process of setting up the Azure OpenAI service consists of two phases.

1. In the first phase, do the following:

   I.   You must complete a request form to gain access to the Azure OpenAI service. To find the request form, follow the first two steps outlined in the *How to do it* section that follows.

   II. After submitting the form, you will need to wait for approval from the **Azure Cognitive Services team**. You will receive a confirmation email once your request has been approved, marking the end of the first phase.

2. We will walk through the second phase in the *How to do it* section.

How to do it...

Follow these steps to add the Azure OpenAI service to your Azure resources:

1. Open your resource group in Azure Portal and navigate to the Azure Marketplace by clicking the **Create** button in the top navigation bar.

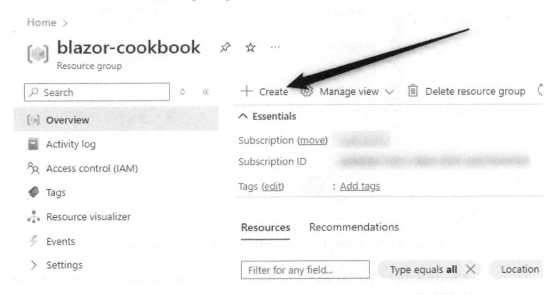

Figure 10.1: Navigating to Azure Marketplace from the resource group overview

2. In the Azure Marketplace, use the search bar in the top panel to find the **Azure OpenAI** service and start the creation process by clicking the **Create** button on the resulting tab.

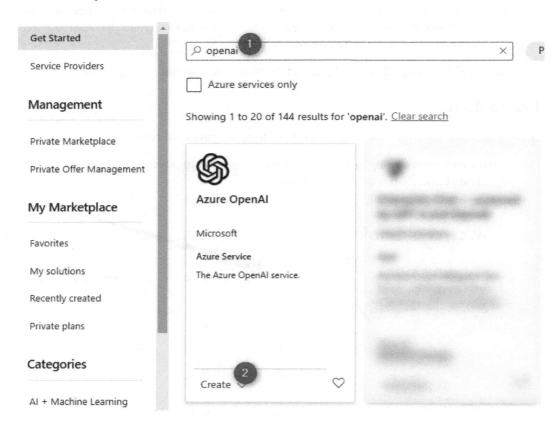

Figure 10.2: Navigating to the Azure OpenAI service creation panel

3. In the **Create Azure OpenAI** panel, provide the necessary details to create an Azure OpenAI instance:

    A. Select the subscription for the service in the **Subscription** field.

    B. Select the resource group where you want to create the service in the **Resource Group** field.

    C. Select the hosting region in the **Region** field.

    D. Provide a unique name for the service in the **Name** field.

    E. Select the pricing plan in the **Pricing tier** field.

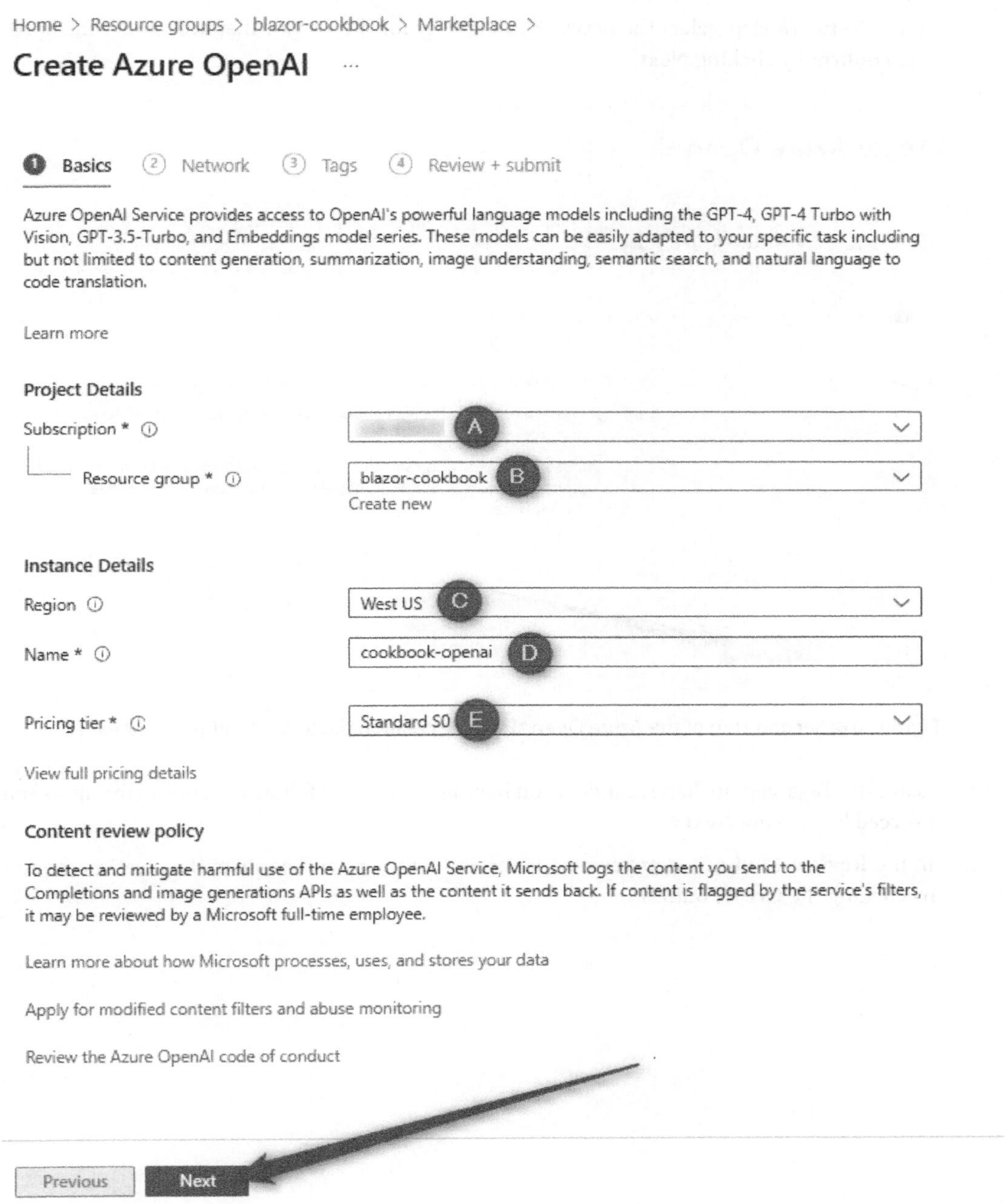

Home > Resource groups > blazor-cookbook > Marketplace >

Create Azure OpenAI   ...

① **Basics**   ② Network   ③ Tags   ④ Review + submit

Azure OpenAI Service provides access to OpenAI's powerful language models including the GPT-4, GPT-4 Turbo with Vision, GPT-3.5-Turbo, and Embeddings model series. These models can be easily adapted to your specific task including but not limited to content generation, summarization, image understanding, semantic search, and natural language to code translation.

Learn more

Project Details

Subscription * ⓘ   [A ▼]

└─── Resource group * ⓘ   [blazor-cookbook B ▼]
Create new

Instance Details

Region ⓘ   [West US C ▼]

Name * ⓘ   [cookbook-openai D]

Pricing tier * ⓘ   [Standard S0 E ▼]

View full pricing details

Content review policy

To detect and mitigate harmful use of the Azure OpenAI Service, Microsoft logs the content you send to the Completions and image generations APIs as well as the content it sends back. If content is flagged by the service's filters, it may be reviewed by a Microsoft full-time employee.

Learn more about how Microsoft processes, uses, and stores your data

Apply for modified content filters and abuse monitoring

Review the Azure OpenAI code of conduct

[Previous]   [**Next**]

Figure 10.3: First step of the Azure OpenAI service creation process – defining instance details

After reviewing the terms and conditions, click **Next** to proceed.

4. In the **Network** step, select the network availability for the service that best suits your needs and confirm by clicking **Next**.

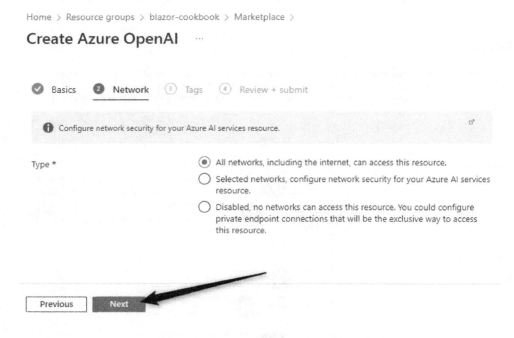

Figure 10.4: Second step of the Azure OpenAI service creation process – configuring network

5. Leave the **Tags** step unchanged unless you have tag policies to follow in your organization and proceed by clicking **Next**.

6. In the **Review + submit** step, review the service summary and confirm the creation request by clicking the **Create** button.

Home > Resource groups > blazor-cookbook > Marketplace >

Create Azure OpenAI ...

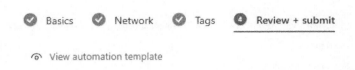

✓ Basics   ✓ Network   ✓ Tags   ④ **Review + submit**

👁 View automation template

TERMS

By clicking "Create", I (a) agree to the legal terms and privacy statement(s) associated with the Marketplace offering(s) listed above; (b) authorize Microsoft to bill my current payment method for the fees associated with the offering(s), with the same billing frequency as my Azure subscription; and (c) agree that Microsoft may share my contact, usage and transactional information with the provider(s) of the offering(s) for support, billing and other transactional activities. Microsoft does not provide rights for third-party offerings. See the Azure Marketplace Terms for additional details.

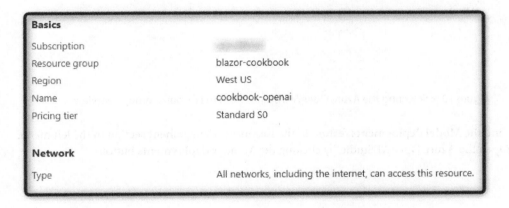

Basics	
Subscription	
Resource group	blazor-cookbook
Region	West US
Name	cookbook-openai
Pricing tier	Standard S0
Network	
Type	All networks, including the internet, can access this resource.

Previous   Next   Create

Figure 10.5: Last step of the Azure OpenAI creation process – reviewing instance details

7. Once the deployment completes, open your resource group overview and select the **Azure OpenAI** service.

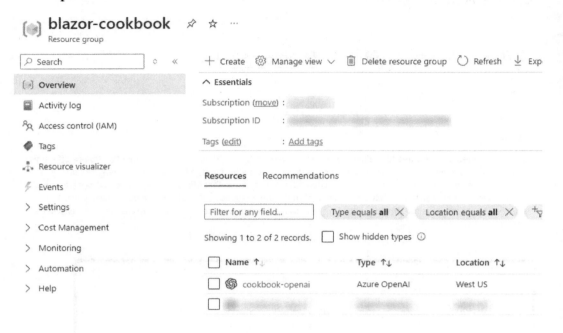

Figure 10.6: Selecting the Azure OpenAI instance from the resource group overview

8. Find the **Model deployments** feature in the **Resource Management** section in the left menu. Open the Azure OpenAI Studio by clicking the **Manage deployments** button.

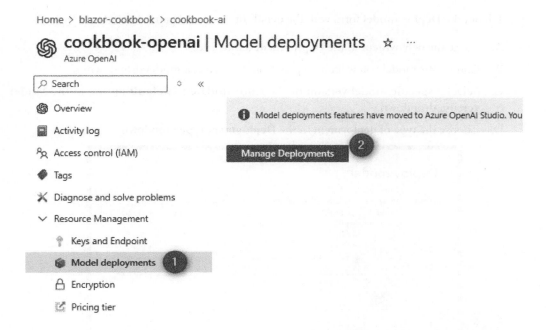

Figure 10.7: Navigating to Azure OpenAI Studio to manage model deployments

9. In the Azure OpenAI Studio, find the **Deployments** feature in the **Management** section on the left menu and start the deployment process by clicking the **Create new deployment** button.

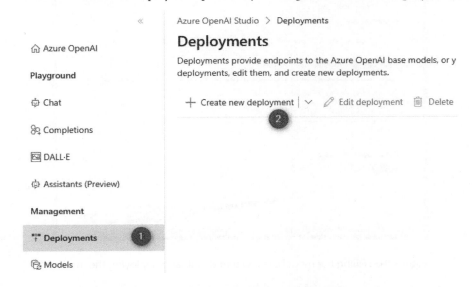

Figure 10.8: Initiating model deployment through the Azure OpenAI Studio

10. Fill out the **Deploy model** form with the details of the model you intend to use:

   A. Name the deployment in the **Deployment name** field.

   B. Choose the model you want to deploy from the **Select a model** dropdown.

   C. Select a specific model version or the **Auto-update to default** option in the **Model version** dropdown.

   D. Choose the type of deployment in the **Deployment type** dropdown.

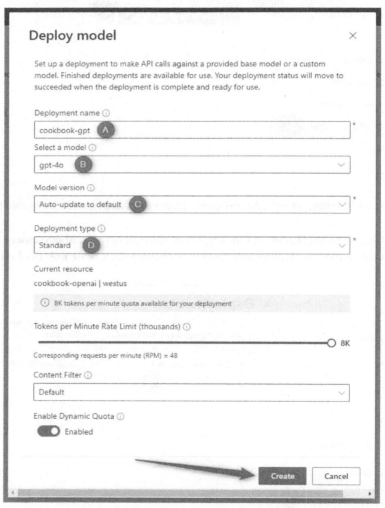

Figure 10.9: Filling the model deployment details and deploying the model

After filling out all required fields, confirm the deployment by clicking **Create**.

How it works...

In *step 1*, we open the Azure Portal and find the resource group where we want to deploy the Azure OpenAI service. From the top bar of the overview panel, we select the **Create** option. Azure will redirect us to the Azure Marketplace, where we can choose the services to install.

In *step 2*, we utilize the search bar at the top of the Azure Marketplace to look for Azure OpenAI. The result tab has a **Create** button, which we use to start the creation process.

In *step 3*, we arrive at the first step of the Azure OpenAI creation – **Basics**. In this step, we fill out all the basic details of the instance we're about to create. We choose the Azure subscription to define the owner of the service. Then, we select the appropriate resource group from the list assigned to the subscription. Next, we define the instance details, such as the hosting region and pricing tier. Be careful, as different areas have different AI models available. Also, depending on the pricing tier you select, you may incur service usage costs. To avoid that, opt for a free pricing tier (it has restricted scalability and request limits but will be enough for the recipes in this chapter). You can review the availability and pricing details by clicking the **View full pricing details** link. Then, we provide the instance name and a pricing tier. Once we have filled in all required fields, we move to the next step by clicking **Next**.

In *step 4*, we arrive at the **Network** step of the Azure OpenAI creation. In the **Network** tab, we define the discoverability of the service. We can disable network access entirely, configure private endpoints, set up network security within Azure, or make the instance publicly accessible. To keep it simple, we allow the instance access from any network, including the internet, and confirm by clicking **Next** to proceed.

In *step 5*, we arrive at the **Tags** step of the Azure OpenAI creation. The **Tags** tab allows defining custom tags describing services. Unless you have tag-based policies defined in your organization, tags won't have any functional impact. Hence, we leave the **Tags** panel unchanged and proceed to the last step by clicking **Next**.

In *step 6*, we arrive at the **Review + submit** panel, where we get the last chance to review the details of the instance we're about to create. When everything checks out, we confirm the creation by clicking **Create**.

It will take some time for the service deployment to complete. When completed, we proceed to *step 7*. We navigate to the overview panel of the resource group and select the Azure OpenAI instance.

In *step 8*, we find the **Resource Management** submenu and navigate to the **Model deployments** feature. In that panel, we click the **Manage Deployments** button and get redirected to the Azure OpenAI Studio for further steps.

In *step 9*, in the Azure OpenAI Studio, we find the **Management** submenu and navigate to the **Deployments** panel. In the **Deployments** navigation bar, we click the **Create new deployment** button to initialize a model deployment for the Azure OpenAI service.

In *step 10*, we arrive at the **Deploy model** submission form, where we must configure the deployment details. First, we define the deployment name – we will later use that name to specify which model to use for executing requests from the Blazor app. Next, we choose the model to deploy. Depending on the region where the Azure OpenAI instance is hosted, we can choose from a different set of AI models provided by Azure. To keep it simple, we opt to deploy GPT-4o. After choosing the model, we specify the version to use. From the dropdown, we can select a specific GPT model version or choose **Auto-update to default** to use the latest stable model. In the deployment form, we can fine-tune a rate limit for requests and a content filter, which we leave at default values. We can also enable **Dynamic quota**, allowing Azure to automatically scale up the tokens per minute limit when there's higher traffic. When we have filled in all deployment details, we can start the process by clicking **Create**.

When the deployment completes, you'll see the model in the **Deployments** panel of Azure OpenAI Studio:

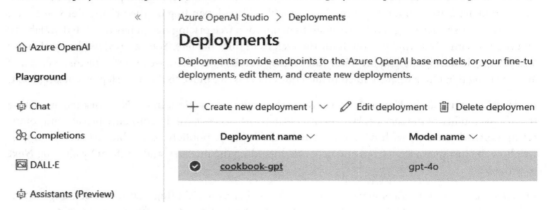

Figure 10.10: Azure OpenAI model deployments overview, showing the deployed model

There's more...

To communicate with the Azure OpenAI instance and the deployed AI model, you will need the model deployment name (which we set in *step 10*) and the Azure OpenAI API access details.

To find those details, navigate to the resource group and the created Azure OpenAI instance. In the menu on the left, select the **Keys and Endpoint** item in the **Resource Management** section.

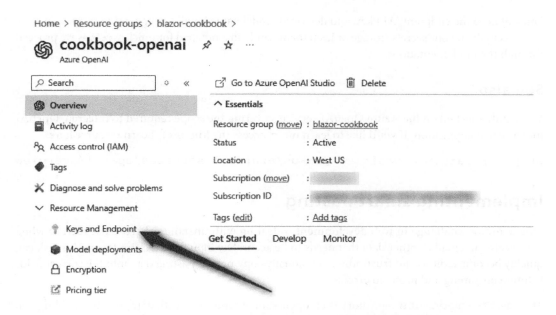

Figure 10.11: Navigating to the panel with the Azure OpenAI instance API access details

You'll arrive at the API details panel, which includes the **Endpoint** pointing to the Azure OpenAI instance, the location where it's hosted, and two API keys. Having two API keys ensures continuous service availability when you need to regenerate one of them.

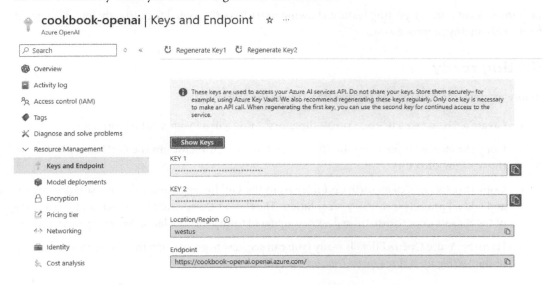

Figure 10.12: API access details panel, with API keys and URI

You will need the endpoint, API key, and deployed model name for all the upcoming recipes, so store them securely in your secrets storage or keep them handy in a notepad for quick access as we proceed through the implementations.

See also

We've only touched on the Azure OpenAI service, covering the scope required to integrate OpenAI into a Blazor application. If you'd like to learn more, access the Microsoft Learn resource here:

https://learn.microsoft.com/en-us/azure/ai-services/openai/overview

Implementing smart pasting

One common challenge in web development is dealing with unstandardized data, such as when you receive an email or other data that needs to be accurately input into a claim form. This task can quickly become tedious and frustrating, as manually copying and pasting data into the correct fields is time-consuming and prone to errors.

The SmartComponents repository is an open-source repository with components enabling you to add AI-driven features to your .NET applications quickly and without an in-depth knowledge of prompt engineering. Among other features, SmartComponents can enhance the pasting of the unstructured data to fit the expected form. Even though SmartComponents is not in the Microsoft namespace, it is under the official .NET Platform GitHub account and is fully endorsed, developed, and maintained by the Microsoft Team.

Let's implement a smart-pasting feature allowing users to paste copied text directly into designated fields without any preprocessing.

Getting ready

Before we dive into making the pasting smarter, do the following:

- Create a Chapter10/Recipe02 directory – this will be your working directory
- Copy the Models file from the Chapter10/Data directory in the GitHub repository to the working directory
- Copy the SmartComponents folder from the GitHub repository to your solution folder, and add all projects inside to your solution. The SmartComponents folder contains a clone of the SmartComponents repository, updated to support the latest Azure OpenAI updates
- Have the Azure OpenAI details ready (you can see how to get them in the *There's more…* section of the *Setting up Azure OpenAI service* recipe)

How to do it...

Follow these instructions to enhance pasting in your application with AI:

1. Navigate to the `csproj` file of the server-side project and include two required `SmartComponents` projects:

    ```
    <ItemGroup>
      <ProjectReference
        Include= "..\SmartComponents\
        SmartComponents.AspNetCore\
        SmartComponents.AspNetCore.csproj" />
      <ProjectReference
        Include= "..\SmartComponents\
        SmartComponents.Inference.OpenAI\
        SmartComponents.Inference.OpenAI.csproj" />
    </ItemGroup>
    ```

2. Still on the server side, open the `Program.cs` file and register `SmartComponents` with the OpenAI backend:

    ```
    using SmartComponents.Inference.OpenAI;
    //...other service registrations
    builder.Services
        .AddSmartComponents()
        .WithInferenceBackend<OpenAIInferenceBackend>();
    ```

3. Locate the `appSettings` file of the server-side project and extend the application settings with an area for `SmartComponents` configuration:

    ```
    {
      "SmartComponents": {
        "ApiKey": "YOUR_API_KEY",
        "Endpoint": "YOUR_ENDPOINT",
        "DeploymentName": "YOUR_MODEL_DEPLOYMENT"
      }
    }
    ```

4. Navigate to the `csproj` file of the client-side project and include the `SmartComponents` project required by the WebAssembly renderer:

    ```
    <ItemGroup>
      <ProjectReference
        Include="..\SmartComponents\
        SmartComponents.AspNetCore.Components\
    ```

```
            SmartComponents.AspNetCore.Components.csproj" />
</ItemGroup>
```

5. Create a new routable `FillClaim` component, referencing the `SmartComponents` assembly:

```
@page "/ch10r02"
@using SmartComponents
```

6. In the `@code` block of the `FillClaim` component, declare a `Claim` form parameter of the `ClaimViewModel` type:

```
@code {
    [SupplyParameterFromForm]
    public ClaimViewModel Claim { get; set; } = new();
}
```

7. In the `FillClaim` markup, construct an `EditForm` frame, binding it to the `Claim` parameter. If `EditForm` is not recognized as a component, include a `@using Microsoft.AspNetCore.Components.Forms` reference at the top of the `FillClaim` component:

```
<EditForm Model="@Claim" FormName="claim-form">
    @* we will continue here *@
</EditForm>
```

8. Inside the `FillClaim` form, add fields for entering event and customer details:

```
<p>
    Event name:
    <InputText @bind-Value="@Claim.Event" />
</p>
<p>Date: <InputText @bind-Value="@Claim.Date" /></p>
<p>
    Customer name:
    <InputText @bind-Value="@Claim.Customer.Name" />
</p>
<p>
    Customer email:
    <InputText @bind-Value="@Claim.Customer.Email" />
</p>
```

9. Add a submit button within the form to confirm the input:

```
<button type="submit">Submit</button>
```

10. Lastly, below the submit button, embed a `SmartPasteButton` component with a default icon:

```
<SmartPasteButton DefaultIcon />
```

How it works...

In *step 1*, we start by configuring the server side of the application. We navigate to the project configuration file and add references to two projects required to make SmartComponents work on the server. The SmartComponents.AspNetCore project contains server components powered by AI, while the SmartComponents.Inference.OpenAI project contains an implementation of services to communicate with OpenAI backend.

In *step 2*, we navigate to the Program.cs file in the server-side project and register SmartComponents in the dependency-injection container. We also register an OpenAIInferenceBackend implementation as the default prompts configuration for SmartComponents to use. Custom inference implementations come in handy when you leverage the AI to generate texts. We will explore that later, in the *Implementing a smart text area* recipe.

In *step 3*, we complete the setup of SmartComponents by navigating to the appSettings.json file on the server side. As appSettings.json is a configuration source of the application, we extend the JSON with a SmartComponents section and key nodes, representing the API key and endpoint and the model deployment name that the SmartComponents components must use.

In *step 4*, we jump to the client side of the application. In-line with default Blazor component packages, SmartComponents also has component counterparts for rendering in WebAssembly mode. We navigate to the configuration file of the client-side project and add a SmartComponents.AspNetCore.Components project reference there.

In *step 5*, we create a routable FillClaim component and reference the SmartComponents assembly. Next, we build a form where the support team can fill in claim details with the help of AI.

In *step 6*, we initialize an @code block and declare a Claim parameter that will also act as the backing model of the claim form. If you're new to form creation in Blazor, we covered that in detail in *Chapter 6*.

In *step 7*, we construct a form frame using EditForm and bind it to the Claim model.

In *step 8*, we build a simple form body, allowing the user to fill in an event name, date, customer name, and email – enough to identify and process the claim.

In *step 9*, we complete the form by adding a submit button.

Lastly, in *step 10*, we enhance the form with AI by embedding the SmartPasteButton component within the form's body. We also declare the SmartPasteButton component to render with a default icon. With that simple setup, you can now transform unstructured data into a ready-to-send form with the help of a (smart) button.

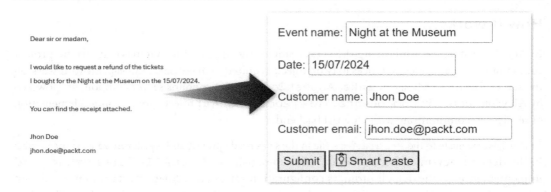

Figure 10.13: A result of smart pasting an e-mail with a claim into a form

There's more...

`SmartComponents` can also work with the OpenAI API key. If you already have an OpenAI account, navigate to the following URL:

`https://platform.openai.com/api-keys`

Here, you'll be able to create an API key that allows you to access the ChatGPT API:

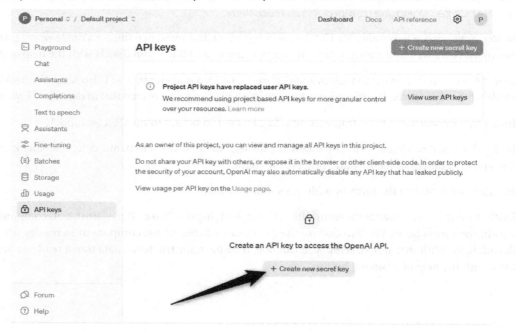

Figure 10.14: Creating an API key to access the OpenAI API

Once you have the API key, open the `appSettings.json` file of the server-side application and update the `SmartComponents` section:

```
{
  "SmartComponents": {
    "ApiKey": "YOUR_API_KEY",
    "DeploymentName": "gpt-4o"
  }
}
```

In the preceding configuration, the `ApiKey` node still represents your API key, while the `DeploymentName` node now defines the GPT model you want to use. Notice that the `Endpoint` node is no longer needed. When you don't provide an `Endpoint` value explicitly, `SmartComponents` will fall back to the default OpenAI API URI.

Implementing a smart text area

You've probably seen the generative power of AI in action – you provide a context, and a wall of sensible text appears. No more writer's block, right? Generative AI is a game-changer for all text-driven features in your application. You can take store item descriptions or event descriptions from a list of bullet points into well-written copy in seconds. With `SmartComponents`, we can easily connect to an AI model and leverage the generative power, making content creation faster and more intuitive.

Let's implement a text area where the support team can fill in a message attached to a response to a client's claim.

Getting ready

Before we explore the AI-powered text area implementation, we must do the following:

- Create a `Chapter10/Recipe03` directory – this will be our working directory
- Copy the `FillClaim` component from the *Implementing smart pasting* recipe or from the `Chapter10/Recipe02` directory in the GitHub repository
- Copy the `Models` from the `Chapter10/Data` directory in the GitHub repository
- If you're starting here, review instructions from *step 1* to *step 4* of the *Implementing smart pasting* recipe for an initial `SmartComponents` configuration

How to do it...

Follow these instructions to add a smart text area to your application:

1. Navigate to the @code block of the FillClaim component and add a replier variable that defines the person filling out the claim form:

```
const string replier =
    "An event organizer support team member replying
    to a claim request.";
```

2. Jump to the EditForm body in the FillClaim markup and extend the form by embedding a SmartTextArea component above the submission button. Attach the replier variable to the UserRole parameter of the SmartTextArea component and bind the text area value to the Message property of the Claim instance:

```
<p>
    <SmartTextArea
        @bind-Value="@Claim.Message"
        rows="5" cols="50"
        UserRole="@replier" />
</p>
```

How it works...

In *step 1*, we jump straight to the FillClaim component. First, we move to the @code block and declare a replier variable, where we put a brief but detailed description of the persona that we want the AI to represent. Considering that AI models learn from content written by humans, you should strive to make the replier description as natural as you would sound when speaking to a friend.

In *step 2*, we locate the EditForm markup in the FillClaim markup. Above the submission button, we embed a SmartTextArea component. The SmartTextArea component supports the bind-value binding pattern (you can learn more about binding in *Chapter 3*) and allows defining standard textarea attributes, such as rows or cols, representing the default size of the text box. It also allows setting a UserRole parameter – that's where we attach our persona definition stored in replier.

That's all it takes to add a generative field to your application:

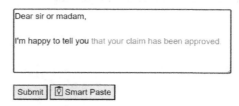

Figure 10.15: AI helping to write a claim response as user types the message

There's more...

So far, we used the default inference configuration provided by the `SmartComponents` package. However, you can customize the prompt and AI behavior by implementing a custom `SmartTextAreaInference` logic. Since AI communication and processing only happen on the server, you must keep prompt customization in the server-side project.

Let's create a `ClaimReplyInference` class, inheriting from `SmartTextAreaInference`, and customize suggestions coming in the `FillClaim` form:

```
public class ClaimReplyInference : SmartTextAreaInference
{
    public override ChatParameters BuildPrompt(
        SmartTextAreaConfig config,
        string textBefore, string textAfter
    )
    {
        var prompt = base.BuildPrompt(
            config, textBefore, textAfter
        );

        var systemMessage = new ChatMessage(
            ChatMessageRole.System,
            "Make suggestions in a professional tone."
        );

        prompt.Messages.Add(systemMessage);
        prompt.Temperature = 0.7f;
        return prompt;
    }
}
```

In `ClaimReplyInference`, we override the `BuildPrompt()` method. We leverage the base implementation to build the prompt but customize it afterward. First, we append an additional `ChatMessage` instance to the `Messages` collection the `prompt` already has. We define that new `ChatMessage` role as `System`. The `System` message sets the overall behavior of the AI model, indicating that we expect a professional tone of suggestions. Lastly, we customize the value of the prompt's `Temperature` property. The `Temperature` setting controls the randomness of the AI responses, with lower values making the output more focused and deterministic and higher values making it more creative and varied.

Having `ClaimReplyInference` in place, we must add it to the dependency injection container:

```
builder.Services.AddSingleton<SmartTextAreaInference,
    ClaimReplyInference>()
```

In the `Program` entry class, we register the `SmartTextAreaInference` class as a singleton. The `SmartTextArea` component will automatically discover the new implementation.

Now, users will get more official-sounding suggestions:

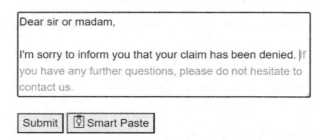

Figure 10.16: AI generating suggestions in a professional tone, to help a user replay to a claim

See also

You can customize all available `SmartComponents` components and fine-tune the AI behavior to your application needs. If you want to learn more, check out the official `SmartComponents` docs on GitHub at `https://github.com/dotnet-smartcomponents/smartcomponents/tree/main`.

Adding a ChatBot

ChatGPT, developed by OpenAI, is an advanced conversational AI model that has gained significant attention since its release. It's designed to understand and generate human-like text based on the input it receives, making interactions with it feel natural and intuitive. The versatility of the GPT models enables their application in numerous contexts, from customer support and personal assistants to educational tools and entertainment.

Let's construct a primitive chat UI and connect it to the Azure OpenAI service to embed a ChatGPT-like chat functionality in the Blazor application.

Getting ready

Similar to `SmartComponents`, which we explored in previous chapters, the chat will require Azure OpenAI API access. To avoid leaking API access details, we move to the server side of the application.

Before we dive into building AI-powered chat, we must do the following:

- Create a `Chapter10/Recipe04` directory – this will be your working directory
- Copy the `InputModel` from the `Chapter10/Data` directory in the GitHub repository
- Prepare the Azure OpenAI Service connection details (you can see how to get them in the *There's more…* section of the *Setting up an Azure OpenAI service* recipe)

How to do it...

Follow these steps to add an AI-powered chat to an application:

1. Navigate to the configuration file of the server-side project and include the latest version of the `Azure.AI.OpenAI` package (at the time of writing, it's still in preview):

```
<ItemGroup>
  <PackageReference
    Include="Azure.AI.OpenAI"
    Version="2.0.0-beta.2" />
</ItemGroup>
```

2. Open the `appsettings.json` file with the server project configuration and add a `ChatBot` section with the required nodes:

```
{
  "ChatBot": {
    "ApiKey": "YOUR_API_KEY",
    "Endpoint": "YOUR_ENDPOINT",
    "DeploymentName": "YOUR_MODEL_DEPLOYMENT"
  }
}
```

3. Move to the `Program.cs` entry file of the server-side project, and right after the `builder` instance is initialized, intercept the chat configuration into variables:

```
var endpoint = builder
    .Configuration["ChatBot:Endpoint"];
var apiKey = builder
    .Configuration["ChatBot:ApiKey"];
var deploymentName = builder
    .Configuration["ChatBot:DeploymentName"];
```

4. Below the configuration variables, register an `AzureOpenAIClient` service as a singleton by passing the `endpoint` and `apiKey` variables into the service constructor:

```
builder.Services.AddSingleton(
    new AzureOpenAIClient(
        new Uri(endpoint),
        new AzureKeyCredential(apiKey)
));
```

5. After registering `AzureOpenAIClient`, add a `ChatClient` service to the dependency injection container as scoped. Leverage the `AzureOpenAIClient` API and `deploymentName` to construct the `ChatClient` instance:

```
builder.Services
    .AddScoped(services =>
    {
        var openAI = services
            .GetRequiredService<AzureOpenAIClient>();
        return openAI.GetChatClient(deploymentName);
    });
```

6. Create a routable `ChatBot` component, rendering in the `InteractiveServer` mode and referencing the `OpenAI.Chat` assembly:

```
@page "/ch10r04"
@rendermode InteractiveServer
@using OpenAI.Chat
```

7. Initialize the `@code` block in the `ChatBot` component and inject the `ChatClient` service as `Chat`:

```
@code {
    [Inject] private ChatClient Chat { get; init; }
}
```

8. Below the service injection, initialize a `Model` instance to bind to the input form and `Messages` collection to persist chat messages to display on the UI:

```
protected InputModel Model = new();
protected List<string> Messages = [];
```

9. Below the `Messages` collection, initialize a `_messages` collection to hold messages in a form transferable to the Azure OpenAI Service. Start the `_messages` collection with a system prompt, defining the chatbot's persona:

```
private List<ChatMessage> _messages =
    [
```

```
    new SystemChatMessage(
        "Act as a friendly salesman for the Blazor Web
        Development Cookbook written by Pawel
        Bazyluk."
    )
];
```

10. Next to the backing variables, implement a `SendMessage()` method. Start by checking the validity of the `Model` state. If the input is valid, convert it to the `UserChatMessage` object and add the message to the backing collections:

```
private async Task SendMessage()
{
    if (!Model.IsValid) return;

    var message = new UserChatMessage(Model.Value);
    Messages.Add($"You: {Model.Value}");
    _messages.Add(message);

    //continue here...
}
```

11. Still within the `SendMessage()` method, request chat completion by passing the `_messages` collection to the `CompleteChatAsync()` method of the `Chat` service and resolve the response payload:

```
var chatResponse = await Chat
    .CompleteChatAsync(_messages);
var response = chatResponse.Value.Content[0].Text;
// continue here...
```

12. Complete the `SendMessage()` method by persisting the received response in the `Messages` collection and in the `_messages` collection as an `AssistantChatMessage` object. Lastly, reset `Value` of the `Model` object:

```
_messages.Add(new AssistantChatMessage(response));
Messages.Add($"OpenAI: {response}");
Model.Value = string.Empty;
```

13. Move to the `ChatBot` markup and construct a simple `EditForm` form with a single input field bound to the `Model` variable, triggering `SendMessage()` when submitted. If `EditForm` is not recognized as a component, include a `@using Microsoft.AspNetCore.Components.Forms` reference at the top of the `FillClaim` component:

```
<h3>What can I help you with?</h3>
<EditForm Model="@Model" FormName="chat-input"
```

```
            OnSubmit="@SendMessage">
    <InputText @bind-Value="@Model.Value" />
    <button type="submit">Send</button>
</EditForm>
```

14. Below the input form, iterate over the elements in the `Messages` collection and render them in separate paragraphs:

```
<hr />
@foreach (var message in Messages)
{
    <p>@message</p>
}
```

How it works...

In *step 1*, we start by adding the `Azure.AI.OpenAI` package to the server side of the application. If you've been using the **NuGet Package Manager**, you'll have to include prerelease versions of the packages, as `Azure.AI.OpenAI` is still in preview at the time of writing.

In *step 2*, we add a chatbot configuration section to the `appsettings.json` file. We will need an `ApiKey` node, an API `Endpoint` node, and a `DeploymentName` node, to specify the name of the model we want to use.

In *step 3*, we navigate to the `Program.cs` file of the server-side project, where we register the necessary services in the dependency injection container. First, we intercept the chatbot configuration values into `endpoint`, `apiKey`, and `deploymentName` by accessing the configuration reader from the `builder` instance.

In *step 4*, we register the `AzureOpenAIClient` service as a singleton, passing the `endpoint` value as the Azure OpenAI URI and initializing `AzureKeyCredentials` with an `apiKey` value. We can have a shared instance of the `AzureOpenAIClient` service as it's thread- and scope-safe by design but consider the memory impact in your implementations.

In *step 5*, we add one more service to the dependency injection container – we register a `ChatClient` service as scoped. We construct the `ChatClient` object by resolving the `AzureOpenAIClient` instance from the services collection and invoking its `GetChatClient()` method with the `deploymentName` value. Having services in place, we construct the UI part.

In *step 6*, we create a routable `ChatBot` component that references the `OpenAI.Chat` assembly, as we will need access to the `ChatClient` class definition. We also need the `ChatBot` component to render in `InteractiveServer` mode, since our users will interact with the chat.

In *step 7*, we initialize the @code block and inject the ChatClient service from the dependency injection.

In *step 8*, we initialize a Model instance to bind the input form where users fill in their messages, as well as a Messages collection, where we persist the text representation of the chat and user messages to render them in the markup.

In *step 9*, we initialize one more collection – _messages. In _messages, we persist messages in the form of ChatMessage objects. With that, we can easily provide the full context of the conversation when requesting a new response from the Azure OpenAI service; without the history of the messages, we would limit the chat context to the last message the user sends. We also start off _messages with a predefined SystemChatMessage object. The SystemChatMessage object allows us to inject a prompt, where we define how the chatbot should behave, but the prompt itself is not a part of the conversation.

In *step 9*, we implement a SendMessage() method where all the chatting logic goes. At the beginning, we check whether the submitted Model value is valid and fast-return when there's nothing to process. Then, we wrap the user input into a UserChatMessage object. We must use the UserChatMessage objects when sending user inputs so the AI can interpret them accordingly. Next, we add the UserChatMessage instance to the _messages context collection and format the user input into a chat-like version to add it to the renderable Messages collection.

In *step 10*, we leverage the Chat instance and its CompleteChatAsync() method to request a new chat response from the Azure OpenAI. Notice that we send the entire _messages collection as part of the request so that GPT in the cloud has the full context of the conversation. Then, we unpack the message from the received response Content property.

In *step 11*, we push the unpacked payload to the backing variables. This time, we wrap the received message in an AssistantChatMessage object before adding it to the _messages collection. The AssistantChatMessage type represents responses from the AI itself. Next, we construct a chat-like message to add to the Messages collection to render it for the user to see. Finally, we clear the Model value to accept another message from the user.

In *step 12*, we implement a primitive markup so the user can interact with the chat. We add a call to action at the top and construct an EditForm form. We bind the form to the Model instance and attach the SendMessage() method to its submission callback. Within the EditForm markup, we add a single InputText field where the user provides their chat requests and a button allowing them to submit the form and trigger the chat generation.

In *step 13*, below the EditForm component, we construct a simple loop where we iterate over the chat-like messages in the Messages collection and render them in separate paragraphs.

With that simple implementation, you already get a ready-to-talk chat prototype:

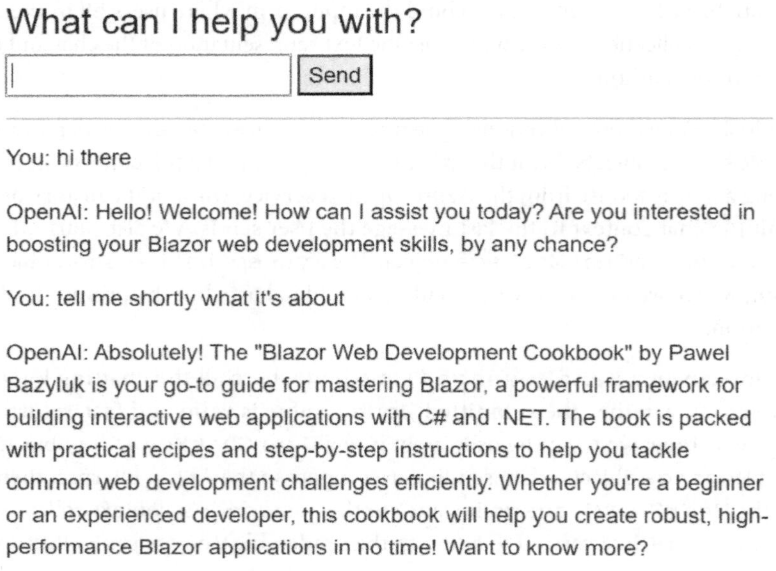

What can I help you with?

| | Send |

You: hi there

OpenAI: Hello! Welcome! How can I assist you today? Are you interested in boosting your Blazor web development skills, by any chance?

You: tell me shortly what it's about

OpenAI: Absolutely! The "Blazor Web Development Cookbook" by Pawel Bazyluk is your go-to guide for mastering Blazor, a powerful framework for building interactive web applications with C# and .NET. The book is packed with practical recipes and step-by-step instructions to help you tackle common web development challenges efficiently. Whether you're a beginner or an experienced developer, this cookbook will help you create robust, high-performance Blazor applications in no time! Want to know more?

Figure 10.17: Primitive chat UI with a powerful AI-powered backend in action

There's more...

Depending on the session or message length that you expect to handle with the chat, you should consider cleaning the context of the conversation periodically. This will help maintain the efficiency and effectiveness of the chat functionality. Managing the length of the chat context impacts both the cost and responsiveness of the chat. Longer contexts can lead to higher costs due to increased API usage and potentially slower response times as more data is processed.

One effective strategy is to implement a **circular buffer** of a fixed size. In a circular buffer, new elements are added to the end of the buffer while the oldest elements are overwritten when the buffer reaches its capacity. This approach ensures that the chat context remains within a manageable size, keeping the conversation relevant and efficient.

See also

If you'd want to explore the `Azure.AI.OpenAI` possibilities further, visit the package docs at `https://github.com/Azure/azure-sdk-for-net/blob/main/sdk/openai/Azure.AI.OpenAI/README.md`.

Connecting an Azure OpenAI service to an existing data index

In Azure, you can have multiple existing data sources, ranging from Azure Cosmos DB to various Azure Cognitive services with tokenized and indexed data. While the Azure OpenAI service works with commonly available GPT models, it also allows you to connect a chosen model to your specific data source. With this integration, you can analyze and extract data more intuitively by interacting with your application through natural language.

Let's connect the Azure OpenAI service to an existing Azure Search service data index. By doing so, we will leverage the power of AI to analyze our internal data seamlessly.

Getting ready

Before we explore connecting Azure Search data to Azure OpenAI, we must do the following:

- On the server-side on your application, create a `Chapter10/Recipe05` directory – this will be your working directory
- Copy the `ChatBot` component from the *Adding a ChatBot* recipe or from the `Chapter10/Recipe04` directory in the GitHub repository
- If you're starting here, register all the Azure services as shown in the `Configure` file, in the `Chapter10/Recipe04` directory in the GitHub repository

How to do it...

Follow these instructions to connect Azure OpenAI to the Azure Search data and enable analyzing the data:

1. Open the `appsettings.json` file on the server side and add a new `Search` section with `ApiKey`, `Endpoint`, and `Index`:

```
"Search": {
  "ApiKey": "YOUR_API_KEY",
  "Endpoint": "YOUR_ENDPOINT",
  "Index": "YOUR_INDEX_NAME"
}
```

2. Move to the `Program.cs` file of the server-side project. Below the builder and Azure OpenAI services initializations, intercept the search data access details into `searchEndpoint`, `searchApiKey`, and `searchIndex` variables:

```
var searchEndpoint = builder
    .Configuration["Search:Endpoint"];
```

```
var searchApiKey = builder
    .Configuration["Search:ApiKey"];
var searchIndex = builder
    .Configuration["Search:Index"];
```

3. Below the intercepted search configuration, register `ChatCompletionOptions` as a singleton. As part of the `ChatCompletionOptions` initialization, build an `AzureSearchChatDataSource` instance and attach it to the constructed completion options:

```
builder.Services.AddSingleton(services =>
{
    var dataSource = new AzureSearchChatDataSource
    {
        Endpoint = new Uri(searchEndpoint),
        IndexName = searchIndex,
        Authentication = DataSourceAuthentication
            .FromApiKey(searchApiKey)
    };

    ChatCompletionOptions completionOptions = new();
    completionOptions.AddDataSource(dataSource);
    return completionOptions;
});
```

4. At the time of writing, the `Azure.AI.OpenAI` package is in preview and your IDE may interpret using the `AddDataSource()` method of the `ChatCompletionOptions` class as a compilation error. To suppress the error, add the required `#pragma` directive at the top of the `Program.cs` file:

```
#pragma warning disable AOAI001
```

5. Navigate to the `@code` block of the `ChatBot` component and inject the `ChatCompletionOptions` instance next to the `Chat` client:

```
[Inject]
private ChatCompletionOptions ChatOptions
{
    get; init;
}
```

6. Still within the `@code` block, inside the `SendMessage()` method, locate where we invoke the `CompleteChatAsync()` method of the `Chat` service and pass `ChatOptions` as a second parameter:

```
var chatResponse = await Chat
    .CompleteChatAsync(_messages, ChatOptions);
```

How it works...

In *step 1*, we navigate to the `appsettings.json` configuration file of the server-side project. We extend the configuration file with a `Search` section where we require the `ApiKey`, `Endpoint`, and `Index` values.

In *step 2*, we stay on the server side but move to the `Program.cs` project entry file. We intercept the search configuration into `searchEndpoint`, `searchApiKey`, and `searchIndex` variables, so we can use them to connect data to the Azure OpenAI.

In *step 3*, we register a singleton `ChatCompletionOptions` object in the application's dependency injection container. `ChatCompletionOptions` is used to configure the behavior of chat completions, allowing us to customize and extend the functionality of our chat service. As part of the `ChatCompletionOptions` initialization logic, we construct an instance of `AzureSearchChatDataSource`, which represents the search data connection details and requires providing an endpoint, API key, and index name. We've intercepted this from the `appsettings.json` file. We use the `AddDataSource()` method of the `ChatCompletionOptions` instance to attach the search data access.

As `Azure.AI.OpenAI` is still in preview at the time of writing, your IDE may flag the use of the `AddDataSource()` method as a compilation error – that's nothing to worry about. The Azure team will adjust this before releasing the stable package. For now, we can suppress the warning by adding a `#pragma` directive at the top of the `Program.cs` file with the `AOAI001` validation code we need to suppress, as we do in *step 4*. Next, we move to the `ChatBot` component and attach the enhanced completion options to our chatbot.

In *step 5*, we go straight to the `@code` block of the `ChatBot` component and inject the `ChatCompletionOptions` instance from the dependency injection container as `ChatOptions`.

In *step 6*, we locate the `SendMessage()` method and find where we invoke the `CompleteChatAsync()` method of the `Chat` service to get a response from the Azure OpenAI. We're already passing a `_messages` collection to the `CompleteChatAsync()` method, but it also accepts a second parameter of the `ChatCompletionOptions` type – that's where we pass the injected `ChatOptions` instance with access to the Azure Search data.

There's more...

You don't have to have the data source and Azure OpenAI in the same resource group. In fact, you don't even have to own the data source. Azure OpenAI will work correctly and generate contextualized results as long as you provide a valid set of configuration details. This flexibility allows you to leverage existing data sources and integrate them with Azure OpenAI seamlessly, enhancing the functionality of your applications without needing to consolidate or migrate resources.

See also

In the recipe implementation, we've used a `#pragma` preprocessor directive. Preprocessor directives have different purposes and allow adjusting your code behavior on a lower level. If you're curious to learn more, check out this Microsoft Learn resource:

`https://learn.microsoft.com/en-us/dotnet/csharp/language-reference/preprocessor-directives`

Index

Symbols

.NET CLI 2

A

B

C

www.packtpub.com

Subscribe to our online digital library for full access to over 7,000 books and videos, as well as industry leading tools to help you plan your personal development and advance your career. For more information, please visit our website.

Why subscribe?

- Spend less time learning and more time coding with practical eBooks and Videos from over 4,000 industry professionals

- Improve your learning with Skill Plans built especially for you

- Get a free eBook or video every month

- Fully searchable for easy access to vital information

- Copy and paste, print, and bookmark content

Did you know that Packt offers eBook versions of every book published, with PDF and ePub files available? You can upgrade to the eBook version at packtpub.com and as a print book customer, you are entitled to a discount on the eBook copy. Get in touch with us at customercare@packtpub.com for more details.

At www.packtpub.com, you can also read a collection of free technical articles, sign up for a range of free newsletters, and receive exclusive discounts and offers on Packt books and eBooks.

Other Books You May Enjoy

If you enjoyed this book, you may be interested in these other books by Packt:

Web Development with Blazor – Third Edition

Jimmy Engström

ISBN: 978-1-83546-591-2

- Understand how and when to use Blazor Server, Blazor WebAssembly, and Blazor Hybrid
- Learn how to build simple and advanced Blazor components
- Explore how Minimal APIs work and build your own API
- Discover how to use streaming rendering and server-side rendering (SSR)
- Mix and match different hosting models to create flexible and scalable Blazor apps
- Familiarise yourself with the new Blazor templates that simplify development
- Debug your Blazor Server and Blazor WebAssembly applications

Web API Development with ASP.NET Core 8

Xiaodi Yan

ISBN: 978-1-80461-095-4

- Build a strong foundation in web API fundamentals
- Explore the ASP.NET Core 8 framework and other industry-standard libraries and tools for high-performance, scalable web APIs
- Apply essential software design patterns such as MVC, dependency injection, and the repository pattern
- Use Entity Framework Core for database operations and complex query creation
- Implement robust security measures to protect against malicious attacks and data breaches
- Deploy your application to the cloud using Azure and leverage Azure DevOps to implement CI/CD

258

Packt is searching for authors like you

If you're interested in becoming an author for Packt, please visit `authors.packtpub.com` and apply today. We have worked with thousands of developers and tech professionals, just like you, to help them share their insight with the global tech community. You can make a general application, apply for a specific hot topic that we are recruiting an author for, or submit your own idea.

Share Your Thoughts

Now you've finished Blazor *Web Development Cookbook*, we'd love to hear your thoughts! Scan the QR code below to go straight to the Amazon review page for this book and share your feedback or leave a review on the site that you purchased it from.

https://packt.link/r/183546078X

Your review is important to us and the tech community and will help us make sure we're delivering excellent quality content.

Download a free PDF copy of this book

Thanks for purchasing this book!

Do you like to read on the go but are unable to carry your print books everywhere?

Is your eBook purchase not compatible with the device of your choice?

Don't worry, now with every Packt book you get a DRM-free PDF version of that book at no cost.

Read anywhere, any place, on any device. Search, copy, and paste code from your favorite technical books directly into your application.

The perks don't stop there, you can get exclusive access to discounts, newsletters, and great free content in your inbox daily

Follow these simple steps to get the benefits:

1. Scan the QR code or visit the link below

https://download.packt.com/free-ebook/9781835460788

2. Submit your proof of purchase
3. That's it! We'll send your free PDF and other benefits to your email directly

Made in United States
North Haven, CT
05 December 2024

61806301R00154